Children in Our Charge

Children in Charge series

Children in Charge
The Child's Right to a Fair Hearing
Edited by Mary John
ISBN 1-85302-368-X
Children in Charge 1

A Charge Against Society
The Child's Right to Protection
Edited by Mary John
ISBN 1-85302-411-2
Children in Charge 3

of related interest

A Voice for Children
Målfrid Grude Flekkøy
ISBN 1-85302-118-0

Children in Charge 2

Children in Our Charge
The Child's Right to Resources

Edited by Mary John

Jessica Kingsley Publishers
London and Bristol, Pennsylvania

Alan Peacock's chapter was originally published in *International Journal of Science Education 17*, 2 (1995) and is reproduced here by kind permission of Taylor and Francis.

Margaret Ralph's chapter was originally published in *Educational and Child Psychology 11*, 4 (1994) pp.35–44 and is reproduced here by kind permission of The British Psychological Society and the author.

First published in the United Kingdom in 1996 by
Jessica Kingsley Publishers Ltd
116 Pentonville Road
London N1 9JB, England
and
1900 Frost Road, Suite 101
Bristol, PA 19007, U S A

Copyright © 1996 Jessica Kingsley Publishers
Alan Peacock's chapter © 1995 Taylor and Francis
Margaret Ralph's chapter © 1994 The British Psychological Society

Library of Congress Cataloging in Publication Data
A CIP catalogue record for this book is available from the Library of Congress

British Library Cataloguing in Publication Data
A CIP catalogue record for this book is available from the British Library

ISBN 1-85302-369-8

Printed and Bound in Great Britain by
Athenaeum Press, Gateshead, Tyne and Wear

Contents

Part One: Children in Our Charge

Part Two: Providing a Conceptual Framework

Part Three: Providing for Children's Rights in a Changing World

Part Four: Providing an Education

Part Five: Providing for Consultation

Part Six: Providing for Children's Rights in New Technological Advances

List of Figures

List of Tables

Editor's Acknowledgements

Many of the chapters included in this collection were first presented in their original form at a 'World Conference on Research and Practice in Children's Rights; a Question of Empowerment?' held at the University of Exeter in September 1992. Other chapters have been inspired by that gathering or report on work that has been developed within the spirit of concerns expressed there. It is only appropriate, therefore, to make acknowledgement here of the support that we received in holding that Conference, held as it was at a time when Children's Rights were not very much on the public agenda in the United Kingdom despite the ratification of the UN Convention by the UK the previous December and the setting up of the Children's Rights Development Unit.

A number of individuals and organisations had the vision to support what, at the time, seemed a high risk venture. Such individuals need to be thanked for inspirational support. The then Assistant Director of Education for Devon County Council, Dr Paul Grey, supported us in concrete and facilitative ways and continued to further the cause of the implementation of the UN Convention of the Rights of the Child imaginatively within the County Council. The Conference Manager, Ron Delve, Co-ordinator Hillary Olek and Graphic Designers Michael and Amanda Still held a risky undertaking together and ensured its success. The Conference Committee made up of colleagues from various Departments in the University; Postgraduate Medical School, Department of Child Health; Psychology Department,; Sociology Department; Law Department; School of Education; Department of Continuing and Adult Education all demonstrated true interdepartmental co-operation and colleagues from the Dartington Social Research Unit of the University of Bristol, from the Faculty of Education at the University of Plymouth and the local Social Services Department reinforced that with real interinstitutional commitment of a high order and continued after the Conference with input into the discussions of the publication possibilities for the Conference papers. There remains only one regret which is that my original Co-Conference organiser, Christina Sachs, from Exeter University Law Department was taken ill fairly early on in the preparations and, although she did manage to attend some of the Conference, sadly she died before the fruits of that Conference could be harvested. We remember her life and work on behalf of children and families with affection and gratitude.

No acknowledgements of the birthing process of this collection would be complete without mention of the children and young people who acted as midwives to much of the work and many of the ideas that have emerged. The work of ten Cornish Schools and their 350 pupils who contributed in a dramatic form their views and feelings about certain Articles of the UN Convention on the Rights of the Child. To them, their adult allies, their teachers and the overall organiser, Rhys Griffith, my thanks for having raised our consciousness in such stimulating ways. To the Young People's Evaluation Panel (Louise Pilcher, Joanne Kestevan, Louise Bridges, Kirstie Randall, Chris Hodder, Natalie Whitelock, Matthew Hendy, Molly Walker, Nicola Gregory, Felicity Thomas, Richard Partridge, Niki Dada, Vicky Maund, Alice Craven, Liz Beardsall, David Mance, Liz Palmer, Charlotte Murphy, Will Woodward and Rachel Bolt) who made the aim of children's participation meaningful, I remain indebted for all they taught us about listening to children. To their schools – Kings School, Ottery St

Mary; Mount St Mary Convent, Exeter; Sands School, Ashburton and the teacher/chauffeurs who believed that what these young people were doing mattered – my appreciation.

The Conference was financially supported by the Bernard Van Leer Foundation, the Elm Grant Trust, the Trustees of Westhill College Birmingham, University of Plymouth Faculty of Education, the School of Education of the University of Exeter, the University of Exeter Research Fund, Devon County Council Education Department and the Social Services Department, the Disabled Young Adults Centre, Cow and Gate Ltd, John Wyeth and Brother Ltd and Milupa.

Having expressed my appreciation for contributions of various kinds to the process of the development of this volume and the one that has preceded it and the one that follows, I wish to make specific acknowledgements for the generous permission I have received from Taylor Francis to reprint Alan Peacock's article which, whilst first presented at the Exeter Conference, appeared in a more developed form in their International Journal of Science Education. The paper by Margaret Ralph, which outlines research work she undertook under my supervision, first appeared in a special issue of *Educational and Child Psychology* published by the Division of Educational and Child Psychology of the British Psychological Society. I am grateful to the British Psychological Society for permission to reprint it here.

I would like to thank the technical and administrative staff within the School of Education for their support and, in particular, Michael Still as Editorial Assistant and my secretary, Angela Garry, for secretarial support, wizardry in all forms of new technologies and an unfailing goodwill when this preoccupation with children's rights began to encroach upon her own rights!

Finally, and by no means least William and Elvira John, my parents: tireless protagonists of my 'best interests'.

PART ONE

Children in Our Charge

In Whose Best Interest?

Mary John

The United Nations Convention on the Rights of the Child[1] was discussed in Volume One of the *Children in Charge* series in relation to one of its most innovative provisions, that of the participation of children in various ways in decision making processes in matters that concerned them. In this volume we turn our attention away from the involvement of children towards *our* responsibilities towards them and the nature of such responsibilities. The balance shifts here from their needs for self-expression and to be taken seriously towards an examination of their quality of life and the part that social structures, social policies, research and intervention play in determining this. Traditional concerns about children have been those relating to the necessity to provide adequately for them. This, at first glance, is a far more predictable and established approach to the rights of the child, an approach which has little concern with them as people in their own right. More recent approaches have, as we shall see, embraced these two aspects.

The Convention provides not only a list for governments of universal minimum requirements, but also embodies the view that countries with more resources must ask more from themselves – and also be prepared to assist poor countries for the benefit of children overseas. It includes the wording 'to the maximum extent of their available resources'. This is a key phrase as governments all over the world are cutting resources with more or less severity and with greater and lesser degrees of impact on the quality of life of that country's children. At the beginning of Article 4 it is made clear that the rights of the child are not primarily dependent on economic resources. Article 4 gives priority to children in stating that:

> States Parties shall undertake all appropriate legislative, administrative, and other measures for the implementation of the rights recognised in

---

1   Information or a copy of the UN Convention on the Rights of the Child is available from UNICEF, 55 Lincoln's Inn Fields, LONDON, WC2A 3NB. Tel: 0171-405-5592. Fax: 0171-405-2332.

the present Convention. With regard to economic, social and cultural rights, States Parties shall undertake such measures to the maximum extent of their available resources and, where needed, within the framework of international co-operation.

There are basic values embedded in the text of the Convention which have relevance for rich and poor countries alike and which mean that girls have the same opportunities as boys, refugee children and children of indigenous or minority groups. The reality that the Convention addresses, however, means that things will not change overnight as the problems on the global scale are enormous. Thomas Hammarberg, a member of the UN Committee on the Rights of the Child observes:

> Ten million children die each year as a result of curable diseases and malnourishment. More than one hundred million children are today deprived of primary education. Almost as many are exploited in harmful jobs. Hundreds and thousands of girls and boys are abused in prostitution. A growing number of children have been infected by HIV. Many children are victimised by war – as soldiers or as part of a terrorised civilian population. Ten million children are refugees inside or outside their own country. Millions of disabled children are forgotten or discriminated against. Children are suffering physical violence in their own homes in most of the world. (Hammarberg 1993, p.302)

To set out to improve the quality of life of the world's children is, as we all acknowledge, a major long-term undertaking. It is a common mistake amongst the uninitiated to think of the Convention on the Rights of the Child as only applicable to countries in the Third World. Gerison Lansdown in Chapter 6 rapidly disabuses us of that notion by outlining how far short of its commitment to the implementation of children's rights the United Kingdom has come since it ratified the Convention in December 1991. The United States has been amongst a handful of countries to sign the Convention only very recently. It has, however, *signed* the Convention – which is the very first stage at which a country starts enquiries as to whether the Convention is compatible with national legislation. When such enquiries have been satisfied the next stage is ratification. It seems unlikely, given the huge opposition to the Convention within the United States, that ratification will be speedy. Bernardine Dohrn (1993) observes that the implementation of the Convention in the United States could dramatically improve the lives of children there. She points out that the Convention requires a standard of health care that 'would put Chicago to shame' in that in Chicago children are more likely to die in the first year of life than in 18 other countries. African-American babies there suffer an infant mortality rate which is higher than in 33 other nations (Children's Defence Fund 1991). Providing for children, however, is not just about minimal resources. As we have already intimated, it includes rights to a certain quality of life. Whilst Cynthia

Price Cohen (1995) summarises in disturbing detail the shortcomings of the United States as one industrialised country which fails to provide for its children, Bernardine Dohrn illustrates, by reference to specific examples, that this shortfall in provision does not only relate to the basic necessities of life but is also evidenced in the way that children are treated, which is in contravention of some of the provisions of the Convention. Article 37 states: 'Accused children have the right to be treated with dignity, presumed innocent until proven guilty in a prompt and fair trial, and detained separately from adults... Alternatives to institutional care shall be made available'. The separation of adult and child prisoners has been one of the aspects of the Convention that the United Kingdom has exempted from its ratification. Dohrn indicates that Chicago's juvenile jail incarcerates the largest population of children under one roof in the United States, and perhaps the world, its intake having increased by 50 per cent in seven years:

> Every day, children, overwhelmingly African-American children, are brought downstairs from the jail to the court chained to each other in long lines, paraded past other children who are in court as victims of violence or neglect, in a scene of humiliation and degradation reminiscent of slavery chain gangs. Does transporting Chicago's children to court in chains presume innocence? Does it promote dignity? (Dohrn 1993, p.29)

Recent reports by the Children's Defence Fund: *America's Children Falling Behind: The USA and the Convention on the Rights of the Child* (CDF 1992) and the American Bar Association Survey: *America's Children at Risk* (ABA 1993) which add to the disquieting picture of the lives of children in one of the World's largest industrialised countries, were, in evaluating the situation, primarily concerned with the child's material well-being and quality of life and not with the child's right to be recognised as a person. Price Cohen draws our attention to the two-fold significance of this. In 1959, the UN Declaration of the Rights of the Child stressed the needs of the child for care and support. This uses the traditional view which does not incorporate the newer perspectives of self-advocacy. Second, she claims, the American view of rights can 'best be described as claims by citizens for protection from undue interference by the State rather than claims for services or benefits'. She explains this fragmented picture by reference to two influences: one being the fact that the USA has no overall children's policy and the second being that the tendency is for America to define its laws through litigation. This situation is also true in the case of rights which are only finally upheld by reference to definitive judicial decisions. As the subject of children's rights is relatively new this will take some time. So the Convention, as it concerns the quality of life of the child, does not relate only to children in Third World countries. Children's needs, it seems, are not necessarily met regardless of the state of development of the country in which they live. Let us consider further the relationship between needs and rights.

NEEDS AND RIGHTS

The relationship between children's needs and their rights is by no means straightforward. As we have seen in the United States, the traditional view of rights has been on 'rights from' rather than on 'rights to'. Colin Wringe, in Chapter One, introduces a philosopher's reminder of the importance of approaching the fabric of the child's welfare rights with a clear understanding of what, theoretically and conceptually, is involved in such considerations. He points out that, as in the United States, rights are often approached from the point of view of abuses or violations of rights, i.e. from the point of view of wrongs rather than rights. Philosophers, he claims, have to confront the issue of *what ought to be* and 'more particularly whether something ought to be because it is a right, which should be implemented in the here and now, or whether it is desirable for some other reason and may therefore take its turn amongst our other priorities'. He sees amongst the three broad elements of the UN Convention – rights to freedom, rights of protection and the rights to have certain basic needs met – a useful division as he argues that the justification of a right depends on the kind of right it is. He goes on, somewhat alarmingly, to point out that although one might justify children's welfare rights in terms of children's vulnerability and inability to fend for themselves – which means that this category of rights is of particular importance to them, while rights to a standard of living to ensure proper development, and rights to education apply to the conditions of youth and childhood specifically – the philosophical problem arises from the fact that need, even extreme need, has not traditionally been regarded as sufficient to justify a right. This piece shakes many of our preconceptions about what a child's rights in the area of resource allocation should be. It makes us think about how we justify such rights. Roche, in Chapter Two, explores some of the arguments from a lawyers point of view. For example, that children's needs are not necessarily well met by the divisive language of rights.

THE 'BEST INTERESTS' PRINCIPLE

The relationship between quality of life issues and the status of the child are in some senses paradoxical. Whilst Article Four of the Convention lays bare the need to prioritise children it also stresses that children are to be seen as equals in that it gives children and teenagers the status of human beings with full rights, giving them the same value as adults. The fact that they are valued and that childhood itself has a value, independent of it as an apprenticeship period to the adult world, is underscored by the rights, for example, to play, embodied in the Convention (and taken up in this Volume in Chapter Twelve by Viv

Hogan). The acknowledgement of the child's equal status, yet at the same time their vulnerability and need for protection particularly whilst young, is in some sense reconciled in the Convention by the principle clearly formulated in Article 3.1. of the Convention. 'In all actions concerning children, whether undertaken by public or private social welfare institutions, courts of law, administrative authorities or legislative bodies, the best interests of the child shall be a primary consideration.'

This is one of the central themes running through the Convention which relates to the nature of the provision and treatment of children and has come to be known as the 'best interests principle'. At first glance this seems relatively straightforward but contained within this are a number of complex assumptions about the relationship between culture and human rights, about the universality of the child's 'best interests' — what constitutes 'best' — and who decides. As John Eekelaar and Robert Dingwall (1994) point out:

> The relationship between the principle that proclaims the best interests of the child as a guide (of varying degrees of force) for actions and decisions regarding children and the idea that children have rights is by no means straightforward. For example, some might see the principle as antithetical to the concept of children's right; others might see it as being complementary to such rights; some might regard the principle as so conditioned by cultural relativism as to be completely vacuous. (p.i)

This may be the case, but a reading of the United Nations Convention on the Rights of the Child makes it clear that this principle holds a very important place in that Convention. In Volume One, the voice of the child in matters that concerned him/her was a primary focus with Articles 12 and 13 forming the co-ordinating framework. Here, when attention is turned to the best interests principle as a primary consideration in providing for children, it is rare to find the voice of the child in the debates surrounding what those interests are. In Chapter Two, Jeremy Roche explores, within the context of particular developments within the legal system of the United Kingdom, the child's right to decide. This sophisticated analysis of the relationship between the agent/agencies who decide what is best for the child and the child's welfare is contrasted with simpler, more straightforward approaches to consulting children later in the book (Chapters Eleven and Twelve). Consulting children about what their interests are can also be undertaken in ways which illustrate the patriarchal approach (as in the 'Just a tick method') to involving children in decisions about the curriculum or in rather more detailed attempts, as in Chapter Twelve, to get at what children's views are and involve them far more substantially in the decision making process in an area where children clearly know best, that is, about their play needs. The best interests principle, however, goes beyond finding ways of establishing what children's views are about various aspects of their quality of life.

The complex nature of the best interest principle that threads its way through the Convention has been analysed by Philip Alston (1994) in a seminal paper which focuses on the broad relationship between culture and human rights. This is a relationship that is illustrated and explored in this collection with chapters from Latin America, Eastern Europe, Africa and the UK – demonstrating, in some ways, resonances that underscore the aspiration for a universality of human rights standards and at the same time look to the local dimensions of the influence of culture. The Convention, because of its aim of universal ratification and universally applicable standards, has been highly important in focusing the debate as to whether human rights norms are capable of this sort of transcultural generality or whether they are inevitably relative to each individual society. The sophisticated diplomacy that has surrounded the Convention in high places, however, has meant that much of the debate has been abstract and highly generalised. It is important to look at specific examples in order to really grasp the implications of its provisions and nowhere is this more important than in the case of illustrations of various aspects of the 'best interests' principle. In Volume One the emphasis was on thinking globally and looking at local activities. Here too this is important. The counterpoint between the global dimension and the specific national activities provide a universal meaning and setting the national or local work in the broader context is a guard against a too narrow view of cultural relativism.

Since 1959, when the principle was first put forward in the Declaration of the Rights of the Child, it has been reflected in a variety of international instruments including the 1979 Convention on the Elimination of All Forms of Discrimination Against Women and the Declaration on Social and Legal Principles relating to the Protection and Welfare of Children with Special Reference to Foster Placement and Adoption Nationally and Internationally. There is evidence of a general acceptance of the principle – both in its specific terms and, more generally, in such forms as 'the paramount interest of the child' – provided by the frequency with which it has been used and referred to internationally in legal analyses. Although this general level of acceptance is important to note, it is worth underlining the very specific emphasis this term has been given when interpreted within the whole context and tenor of the UN Convention on the Rights of the Child. As first introduced in the Declaration of the Rights of the Child, the context within which it was used was one in which, unlike the Convention, the child is seen more as the object rather than the subject of rights. In addition, some of the other international instruments in which the principle occurs are primarily focused on the rights of others. The most important point of departure is that in the Convention it is made clear that the principle is not narrowly confined to the context of legal or administrative proceedings but 'in relation to *all* actions concerning children'.

Alston's analysis (1994) of Article 3.1 puts forward a number of aspects of this guiding principle in the Convention.

Complex and multidimensional

He points out that many people have falsely assumed that the Convention is a 'unidimensional document that reflects a single unified philosophy of children's rights and contains a specific readily ascertainable recipe for resolving the inevitable tensions and conflicts that arise in a given situation among the different rights recognized'. He points, in contrast, to the very multidimensional and complex nature of the Convention. In a similar vein there has been a misunderstanding as to the extent to which the relative and reciprocal rights of the various actors – child, parent, family, community, etc – are specified and defined. Chapter Seventeen, by Monica Cockett and John Tripp, explores some of the complex interplay of rights in relation to mediation work with children of divorcing parents. The principle of 'best interests of the child' is mentioned in a number of Articles of the Convention: in Article 9 with reference to the separation of the child from the family settings; in Article 18 with reference to parental responsibility for the upbringing and socialisation of the child; Articles 20 and 21 in relation to adoption and comparable practices; Articles 37 and 40 in the context of the child's involvement with the police and justice system. The complex and multidimensional aspects of the Convention are well amplified in the broad range of apparently disparate themes that are held together in this Volume around a concern with providing for children and having at the centre of that provision, their 'best interests'.

Commonalty

The origins of the principle were limited in terms of its roots in jurisprudence. Nevertheless, the principle, in general terms, has come to be recognised and acknowledged in providing for children by many legal systems and is mirrored in various ways in diverse cultural, religious and other traditions.

THE 'BEST INTERESTS OF THE CHILD' IN A CHANGING WORLD

Whilst the principle has come to be recognised by lawyers, professionals and service providers in the caring services throughout the world, its impact on policies and policy development has been questionable given that 'bigger' issues often cast a shadow over the child's welfare. Hammarberg (1993) – from a position of some considerable insight in lodging a case for a political awakening leading to increased political attention to children and young people which he feels is necessary if we are to change their actual circumstances – claims:

> Children have always been, and still are, the victims of hypocrisy.
> Politicians often pay lip service to the well-being of children, many of
> them are eager to be seen as child friendly. But in real terms when other
> interests come into the picture, children tend to be let down (p.296)

Hammarberg goes on to explain that he feels that this hypocrisy has developed
within a climate of the de-politicisation of children, which is based on the
mistaken belief that problems related to them are non-controversial and lie
outside the political agenda. If we look for a moment at the situation in Latin
America we see immediately that when it comes to resource allocation issues
then the best interests of the child *vis-à-vis* other interests are immediately
controversial and implicitly, if not explicitly, political. Chapter Three looks at
the situation in Uruguay. To fully understand the significance of this brief paper
it is worth stepping back and looking at issues relating to foreign aid which
have affected much of poverty stricken Latin America.

Chavarria, Director General of the Inter-American Children's Institute,
believes, for instance, that the already dreadful living conditions of many Latin
American children has been worsened by government policies adopted in
response to massive economic problems which have been the consequence of
carrying a huge foreign debt. Chavarria (1992) describes the impact of cuts in
public spending on the quality of care available to children living in extreme
poverty with child survival being a major problem in the region with infant
mortality reaching alarmingly high levels. Duron Segovia's (1993) work reinforces these concerns, demonstrating that structural adjustment can have an
adverse impact on children, as measured by various social indicators, and she
asks, on the basis of her very extensive research, whether issues such as child
care and infant malnutrition are sufficiently high on national agendas. She
explores whether the child's welfare is sufficiently high on the agendas
world-wide and the extent to which the financial policies adopted put children
further and further on the margins of society. She questions whether the fact
that millions of children are suffering from malnutrition and its consequences
and millions more are dying is even an issue for the International Monetary
Fund and the leaders who are pre-occupied with a country's external debt. In
Chapter Three, Juan Petit argues for a greater degree of community participation and integration in the social structures in the move towards family
empowerment and from this he argues for a realistic and operational menu for
children's policies. His chapter contextualises within the rapid changes that have
taken place in his country what needs to be put in place so that the best interests
of the child can be recognised and eventually provided for.

Turning from Latin America to Eastern Europe we see some of the consequences of the collapse of totalitarian regimes from the inside in Jana Ondráck-
ová's account (Chapter Four) and in terms of foreign aid and intervention in
Margaret Ralph's (Chapter Ten). Eastern Europe and the Cold War played a
very significant part in shaping the UN Convention on the Rights of the Child

and indeed contributed much, by way of example, to the debate on cultural relativism. Alston (1994), in his fascinating account of the politics that lay behind the drafting of the Convention itself, points out that this debate was initially overshadowed, if not silenced, by an ideologically dominated East-West dispute as to whether civil and political rights should be accorded priority over social, economic and cultural rights or the other way around. The UN itself has always insisted that these are of equal importance. The development of an independent stance by Third World nations – who might well have argued that many of the rights, or indeed, the very notion of human rights, were Euro-centric – was deflected by pressure to side with either East or West. One of the results of the ending of the Cold War has, therefore, been the re-opening of the cultural relativism debate, that is the extent to which the situation of children and their entitlements can only be understood and evaluated within their own national context.

The Cold War, furthermore, affected, in significant ways, the drafting and the adoption of the Convention. The submission by Poland in 1978 of the original draft of the UN Convention to the UN Commission on Human Rights in preparation for the 1979 International Year of the Child 'constituted a quintessentially political gesture...the Polish Government was probably motivated more by a desire to seize at least some of the human rights initiatives of Jimmy Carter. The rights of the child seemed to be the ideal topic for this purpose, not only because of a long association between Poland and the promotion of the concept at the international level, but more importantly because it was assumed that such a convention could justifiably be confined to the economic, social and cultural rights to which Communist countries wanted to accord priority' (Alston 1993, p.6). Initially the West played down the significance of this initiative and tried to drag out the process of drafting although it became apparent by the mid 1980s that significant levels of support were building up for the draft Convention such that it was likely to be adopted. The response of the Reagan administration to this was to press for the inclusion of the sort of civil and political rights that it accused Communist countries of trying to deny or minimise. Essentially this was a manoeuvre aimed to try to make the document lose support from the original sponsor, Poland and her allies. Alston believes that, by chance, a number of factors played a significant part at this point which meant that this ploy did not work. The most significant factor was the beginning of the end of the Cold war coupled with the encouragement by UNICEF, which by 1986 had begun to play an active role in the drafting process, in encouraging and facilitating the active participation of developing countries. This latter development not only extended the raft of support but ensured the acceptability of the Convention to many of those countries, thus gaining much more widespread acceptability. The replacement of Ronald Regan in 1989 removed the possibility of any further delays or obstacles in the final stages of the drafting and, at about this time, former

Communist countries were anxious to demonstrate their new commitments to comprehensive and international human rights norms. The result of this history is that the Convention is claimed to be more sensitive to different approaches and perspectives than most of the human rights treaties which preceded it. There have been attacks on human rights norms by the cultural relativists and there will continue to be. The extent to which, given its particular history, the Convention on the Rights of the Child will stand up to such attacks rather more robustly and the role the best interests principle will play in this will be interesting to monitor.

The chapters by Jana Ondráčková and Margaret Ralph need to be read with this particular history and its legacy in mind. The uneasy transitions from traditional perceptions of children, particularly underprivileged or minority children, to a sense of equal rights and appropriate provision is slow on the ground even for such countries which have ratified the Convention and old habits and traditional thinking die hard and the new learning is slow and often reluctant.

Developing countries, as was indicated above, were brought into the final stages of the development of the Convention and many have enthusiastically embraced it. Rapid transformations were witnessed in Eastern Europe. Africa has also experienced a period of upheavals related to independence from colonial rule. The majority of African countries embarked upon policies of mass primary and secondary education. In Zimbabwe, for example, Fay Chung, the Minister of Primary and Secondary Education, reports (Chung 1993) that only one-third of school age children were able to attend primary school before independence. By 1993 there was virtually a 100 per cent entry, although only 4 per cent of the age group were able to enjoy the privilege of secondary education. By 1993, 42 per cent of the girls and 49 per cent of the boys reached secondary school. Alan Peacock, in Chapter Eight, discusses, in the case of teaching of science in rural Africa, the influence of post-colonial pressures and goals; the most important of which, for education, was providing the kind of education they had been denied by colonial powers (i.e. universal primary education, formal, academic, geared to certification) accompanied by a need for a rapid increase in 'high-level manpower' with technical skills to implement development plans. He explains how these pressures often worked in conflict and the tensions existing between different perceptions of science varying from highly traditional models to Anglo-American models and un-revised pre-inde-pendence models of the subject area itself and teaching methods. In relation to the 'best interests' principle, he addresses the importance of the cultural relevance of the education the child receives. In some senses it is true that the world is becoming increasingly smaller and more interconnected with events in one part of the world affecting that of another very rapidly. Fay Chung (1993) points out that it is also true that small ethnic and cultural groups are increasingly feeling the need to express their cultural and historical individualism:

> Without the advantages of universal knowledge and skills, particularly in science and technology, a nation or an individual is doomed to servitude. On the other hand, without cultural specificity, education can become an alienating force removing the educated elite from their roots, thus ruling out any possible contribution they might have been able to make in the transformation of their societies. Education must, therefore, be firmly based on the historical culture as well as future aspirations of the people. It must take into account the present stage of world knowledge but must be able to apply such knowledge to the actual situation of their lives. Knowledge must be relevant. Knowledge must bring palpable improvement to people's lives. (p.35)

This sentiment resonates through a number of chapters dealing, in a variety of ways, with education inside and outside Africa. Andrew Hannan's emphasis on equality of opportunity in a multiracial society in the United Kingdom (Chapter Seven), Cathie Holden looking at the development of the new Europeans (Chapter Nine), Niki Davis examining the relationship between children's education and the changing technological culture world wide (Chapter Fourteen) and Rhys Griffiths looking at the development of the world citizen through the lenses of the nature of power relationships in the educational process (Chapter Eighteen).

Looking at development in Africa and the significance of those developments in alerting us to the importance of cultural relativity, particularly in relation to education, has not been the only influence on our thinking about the best interests of the child that has been focused by what has happened in countries in the Third World. In the early 1960s it was becoming evident to people concerned about poverty in the Third World, including UNICEF, that the beginning of a process of massive urbanisation of unprecedented proportions was under way. Two decades later, we find that two-thirds of the world's urban population is now concentrated in developing countries and by the year 2000, the developing world's urban population will be twice its 1980 level, and possibly triple by 2010 (Donohue 1982). Urban poverty, with all its attendant problems, has had to be focused by various child support agencies in the developing world. In Chapter Five, Munene Kahiro outlines how the Child Welfare Society of Kenya has been a leading force in advocating and promoting the UN Convention on the Rights of the Child and, in particular, in relation to children infected with the HIV virus. He explains how, with the influence of western civilisation, most of the customs which held extended families and communities together have eroded. The work of the Child Welfare Society of Kenya in co-ordinating the setting up of the National Alliance for Advocacy on Children's Rights (NAACR) is outlined. It is worth comparing the work of this Alliance, in terms of its plans to publicise the Convention and the activities it has undertaken and the support that has been received, with the work and situation of the Children's Rights Development Unit in the United Kingdom which is described by Gerison Lansown in Chapter Six.

Supporting children and ensuring their best interests are protected in the UK has been undertaken on the ground by Children's Rights Officers. Rosemary Rae has examined, through her research, the effectiveness of such an approach to protecting the child's rights. In Chapter Fifteen, she illustrates how very important it is that when we do provide for the children in our charge, we also monitor how well we are doing and examine critically where experience falls short of our aims. Support for children in very troubled areas of the world sometimes has to be provided in particularly harrowing and sometimes compromising situations. Michael Singer (Chapter Sixteen) illustrates, through a composite case history, the complexity of the 'best interests' principle as it relates to child refugees seeking not only political asylum but a 'voice' in the process.

In complete contrast, both Bob Snowden and Niki Davis deal with issues that are part of an industrialised and highly developed world. In Chapter Thirteen, Bob Snowden deals with all the complex issues surrounding the child's rights in relation to new forms of reproductive technologies. He looks at the 'best interests' theme from the point of view of the child's right to know about his or her parentage and all the moral, ethical and practical difficulties and dilemmas this entails. In Chapter Fouteen, Niki Davis briefly describes the increasing range of electronic communication available today with examples of applications in education. She demonstrates the benefits of communication across countries, regardless of time and distance, which enable individual children to link with others. They can share geographical, cultural and commercial differences with the curiosity common to children. New technology can extend access for those with special educational needs without making their difference apparent. She describes the curriculum development to support the new learning styles, professional development of teachers and increased research in the classroom. Not only is post modern society changing by the introduction of new technologies, but also demographic data reveals the strain that many societies are under if divorce statistics are any indicator. Monica Cockett and John Tripp report, in Chapter Seventeen, on their work of supporting children through the mediation process in divorce, focusing the child's best interests in helping parents to think constructively about parenting issues in newly restructured lives.

In looking at children in a changing world, in the context of a new emphasis on their rights to a decent quality of life and a certain degree of self determination, we complete our 'tour' by looking again at the nature of the education provided in the United Kingdom; considering the process of education as being the means by which the child learns about power relations and, most importantly, their own power in a changing world. Education is supposed to be, according to the rhetoric of many a school prospectus, a process in which children are empowered but is it? Roger Hart (1992) suggested that whilst schools seem the obvious places few of them, in his international researches, show any evidence of democratic participation. Jeffs (1995) argues that, following the example of some Australian federal education programmes, state funding for education in the UK should be linked to the establishment of administrative structures that guarantee the rights of parents, teachers and young people to make a full contribution to the management of their schools. This issue is taken up in Chapter Eighteen by Rhys Griffith. How do children become powerful agents in their own society? How can the balance be struck between rights and responsibilities? To what extent do children really enjoy equality of opportunity? Rhys Griffith reminds us that maybe, in serving the 'best interests' of the child, the one resource that we should share with the child throughout the educational process is that fundamental to any society – that of power.

REFERENCES

Alston, P. (1994) 'Reconciliation of culture and human rights.' In J. Eekelaar and R. Dingwall (eds) *The Best Interests of the Child. Special Issue of the International Journal of Law and the Family, 8.* Oxford: Oxford University Press.

American Bar Association (1993) *America's Children at Risk.* Washington DC: American Bar Association.

Chavarria, E.M.Z. (1992) 'The rights of children in democratic societies.' In M.D. Fortuyn and M.de Langen (eds) *Towards the Realisation of the Human Rights of Children: Lectures given at the Second International Conference on Children's Ombudswork.* Netherlands: Children's Ombudswork Foundation and Defence for Children International.

Children's Defence Fund (1991) *Leave No Child Behind.* Washington, DC: Children's Defence Fund Report.

Children's Defence Fund (1992) *America's Children Falling Behind: The USA and the Convention on the Rights of the Child.* Washington DC: Children's Defence Fund.

Chung, F. (1993) 'Education in a changing society.' In K. Ekberg and P.E. Mjaavatn (eds) *Children at Risk: Selected Papers.* Trondheim: Norwegian Centre for Child Research.

Cohen, C.P.(1995) 'Children's Rights: an American Perspective.' In B. Franklin (ed) *The Handbook of Children's Rights; Comparative Policy and Practice.* London: Routledge.

Dohrn, B. (1993) 'Leastwise of the land: Children and the Law.' In K. Ekberg and P.E. Mjaavatn (eds) *Children at Risk: Selected Papers.* Trondheim: Norwegian Centre for Child Research.

Donohue, J. (1994) 'Facts and figures on urbanization in the developing world.'
    Assignment Children, nos 57/58. Quoted in Cristina Szanton Blanc (ed) (1994)
    Urban Children in Distress. Reading: Gordon and Breach and UNICEF.

Duron Segovia, M. de. J. (1993) Sindrome de maltrado social del menor en los paises
    deudores deAmerica Latina (Syndrome of the social maltreatment of minors in the
    indebted countries of Latin America). *Revista de la Universidad del Valle de Atemajac,
    Guadalarajara, Issue 19,* April-July 1993. Summarised in Structural Adjustment,
    Modernisation and Children. *Bernard Van Leer Foundation Newsletter, No 74,* April
    1994, The Hague.

Eekelaar, J. and Dingwall, R. (eds) (1994) *The Best Interests of the Child. Special Issue of
    the International Journal of Law and the Family, 8.* Oxford: Oxford University Press.

Hammarberg, T. (1993) 'The rights of the child and the industrialised countries.' In
    K. Ekberg and P.E. Mjaavatn (eds) *Children at Risk: Selected Papers.* Trondheim:
    Norwegian Centre for Child Research.

Hart, R. (1992) *Children's Participation: from Tokenism to Citizenship. Innocenti Essays. No.
    4.* Florence: UNICEF International Child Development Centre.

Jeffs, T. (1995) 'Children's educational rights in a new ERA?' In B. Franklin (ed) *The
    Handbook of Children's Rights; Comparative Policy and Practice.* London: Routledge.

PART TWO

Providing a Conceptual Framework

CHAPTER ONE

Children's Welfare Rights
A Philosopher's View

Colin Wringe

A common complaint of philosophers is that discussions of the rights of children or other classes of oppressed beings tend not to be about rights at all but about wrongs, that is about abuses of rights. These may include harrowing descriptions of how children are constrained and oppressed, humiliated or hurt or not given the things they desperately need for their bare survival, health or well-being. Little, however, is said about the rights which these actions or deprivations actually infringe. The reason for this is that many of those working in the field of rights belong to the empirical disciplines of the social sciences and are concerned with what is rather than what ought to be, or are actively involved in working for children and are therefore more interested in practicalities than in the niceties of justification. Philosophers, however, must confront the issue of what ought to be and more particularly whether something ought to be because it is a right, which should be implemented here and now, or whether it is desirable for some other reason and may therefore take its turn among our other priorities.

If we look at the 1989 Convention on Children's Rights, or any other twentieth century statement of rights, we see that the rights claimed do indeed correspond to the three categories of abuses or wrongs mentioned above. There are rights to do the things one wants to do without unreasonable constraint (rights of freedom), rights not to be hurt or injured (rights of protection), and rights to have certain basic needs met (welfare rights).

It is useful to divide rights up in this way because the justification of a right depends on the kind of right it is. This is important because those who oppose rights claims often demand an inappropriate form of justification which, in the nature of the case, cannot be provided. Thus, in the past, it was sometimes asked whether children were sufficiently rational to possess rights. The question of rationality, however, is only relevant in the case of rights of freedom in so far as a right of freedom may be useless or positively dangerous if we do not have the capacity to use it wisely. Alternatively, it may be asked what children, or the poor, or the sick, have done to deserve any rights. But desert is only relevant to transactional rights like rights to have promises kept, benefits repaid or services rewarded. These are quite different from the general or universal rights mentioned in the Convention on Children's Rights or other rights declarations.

The first two categories of rights mentioned above may be fairly easily accounted for in terms of traditional doctrines of Natural Rights. According to that tradition, individuals enter the world without obvious grounds of subordination one to another (Locke 1690, p.298). We are at least born equal, even though we may very soon find ourselves in chains (Rousseau 1762, p.3). No one denies that differences of gender, race, strength, place and order of birth and so on are real enough in their way, but they do nothing to justify domination or excuse injury. It was sometimes argued (Mill 1859, p.73) that children and primitive peoples could not possess rights of the first category (rights of freedom) because they lacked rationality and, therefore, the ability to make choices for themselves. This failing, however, was frequently exaggerated and was, no doubt, often little more than an excuse for adult over-protectiveness or imperialist exploitation.

The third category of rights claims in various declarations and charters (welfare rights) is somewhat more problematic, for these are not rights to be let alone (justified by the absence of any grounds for interfering with people), but rights to receive the necessities of an acceptable life from others when people are not able to produce or obtain them for themselves. In the Convention on Children's Rights these are mentioned in Article 6, the right to sustenance, Article 24, the right to health care, Article 26, the right to social security, Article 27, the right to a sufficient standard of living adequate for physical, mental, moral and social development and Articles 28 and 29, rights to education.

Unlike rights of freedom, but similar to rights of protection, welfare rights may not be denied on the grounds that some children are not yet fully rational beings, for we do not need to be rational to suffer if we are harmed or do not have the things we need. Children's vulnerability and inability to fend for themselves mean that this category of rights is of particular importance to them, while rights to a standard of living adequate to ensure proper development and rights to education apply to the conditions of youth and childhood specifically.

The philosophical problem arises from the fact that need, even extreme need, has not traditionally been regarded as sufficient to justify a right however much pictures of sick, starving or unsocialised children may clutch at our heart-strings or appeal to our feelings of human kindness. Any obligation to respond to the needs of others is held by many liberal philosophers, as well as by right-wing politicians, to be a so-called duty of imperfect obligation to be attended to as time, resources and other commitments allow, rather than one of perfect obligation, calling for immediate implementation.

We could, of course, accept that Articles 6, 24 and 26–29 of the Convention, unlike the other articles, do not refer to rights at all but are simply appeals to our charity or attempts to persuade governments to enshrine them in their legislations and thus create legal rights. That would be to admit that these articles do not at present refer to rights at all but rather to pious hopes. We are not, however, obliged to accept this position. The alternative requires us to look at a further category of rights, not mentioned so far, namely property rights, for the controversy about welfare rights is essentially a controversy about the rights governing property and its distribution.

Philosophers of the Enlightenment such as Locke (1690, p.329) appear to be against those seeking to justify welfare rights when they argue that rights of property are created by mixing our labour with previously unowned objects taken from the state of nature. Sick or starving children are in no position to mix their labour with anything. As for the destitute generally, their problem is that they have no access to things in the state of nature to mix their labour with. The resources of nature, land and materials have already been claimed as property by others who either will not allow them access at all – this, essentially, is what immigration laws are all about – or will only do so on the condition that most or all of what is produced belongs to the owners of the resources or the means by which they are transformed into something useful, rather than to those who contribute their labour.

More recently, Robert Nozick (1974, pp.150–3), whose *Anarchy, State and Utopia* may be regarded as the most emphatic and detailed statement of the case against welfare rights, recognises only three ways in which the right of access to resources may be gained:

- just acquisition by mingling one's labour with objects taken from a state of nature
- just transfer as a result, for example, of voluntary gift sale or legacy
- compensation for previous injustices.

The right to a share in the world's resources on grounds of need is specifically ruled out and Nozick recognises that the effect of his three modes of just acquisition may well leave some individuals with no right of access to any of the world's resources. Such individuals would presumably be unable to survive except by the grace and favour of others, which those others would have a perfect right to withhold if they so chose.

This appalling conclusion would imply that our established laws, rights and conventions relating to property are a kind of absolute, rather than a natural consequence of the fact that human beings, having entered the world in a state of non-subordination to each other, are obliged to come to certain agreements among themselves in order to make life tolerable. If we enter the world without obligation to others, there is no reason why we should accept the laws, rights and conventions already existing in the world we enter, unless there is at least some minimal advantage to us in doing so. In the contractarian tradition, to which talk of rights naturally belongs, our primitive liberty is traded for the advantages of society, and this is the justification for requiring individuals to obey the law.

For this justification to be valid, the individual must at least gain some benefit from his or her membership of society. Those who die of starvation, easily preventable disease or exposure, or are so lacking in minimal education and socialisation that they grow up no better than brutes or someone else's slave labour, beasts of burden or stengun fodder gain nothing from their membership of society. In their case, the obligation to obey the law does not apply. In other words, minimal welfare rights and protection from gross harms of the kind described above is the condition of our obligation to obey the law and respect the rights of others.

This conclusion will be a cause of indignation and accusations of irresponsibility by some, since it seems to imply that if those who have little to gain from society engage in violence, looting, pillage and arson in certain inner cities, then good bourgeois property owners like ourselves are in no moral position to complain or say that there is no excuse for these things. There is, in fact, every excuse, for those who have nothing to gain from society do only what is their right. They are under no obligation to obey society's rules for they are not members of society at all but literally at war with it in the struggle for survival, for it is society's rules that forbid them access to what they need to survive.

Needless to say, my purpose is not to foment violence on the streets, but to show that the Natural Rights tradition which underlies widely recognised rights of freedom and protection, may also be shown to justify the welfare rights of both adults and children who, for whatever reason, are unable to make minimum provision for themselves. Put briefly, if there are any rights at all, then there are also welfare rights, so that those rights claimed in articles 6, 24 and 26–29 of the 1989 Convention on Children's Rights are not mere appeals to charity but are entitled to the same urgency of implementation as those others which claim protection from oppression and abuse.

REFERENCES

Locke, J. (1690) 'Two treatises of government.' In P. Laslett (ed) Cambridge: Cambridge University Press, 1960.

Mill, J.S. (1859) 'On liberty.' In A.D. Lindsay (ed) *Utilitarianism, Liberty, Representative Government*. London: Dent, 1910.

Nozick. R. (1974) *Anarchy, State and Utopia*. Oxford: Blackwells.

Rousseau, J.J. (1762) 'The social contract.' In G.D.H. Cole (ed) *The Social Contract and Discourses*. London: Dent, 1913.

CHAPTER TWO

Children's Rights

A Lawyer's View

Jeremy Roche

INTRODUCTION

The past fifteen years have witnessed significant changes in the debates surrounding childhood. Numerous legal and organisational initiatives reflect a transformed politics of childhood (as seen in the setting up of the Children's Legal Centre, Childline, the Children Act 1989 and the UK government's ratification of the UN Convention on the Rights of the Child). At the same time it has been argued that the increased role of law in matters affecting children works to their disadvantage – children's needs are not met by the divisive language of rights and the increased possibility of recourse to the law. (King and Trowell 1992) This can be seen as part of a general critique of rights with an added emphasis on the inappropriateness of law's formality for dealing with children's issues.

Other commentators, albeit in a different context, have seen struggles for rights as being of critical value to those on the margins of society, for example, women and people of colour, as part of a strategy of meaningful inclusion rather than exclusion (Minow 1987; Williams 1991). In summary, their argument is that the reality of the distribution of social power results in the law and legal processes having potentially very different meanings for people, and for some, law's formality is its most valuable asset.

Here, I argue that children can also be seen as 'on the margin' and that their struggles for rights are important in that they require us to reflect on, and argue over, where we are and how we want to be in the future. Within such struggles, the child's right to participate in decisions that affect his or her own life is central; it is only through respect for children and their perspectives that a real community of interests, which includes all those who live within it, can come into being. This is not a case of our agreeing a new rights agenda but of our sharing a commitment to taking all children seriously and as seeing them as citizens too.

WHY RIGHTS ARE IMPORTANT

It might seem strange to argue that children, who loom so large in the private lives of parents, over whom bitter legal battles are fought and who constitute a very significant proportion of the population, can be properly described as being on the margin. Their marginality derives from the denial of their subjectivity (see James and Prout 1990 and Stainton Rogers 1992). It is their relative lack of power, typically expressed via 'their right to be protected' from others and themselves, that excludes them from public dialogue and renders them marginal to important decisions, public as well as private, in our society.

In liberal social theory the emphasis has been on the necessity and value of a sphere of privacy. This is a central image of liberal society – that there is and ought to be a place where one is free of public power as long as one is not harming others. J.S. Mill argued this as a principle of good government and his influence can be heard in modern debates about law and the family constructed in terms of family privacy versus state power.

This idea that children are best looked after in their own families is one of the central propositions of the Children Act 1989. The political objection to burgeoning state power often links with a welfare based one – children can suffer more, not less, as the result of any legal intervention. Yet while there is much to support such a position, for example recent scandals surrounding the residential care system such as 'Pindown' and the Beck trial, such an argument tends to minimise the damage that can be done to children in the home. What is not addressed is the idea that there might be a multiplicity of interests in the family and that victory for the family might mean defeat for the children. (Freeman 1983a). Law's silence did not, and does not, mean an absence of power. Law for sure is an expression of public power but it does not have a monopoly on power in society. The silence of law meant, and means, the absence of a mechanism to challenge private power.

For many women and children the silence of the law on domestic relations meant subjection to the power and violence of fathers and husbands. Part of the story of progress in this century has been that of law's incursion into the family. This is not a romantic tale of betterment but, nonetheless, significant changes have occurred. Law, and struggles around law, have, from time to time, been central to this process: it has been a mechanism for raising public consciousness and for conducting a public conversation for change. Feminists and others have argued to fill the silences, to tell the stories so that the quiet, undisturbed exercise of patriarchal power is brought to an end. In relation to children the argument is not so much that 'their historical moment has come' rather that once we refuse to relate to the child simply as an object, certain consequences flow. Writing of children's rights the Stainton Rogers (1992) observe: 'It is not just a plea that they should be seen as persons, that their voice should be heard but an assertion of their own self-constructive powers of personhood (that they are persons)...the child cannot be constructed as a commodity, the object of policy...' (p.84).

Those without the privilege of economic wealth and power have only words and bodies with which to resist power's claims. The language of rights and democracy may be the only resource many have. Rights and the idea of citizenship have the potential to be levellers: they have the 'promise' of restraining the powerful. So my concern with those who reject the language of rights is not one simply of analytical disagreement but of practical consequences. Patricia Williams (1991) writes: 'For the historically disempowered, the conferring of rights is symbolic of all the denied aspects of their humanity: rights imply a respect that places one in the referential range of self and others, that elevates one's status from human body to social being' (p.153).

The language of rights, in the context of Europe and North America, has been a central mechanism of social communication and solidarity since the Enlightenment. It is arguable that as a critical public language it does not 'belong' to any one group or class, nor does it express a unified world view. Rather the language of rights is the constantly contested language whereby private and public experiences and interests are exchanged. Bowles and Gintis (1986) write: 'In society meanings are not fixed, they are prizes in a pitched conflict among groups attempting to constitute their social identity by transforming the communicative tools that link their members together and set them apart from others.' (p.157)

The language of rights is only one mechanism which permits the constitution of community. It is not the only one nor will it flourish outside of other developments, for example in the case of children's rights the activities of a range of organisations committed to promoting the interests of different children may dictate the direction and pace of change, but it is an essential part of the process.

CHILDREN'S RIGHTS

Given the above defence of the value of rights, is there anything about the issue of children's rights which requires special argument or justification? Freeman recommended that a distinction be made between adolescents and younger children, and major and minor decisions (Freeman 1983b). In this he anticipated the judgment of Lord Scarman in Gillick v West Norfolk and Wisbech Area Health Authority [1986] A.C. 112, where he refers to the 'mature minor' being able to make his or her own decision depending on their understanding of the particular question at issue.

More recently Freeman (1992) has commented: 'The passing of laws, the implementation of conventions, is only a beginning... The importance of legislation as a symbol cannot be underestimated, but the true recognition of children's rights requires implementation in practice' (p.60).

Children's rights, if they are to be socially meaningful, require not just a shift in values and social organisation but resources and a clear allocation of responsibility for their delivery. Today emphasis is placed on rethinking the contexts in which issues of children's rights arise and on the key attitudinal changes on the part of adults and professionals that any further progress on the children's rights front requires. This change indicates that, in part, the early arguments have been successful, for example children can no longer be beaten lawfully in state schools, they are entitled to legal representation in proceedings under the Children Act 1989 and their 'wishes and feelings' must be taken into account in a wide range of decision-making contexts. The issue now is not one of establishing the principle of children's rights but of extending the range of situations where the language is perceived as legitimate, for example the operation of local authority social services departments have to take cognizance of this language, education authorities do not.

Here the breadth of the U.N. Convention on the Rights of the Child is valuable. It provides, leaving aside the reservations entered by the UK govern-ment, a useful yardstick by which progress on the condition of childhood in the UK can be measured. While such an audit might not make pleasant reading (see Bradshaw 1990; Children's Rights Development Unit 1994) it will provide a basis for considering the impact of public policy and legislation on different childhoods. In Article 12 the Convention provides a key right which promises a more turbulent future. Article 12 states: 'State parties shall assure to the child who is capable of forming his or her own views the right to express those views freely in all matters affecting the child, the views of the child being given due weight in accordance with the age and maturity of the child'.

Gerison Lansdown (1992) comments on article 12:

> Consulting with children means more than just asking them what they think. It means ensuring that they have adequate information appropriate to their age with which to form opinions. It means being provided with meaningful opportunities to express their views and explore options open to them and it means having those views listened to, respected and considered seriously. (p.4)

This opens up the prospect of radically different ways of relating to children, disturbing some patterns of adult-child relations and particular visions of community at the same time as raising new images of inclusion.

THE CHILD'S RIGHT TO DECIDE?

If a child's stated preferences are going to be an issue, the question then arises 'at what stage in her development will her wishes be taken into account, and might they ever be determinative?' This appeared to have been settled by the judgment of the House of Lords in Gillick. A child or young person, so long as they satisfied Lord Scarman's 'mature minor' test, would be able to make their own decisions. Lord Scarman had held that the parents' right to consent to medical treatment on behalf of their child yielded 'to the child's right to make his own decisions when he reaches a sufficient understanding and intelligence to be capable of making up his own mind on the matter requiring decision'.

The case was heralded as a victory for children's rights. Certainly if the House of Lords had found in favour of Mrs Gillick things would have been very different: young people would have been denied access to information and services on contraception and thus would not have enjoyed the right to make decisions about their own bodies. Provisions contained in the Children Act 1989 also seemed to be within the spirit of the Gillick decision, for example section 43(8) which allows a child, if she is 'of sufficient understanding to make an informed decision', to refuse to submit to a medical or psychiatric examination or other assessment.

However, some commentators took a less optimistic view of the decision. Bainham (1986) argued:

> The ultimate decision on whether contraceptives are to be made available is one for the medical profession, applying the guidelines laid down by the House. From the child's point of view the effect is the substitution of one adult decision-maker (the doctor) in place of another (the parent). In this sense the decision is entirely consistent with the paternalistic and protectionist orientation of family law. (pp.273–4)

One might add that, from the child's point of view, this substitution could make a significant difference. However, recent legal developments seem to support Bainham's broad conclusion. First, in the case of Re R [1991] 3 W.L.R. 592, Lord Donaldson M.R. provided a new gloss on the Gillick decision. This case involved a 15-year-old girl in local authority care. She suffered periodically from bouts of mental illness characterised by violent and suicidal behaviour. The matter came before the High Court after she was admitted to an adolescent psychiatric unit which operated a programme of treatment involving the compulsory use of anti-psychotic drugs. The local authority consented to the proposed course of treatment on R's behalf. When R, in a lucid period, indicated that she would refuse such treatment the local authority withdrew its consent and began wardship proceedings, applying for leave to permit the unit to administer the proposed medication without R's consent. In the High Court, Waite J. granted the application finding that R was not 'Gillick competent' because of her mental condition and that the proposed course of treatment was in her best interests.

However, in the course of his judgment, Waite J. observed that if R had had sufficient understanding and intelligence to enable her to understand fully what was proposed and to be capable of making up her own mind on the matter (i.e. if she was 'Gillick competent'), the parents' right and the court's right yielded to the child's right to make her own decision. In this he was following a widely accepted reading of Lord Scarman's judgment in Gillick.

In the Court of Appeal, Lord Donaldson M.R. specifically rejected this line of reasoning. There are two distinct strands in his judgment. First, he observed that a 'right of determination was wider than a right to consent'. He argued:

> I do not understand Lord Scarman to be saying that, if a child was 'Gillick competent',...the parents ceased to have an independent right of consent as contrasted with ceasing to have a right of determination, that is, a veto. In a case in which the 'Gillick competent' child refuses treatment, but the parents consent, that consent enables treatment to be undertaken lawfully, but in no way determines that the child shall be so treated. (p.600)

So the first line of attack on the broad reading of Gillick is to draw a distinction between the 'Gillick competent' child's right to consent to treatment and her right to withhold consent to medical treatment. The difficulty with this argument is its subordination of the decision-making power of the 'Gillick competent' child to the court's (or the doctor's) perception of what is in her best interests. At this stage it is important to note just how onerous Lord Scarman's competency test is. He had stated:

> ...I would hold that as a matter of law the parental right to determine whether or not their minor child below the age of 16 will have medical treatment terminates if and when the child achieves a sufficient understanding and intelligence to enable him or her to understand fully what is proposed. It is not enough that she should understand the nature of the advice which is being given: she must also have a sufficient maturity to understand what is involved. There are moral and family questions, especially her relationship with her parents; long-term problems associated with the emotional impact of pregnancy and its termination; and there are the risks to health of sexual intercourse at her age, risks which contraception may diminish but cannot eliminate. (pp.188–9)

Given the difficulty in satisfying this test, a difficulty which clearly increases the more serious the matter in question, Lord Donaldson M.R.'s argument becomes hard to justify. If a young person satisfies this competency test, i.e. if they are adjudged by adults to be competent to make the decision in question, on what basis can their decision-making power be taken away from them? The judicial reply to this is that the court is only concerned with the child's welfare and that the court's overriding concern is with the protection of children from their (misguided) selves as well as from others.

Second, Lord Donaldson M.R. argued that, irrespective of the right of the parents as 'keyholders' to give effective consent to medical treatment for their child (thus by-passing their child's refusal to give such consent), the powers of the court in the exercise of its wardship jurisdiction are 'wider than that of parents'. He acknowledged that the function of the court is to 'act as the judicial reasonable parent' but that this is not the same thing as saying that the jurisdiction is 'derived from, or in any way limited by, that of the parents'. He concludes:

> If it can override such consents (i.e. those of the parents), as it undoubtedly can, I see no reason whatsoever why it should not be able, and in an appropriate case willing, to override decisions by 'Gillick competent' children who are its wards or in respect of whom applications are made for, for example, section 8 orders under the Children Act 1989. (p.602)

This line of argument was confirmed by Lord Donaldson in Re W (A Minor)(Consent to Medical treatment) [1993] 1 F.L.R. 1. The recent case of South Glamorgan County Council v W and B [1993] 1 F.L.R 574 further illustrates this protectionist approach. Here the High Court gave leave to the local authority under s.100(3) of the Children Act 1989 to bring proceedings to invoke the High Court's inherent jurisdiction in the event of the 15-year-old's refusal to submit to the medical assessment ordered under an interim care order (see s.38(6) of the Act). The High Court had decided that it could not find on the evidence that she was not of sufficient understanding to make an informed decision. The 15-year-old did not consent and the local authority came back and asked the court to exercise its inherent jurisdiction to order that the assessment proceed – thereby by-passing the 'right' given to 'mature minors' by the Children Act 1989 to refuse to submit to unwanted medical interventions. Brown J. stated:

> In my judgment, the court can, in an appropriate case – and they will be rare cases – but in an appropriate case, when other remedies within the Children Act have been used and exhausted and found not to bring the desired result, can resort to other remedies, and the particular remedy here is the remedy of providing authority for doctors to treat this child and authority, if it is needed, for the local authority to take all necessary steps to bring the child to the doctors so that she can be assessed and treated.

This paternalism and caution (O'Donovan 1993) is also evident in the recent controversy over children applying for leave to apply for a 'section 8 order' under the Children Act 1989. If the child does have the requisite understanding to make the proposed application for a section 8 order, for example a residence order, thereby enabling her to live in a particular household, why should we object? Quite apart from the autonomy argument, there is a child protection issue here: many children end up running away from home because they have no other way of escaping from circumstances they see as fundamentally unsatisfactory if not harmful. While courts operate as a filter – to make sure that the test in section 10(8) of the Children Act 1989 is met (see Practice Direction [1993] 1 FLR 668; and Re C (a minor) (leave to seek s.8 orders)[1994] 1 F.L.R. 26) – their approach in these mis-named 'child divorce' cases reveal the continuing difficulty experienced by them when faced with a mature, participating child.

CHILDREN'S RIGHTS AND THE PROBLEM OF AUTHORITY

Mrs Victoria Gillick had wanted the law to declare unlawful the advice given by the DHSS regarding the circumstances in which a medical practitioner could give confidential contraceptive advice and treatment to a minor. The complaint, in essence, was that the law should uphold her position as a parent, not undermine it. *The Times* (1985) editorial (entitled 'Gillick's Law') observed:

> The main contention on one side is that the law ought to be arranged so as to lend support to those parents who are conscientiously doing their duty to care for the health and morals of their children...to lead them to a proper understanding and right use of the sexual drive, as the parents understand these things.

The American case of Goss v Lopez, 419 U.S. 565 (1975), illustrates that this issue of authority extends beyond the family. This case concerned school disturbances which resulted in the suspension of a number of students from their schools. The Ohio statute provided for suspensions of up to ten days without any procedural safeguards either before or after the suspension.

Zimring and Soloman (1985) writing about this case state:

> In this case, the central issue was whether secondary school pupils standing on their own were citizens or merely minions of the school...
> The issue was no less than the legitimate authority of the school principal to rule his educational flock *as a father*. (emphasis added) (pp.457–8)

This metaphor, given the facts of this case, warrants two observations. First, this imagery was consistent with prevailing conservative opinion – to tinker with the school-family would be to invite disorder in school and society. In his dissenting judgment, Justice Powell argued:

> When an immature student merits censure for his conduct, he is rendered a disservice if appropriate sanctions are not applied or if procedures for their application are so formalised as to invite a challenge to the teacher's authority... School discipline, like parental discipline, is an integral and

important part of training our children to be good citizens – to be better citizens. (419 U.S. at 593)

There are echoes here of the arguments deployed in the 1920s to prevent mothers from acquiring equal rights of guardianship over their children. To open up the possibility of challenge to the authority of the father would be to court familial and social disaster (See Brophy 1985).

Second, even if this way of seeing the school normally has a claim on our thinking (and this is a big 'even if'), in the case of Goss v Lopez there was also the issue of race. The background to the disturbances which resulted in the suspensions was that in these schools the teachers were white and the pupils were black. The pupils' assembly programme for Black History Week was cancelled by school administrators. On the night before the disturbances, two black pupils were shot. The community here was quite clearly an angry and divided one. The Supreme Court found the statute unconstitutional by a five to four majority. The majority held that students facing suspension 'must be given some kind of notice and afforded some kind of hearing'. What kind of notice and what kind of hearing were to be left to the schools themselves to determine.

While Justice Powell had seen it to be important to allow the teacher to be free to 'discipline without frustrating formalities' Minow (1987) has a different perspective:

> Legal language translates, but does not initiate, conflict. The fear that judicial recognition of rights for children would inject conflict and invite rebelliousness is mistaken in two ways... First, conflict was present long before anyone asserted in court that students had rights... Second,...rights arguments, in essence, reconfirm community. The particular right ultimately announced in Goss amounted to no more than minimal notice and an opportunity for the student to have a conversation with a school official, much as any sensitive school official or parent would talk to a child before punishing her. This right to a conversation is a good example of the way in which asserting rights may actually affirm, rather than disturb, community. (pp.1871–74)

The language of children's rights is one vehicle whereby the reality of conflict, be it in the home, the school or wherever, will be voiced and alternative images made visible. The concern is that if we pretend that the community is a harmonious one, if we deny the existence of conflicts within it, the result might be that the position of the 'marginal' members in the 'community' will deteriorate. As already argued, to acknowledge conflict and to seek the use of law may 'shift the balance of power in an already violent situation' (Minow 1987, p.1902).

By way of a contrast, in England and Wales in the sphere of education the language is not one of children's rights but rather rights of the parents. It is parents who have a right of appeal if their child is refused a place at the school of their choice (Education Act 1980). It is parents who appeal to the local education authority if their child is excluded – unless the pupil is 18 when she can appeal in her own right (Education Act [No.2] 1986). It is parents who appeal against the expulsion of their child. While the Education Act 1993 has removed the power of the Headteacher to exclude a pupil for an indefinite period of time, there is no formal mechanism which requires a headteacher to consult parent or pupil before arriving at a decision to exclude. The Advisory Centre for Education stated in a report that exclusions have increased and that the procedure by which decisions to exclude are reached are characterised by inconsistency and delay (ACE 1993).

When you consider who gets excluded the picture is more alarming. According to a Department for Education survey, not only have exclusions increased but a disproportionate number of pupils of Afro-Carribean origin are being excluded (DFE 1993). At the same time a number of reports indicate problems of racism and racial harassment among pupils in schools (see Commission for Racial Equality 1985; Nottingham County Council 1991; Troyna and Hatcher 1992).

This failure to consider the differing interests within the educational system and to set up mechanisms whereby children's interests and views can be expressed and considered shows the limited purchase that the language and imagery of children's rights has in our society. The silencing of the child save through the voice of her parents conflicts with the language of Article 12 of the UN Convention on the Rights of the Child. The school, it seems, is even more impregnable than the English parent's castle. The commitment to treating children with respect, consulting them and listening to their views stops at the school gates.

CONCLUSION

> I find something terribly lacking in rights for children that speak only of autonomy rather than need, especially the central need for relationships with adults who are themselves enabled to create settings where children can thrive. (Minow 1987, p.1910)

It seems strange perhaps, given the argument of this paper, that I should start the conclusion with a quotation which declares how unsatisfactory a theory of children's rights, based exclusively on the idea of the autonomy of the child, would be. I must explain. To place emphasis on the right of the child to participate does not preclude our recognising that children also need support. It is the manner in which such things are done that is important. It should not be a question of adult imposition versus child autonomy: rather a matter of acknowledging the interconnectedness of our lives, of no longer seeing the relationships that children have with significant adults as naturally and necessarily hierarchic. There may be times when the child does not want the burden of taking the decision – but this is very different from never having been asked, from being ignored. We, as adults, might also benefit from a genuine dialogue with children in confronting our dilemmas. As in other spheres of our lives, it is not just what we do that is important but how we do it.

While the UN Convention on the Rights of the Child provides a new set of symbols, the practical difficulties will not disappear as a result – on the contrary. Article 12 refers to the child's right to express herself on all matters affecting her – are we ready to meet this challenge? It is one thing to say that the rights of the child are important. It is quite another to follow through the implications of that position.

While the Children Act 1989 can be seen as providing new avenues whereby children can express and act on their own wishes, the approach of the courts to child litigants has been one of extreme caution. Furthermore, it is self-evidently the case that not all children will be able to do so. Either because of their age or a disability, many children will not be able to take decisions let alone directly participate in proceedings which concern them. The practice of some lawyers and welfare professionals working with children reveals changes are taking place. The new Law Society Handbook for Solicitors and Guardians ad Litem emphasises the need for lawyers to recognise the different skills that working with children requires: the language used must be readily understood by the child client, the need to respect the child client's autonomy and to pay proper regard to the views of the child client (Liddle 1992, p.12; see also King and Young 1992).

Critically, once we genuinely allow children to exercise their right to speak and be heard, we might have to participate in new conversations. Children of different backgrounds might make varying demands of adults regarding education, health, religion, marriage as well as with whom they are able to associate. There is no single voice of childhood. Their voices may or may not make claims on the law. Yet any commitment to children's rights, as noted earlier, is part of a larger project regarding citizenship. Held (1991) writes:

> If citizenship entails membership in the community and membership implies forms of social participation, then citizenship is above all about the involvement of people in the community in which they live; and people have been barred from citizenship on grounds of class, gender, race and age among many other factors. Accordingly, the debate on citizenship requires us to think about the very nature of the conditions of membership and political participations. (p.20)

At the very least, in order to participate children must have access to resources and services which allow them to articulate their interests and choices, whatever the context, and society must be willing to consider and act on the argued-for outcomes. The language of rights is a key part of this project.

REFERENCES

Advisory Centre for Education (1993) *Fair Play*. Bulletin No.53

Alston, P., Parker, S. and Seymour, J. (1992) *Children, Rights and the Law*. Oxford: Clarendon Press.

Bainham, A. (1986) 'The balance of power in family decisions.' *45 Cambridge Law Journal 2*, 262.

Bowles, S. and Gintis, H. (1986) *Democracy and Capitalism*. New York: Basic Books.

Bradshaw, J. (1990) *Child Poverty and Deprivation in the U.K.* London: National Children's Bureau.

Brophy, J. (1985) 'Child care and the growth of power: the status of mothers in custody disputes.' In C. Smart and J. Brophy (eds) *Women in Law*. London: Routledge.

Children's Rights Development Unit (1994) *UK Agenda for Children*. London: CRDU.

Commission for Racial Equality (1985) *Birmingham Education Authority and Schools: Referral and Suspension of Pupils*.

Department for Education (1993) *National School Reporting Survey*. London: DfE.

Freeman, M.D.A. (1983a) 'Freedom and the welfare state: child-rearing, parental autonomy and state intervention.' *Journal of Social Welfare Law*, 70–91.

Freeman, M.D.A. (1983b) *The Rights and the Wrongs of Children*. London: Frances Pinter.

Held, D. (1991) 'Between state and civil society: citizenship.' In G. Andrews (ed) *Citizenship*. London: Lawrence and Wishart.

James, A. and Prout, A. (eds) (1990) *Constructing and Reconstructing Childhood Contemporary Issues in the Sociological Study of Childhood*. London: Falmer.

King, M. and Trowell, J. (1992) *Children's Welfare and the Law: The Limits of Legal Intervention*. London: Sage.

King, P. and Young, I. (1992) *The Child Client*. Bristol: Jordans.

Lansdown, G. (1992) 'Key right is the child's right to be heard.' *Childright 91*, (November), 4.

Liddle, C. (1992) *Acting for Children The Law Society's Handbook for Solicitors and Guardians ad Litem Working with Children*. London: Law Society.

Minow, M. (1987) 'Interpreting rights: an essay for Robert Cover.' *96 Yale Law Journal 8*, 1860.

Nottingham County Council (1991) *Pupil Exclusion from Secondary Schools*. Nottingham: Nottingham County Council.

O'Donovan, K. (1993) *Family Law Matters*. London: Pluto.

Stainton Rogers, R. and W. (1992) *Stories of Childhood Shifting Agendas of Child Concern Hemel Hempstead, Harvester Wheatsheaf*. The Times (1985) 18th October.

The Times (1985) Editorial – 'Gillicks Law.' 18 October 1985.

Troyna, B. and Hatcher, R. (1992) *Racism in Children's Lives: A Study of Mainly White Primary Schools.* London: National Children's Bureau.

William, P. (1991) *The Alchemy of Race and Rights.* Cambridge: Harvard University Press.

Zimring, F. and Soloman, R. (1985) 'Goss v Lopez: The principle of the thing.' In R. Mnookin *In the Interests of Children.* New York: Freeman.

PART THREE

Providing for Children's Rights in a Changing World

CHAPTER THREE

World Changes and Social Policies in Uruguay

Juan Miguel Petit

Scarcely ever could it be asserted, as nowadays, that 'everything moves, everything changes, and nothing is as it seems to be' (Berman 1983). By the end of this century many things appear to be ending, and others just starting. Monolithic systems collapse in some hours, leaving no remnants. Many dogmas and principles struggle in the face of new realities and behaviours. Social sciences have little or no answer to the emergence of phenomena that go beyond the existing categories.

Unassured, and at the mercy of elements, we stare at a swiftly changing world whose meaning we are unable to figure out. The expectations of economic thriving, together with the stunning scientific and technological progress, are pervasive. But euphoria for a new international order cannot conceal the fragility of development: much of the world population fail to meet their basic needs, new conflicts and social tensions burst out and the environment is being irreparably damaged. We are urged to think over our ways of living together.

The present century has seen the horrors of totalitarianism and dictatorship under different signs and banners though with identical methods, the annihilation in concentration camps, and the negation of liberties. However, it has also seen the steady and irreversible acquisition of new citizen's rights, and the revalue of freedom and democracy as essential requisites for social justice and development.

In this context of upheaval and uncertainty, many of the tools that used to be appropriate for social action are now found to be obsolete. Citizens no longer expect abstractions of generic statements, but definitions that make them feel they are enjoying their rights.

In Latin America, social problems and impoverishment of vast sectors coexist with crises in the government viewed as responsible for overall welfare. Questions proliferate at the time of framing social policies. Indeed, as political, social and cultural transformations rushed forward in the recent years, many models that boasted understanding the society and its evolution have been abandoned. The challenge of today is less overwhelming than the ideologies that believed they could understand and anticipate everything. What is at stake is the development of all the inhabitants of our countries. Thus, by participating in the creation of their own society – enjoying their rights, and complying with their obligations – they will be able to construct their own happiness.

It is worth remembering that 'changing the world is a rarely harmless dream, changing its behaviours is the point of departure for any progress' (Crozier 1992).

LATIN AMERICA IN THE STORM

Between 1950 and 1980, most Latin American countries reached considerable rates of growth and urbanisation, while the structures of production and employment underwent considerable changes. But the economic crisis of the 1980s reversed the previous decrease in poverty, multiplying the number of the poor, in both absolute and proportional terms, up to the striking present figures of 200 million people, that is, 38 per cent of households.

If trends do not shift, by the threshold of the twenty-first century, 47 per cent of the region's population will live in conditions of extreme poverty. This calls us to modify 'the inertia of history, that, as shown by the stunning changes occurred recently world-wide, does not respond to any determinism or fatality, but depends on men, it depends on ourselves' (Ottone 1990).

The fragmentation and disarticulation of Latin American society do not stem only from the depth of social and economic exclusion. They also arise from the contrast and odd coexistence of an obvious modernisation of the upper and some middle sectors with a stagnation or backward movement of the marginalised sectors. A common experience consists in 'being immersed in three or more cities with no communication, whereas it is the same city we are speaking about. The linked relationships between those different cultures are increasingly infrequent, and if any, violent' (Ottone 1990).

The cities in the region, rather than a reflection of cultural heterogeneity, show the sharp contradiction of the dual economic and social structures. 'On one hand, the islands of modernism, the paradigms of the progress of formal society, containing the formal city, the formal economy. On the other hand, the mare nostrum of poverty, where economic, social, political and urban informality prevail' (Neuva Sociedad 1991).

Efforts to integrate into the international economy produce a productive dynamism that drives social sectors which assume the guidelines of both industrial societies, and highly competitive environments. This results in unsatisfied basic needs, critical conditions of living, pollution, marginalisation or isolation.

These two perspectives summarise the ambivalence of Latin American societies, shared by many other underdeveloped regions. Wealth and misery, affluence and poverty, dynamism and isolation: those integrated members of the system interact daily with the inhabitants of the borders, the margin, those outcast. They coexist in a reality whose integration and participation mechanisms are blocked, making that inter-cultural relation riven with conflict.

CRISIS AND OPPOSITIONS

In the middle of the storm, many governments of the region try to be up to date and in tune with the international economic tendency. They either undertake structural reform, adjustment programmes, or they merely administer the present realities as much as they can. In any case, it is expected that economic growth will solve, automatically, the social problems involving children and their families.

It is often said that the 1980s were a 'lost decade for development' on the Continent. By its end, however, the restoration of democracy in most of the region multiplied citizens' expectations and also increased the pressure for such democracies to assure decent living conditions for all their members. Failing to do that jeopardises – by explosion, social decline, or corrosion – the survival of the systems and nations themselves.

The public sector crisis has shown the State's failure to respond to the new social claims and chronic outstanding problems. Cultural heterogeneity, new problems and social fragmentation have caused 'perplexity' in the traditional social policy makers. Informality, massive impoverishment, ghettoisation and chaotic proliferation of claims have all evidenced the insufficiency of present services, revealing them as paternalistic suppliers of indiscriminate care.

Although the crisis of the State and its social policies for children is notorious, that undergone by many non-governmental organisations has not been so extreme. Although they emerged as an alternative to the official policies during the obscure time of military dictatorship, their activities are now considerably constrained. Many of them, together with social movements and grass-root activists, have developed pilot programmes or experiences with an innovative methodology, but a limited impact. Not but a few of them have given birth to their own bureaucracies that risk becoming ends in themselves. Thus international co-operation for development is denaturalised, and moves apart from its target population.

The opposition between the public and the private brings about a waste of resources, reinforces isolation, and prevents efficient methodologies from generalising under stable policies. A remarkable example is the effort made in Brazil to obtain enactment of the new Statute for Children and Adolescents, derived from the the dynamic and creative interaction between the social movement, public policies, and the legal world.

Many non-government organisations are tempted to stick to a testimonial function, and become isolated. Distrust and bureaucratisation bar the State from opening up to new actors and approaches. One of democracy's challenges is to overcome this blockade.

CONTROVERSY, THE CHILDREN, AND...

The attitudes towards social policies are twofold. Although it is felt that they deserve express support, nevertheless they are viewed with distrust.

On the one hand, there are those who believe that 'no social or family policy is better than a good economic wealth-producing policy'. From this viewpoint, social investment brings about scepticism, and its resources are the first to be cut when savings have to be made. Social policies tend to be conceived as palliatives or correctives – necessary, albeit with doubtful results.

On the other hand, the transformative effect of social policies has usually also been denied in the region, and they have been accused, by contrast, of being numb in the face of a painful reality. During the 1960s, 1970s, and early 1980s, actions intended other than to provide for a total change of social structures and to establish a new and revolutionary way of living together without injustice, without oppressors or oppressed were completely scorned. Poor sectors were viewed as 'the urban spearhead of rebellion' (Fanon 1965). Beyond these postures, time has shown that the transformation of reality is an extremely complex process that cannot be explained simply.

The defence of children's rights is founded on an effort to generate mechanisms – diverse, complementary, pluralistic – that, while enabling children to develop their potential, may reduce the social inequalities that undermine the democratic sense of social living. The State must then promote new opportunities for community participation, and accept new forms of action to accomplish its objectives.

Children's rights are conditioned by the way they are brought up. Their growth and development are limited by prevailing material and also cultural and affective deprivation. Deterioration of family relations in marginalised milieus prevent children from assuming their full rights and from becoming active citizens in the future. Paternalistic social policies have a direct influence on those family relations. If direction, support, reinforcement of self-esteem, information, and resources were provided, their beneficiaries might turn into autonomous social actors. They generate, at best, passive 'clients', who grow more and more institutionalised and marginalised, in the face of purely bureaucratic responses. Only new participation and integrative opportunities for social interaction can modify the upbringing conditions of many children in the region. New types of social care and support programmes for the family are required. Ones that are more realistic, decentralised, and appropriate to local realities, mobilising the resources that remain dormant or under-used. To that end, ideas about the rationale of our present policies must be updated.

A NEW ANGLE TO VIEW SOCIAL INTEGRATION POLICIES

According to the ideas expressed above, the decline of the Welfare State calls for an imaginative and innovative redefinition of the role of social policies. When that task is undertaken, the counterpart of paternalistic, over-protective and institutionalising policies becomes apparent: a weak and apathetic civil society, tamed by the public sector. A new style of action must reinforce participation: society's ability to make decisions, organise itself, and manage the actions concerning itself should be developed. Curiously enough, this process is likely to be started up or fostered by the public sector itself, by setting aside its centralised, paternalistic and regulating mode of action. A paradox arises in that the more demands, the more need to take action, the more the difficulties in doing so. 'A more complex social tissue requires more attention, more care. The larger the freedom of participants in the social game, the more necessary the organisation' (Crozier 1992).

This active attitude of civil society can be developed provided that power is not centralised and monopolistic. Present evidence shows that this is an era of the empowerment of new initiatives and organisations. 'Upwards', to supra-national entities, international bodies, common markets, areas of economic and political integration. But also 'downwards', and 'sideways', at the municipal, regional or provincial level under new forms of local administration and management. The key concept is empowerment. It implies decentralisation, the civil society assuming responsibilities and new actors as well as new protago-nists. The people themselves are the best defenders of their own interests, provided that they have a chance to do so. Only an active and lively civil society can generate a protective network for children and their families. Such a network can never work when the answer to a serious situation from public bodies is nothing but institutionalisation.

Relief from poverty, however, should not be considered an objective unre-lated to economic development. Poverty is mostly due to lack of capital, credit and access to appropriate social services. If the poor are to catch up with development, social investment should be a priority and also 'poverty should not be considered a remainder of economic growth to be dealt with separately, without modifying growth strategies. Governments should not approach pov-erty after economic growth. Economic growth models should be adopted that have the elimination of poverty as one of their prime objectives, reasonably combining market efficiency and social responsibility' (UN 1990).

All this change involving public and private actors – the State, social movements, non-governmental organisations, businesses and individuals – is intended to modify traditional social policies under a new social integration policy approach. Its object is overcoming the exclusion of much of the region's population from the social game, from the possibility of building up their own history and of developing their human potentialities. 'The denomination "social integration policies" is more specific and correct than the generic "social policies". These are not policies seeking to improve society on the basis of an ideal model, but rather policies aimed to improve integration of all members of society. By transacting and opting as citizens, they are expected to define what society should be like' (CID 1992).

We conclude after Berman, that 'the modernisation process, even though exploiting and tormenting us, gives rise to new energy and to our imagination, and urges us to understand and face the world, and to strive and turn it into our own world. We and those who come after us will keep on struggling to turn this world into our home, even if those homes we have constructed – the modern street, the modern spirit – keep on vanishing into thin air' (Berman 1983).

OPERATIONAL MENU FOR CHILDREN'S POLICIES

The ideas already outlined must serve as a background for policy-making that assure the recognition of children's rights. Some guidelines for action may be the following:

- Pilot programmes must intend to *generalise* innovations by means of actions that are not limited to a few beneficiaries.

- To achieve the above, it is necessary to overcome the public sector/private sector dichotomy under new relations that give rise to a *network* of social services. The present blockade can only be broken if the identity and proper roles of both sectors are recognised and consensus is reached for a lasting policy.

- Social and community action must be revitalised with new opportunities – regional, local, at the neighbourhood level – for *participation*, by means of *empowerment* of the sectors involved in policies.

- In so far as the community participates, they assume their responsibilities rather than expect everything from somebody else. By doing so, they *take advantage of social resources* available and create answers to their problems. They usually discover many resources and possibilities that remained under-used.

- The civil society thus assumes varied and heterogeneous ways of acting. This is essential to democratic life. And, moreover, it *generates specific answers* to the situations that jeopardise the community's development and rights.

- To achieve *de-institutionalisation* of children's policies, an active society, based on solidarity and social commitment, is required. There is no other way to solve situations of children that are either not being cared for or stigmatised in massive or impersonal institutions.

- Private businesses also qualify for a new role in the civil society. They are not only financially capable, but they have the *infrastructure and unused resources* available to generate programmes and actions. They must not leave anything to charity, but become one of policy's ingredients.

- Children's care systems in the region make us think that our challenge is not simply to improve their situation, but rather *reform* its cultural rationale and *create* something different.

- So that the design of social and educational programmes may be sensitive to changes, it is necessary to forget about the needs of the local or international bureaucracies and suppliers of social services. Marginalisation is expressed through institutionalisation and dependency that derive, in turn, from paternalism and care-giving. They are avoided through *empowerment and information*, that promote processes of self-sufficiency capable of surviving in a changing and competitive world.

- The dimension of Latin American poverty jeopardises both the survival of countries themselves and their democratic existence. Social and educational policy-making must open social participation and mobility channels, as well as *consolidate as cultural values* those of democratic life and social integration of sectors with unsatisfied social needs.

REFERENCES

Berman, M. (1983) *Todo lo Sùlido se Desvanece en el Aire* ('All that is Solid Melts into Thin Air'). London: Verso.

CID (1992) *Politicas de Integración Social.* ('Politics of Social Integration') Montevideo: Centro de Innovación y Desarrollo (CID). Uruguay.

Crozier, M. (1992) 'Estado modesto, estado moderno: estrategia para otro cambio.' Gipuzkoa. Fundacion para la Investigacion en Recursos Humanos: El Departamento de Presidencia y Regimen Juridico de la Diputacion Foral de Gipuzkoa.

Fanon, F. (1965) 'Les damnés de la terre' (The wretched of the earth). *Preface* by Jean-Paul Sartre. London: MacGibbion and Kee.

La Crisis de las Ciudades Latinoamericanas ('The Crisis of Latin American Cities') (1988) Bildner Cnetre for Western Hemisphere Studies. Book reviewed by Alan Gilbert in *Journal of Latin American Studies 24*, February 1992, 228–9.

Nueva Sociedad (1991) 'Enigmáticas, amenazadas.' Special issue about Latin American Cities.

Ottone, E. (1990) 'Hacia un desarrollo sin pobreza en América Latina y el Caribe.' Paper presented at the 1990 United Nations Regional Conference. New York: United Nations Development Programme Publications.

United Nations (1990) *Human Development Report.* New York: OUP for the United Nations Development Programme.

CHAPTER FOUR

The Rights of Children in a Post-Totalitarian Country

Jana Ondráčková

The adoption of the Convention on the Rights of the Child went relatively unnoticed in the countries of the former socialist camp. Considering that these regimes had always presented their young people to the world as bright-eyed, well-fed, happy builders of a glorious socialist future this was not surprising. When socialism crumbled in Central and Eastern Europe the world was shocked by what it saw and heard from Romania, Albania and even Czechoslovakia, which, by economic standards, was comparatively better off than the others. As regards human rights, however, a new dimension was revealed. The world had known countries where human rights were upheld and others where they were violated. When the iron curtain came down it became evident that behind it stretched a vast area where there was very little knowledge, let alone awareness, of the existence of human rights.

The Czechoslovak Federal Parliament ratified the Convention on the Rights of the Child in January 1991. The full text was published in the Collection of Laws. Yet, teachers, students and the general public knew very little of what the convention is about. The text, in accessible form, was being published and disseminated in 'samizdats' by non-government organisations, the government claiming it has no funds for such activities.

One year after the ratification and two years after the velvet revolution, children in Czechoslovakia are no longer discriminated against in the education

---

Since this paper was written and presented at the World Conference on Children's Rights in September 1992 in Exeter, Czechoslovakia has split up into two states, namely the Czech Republic and the Slovak Republic. The author of this paper lives and works in Prague.

Further details of the changes that have taken place in the Czech Republic can be obtained from Jana Ondráčková, Radejovice 48, 251 68 p. Stirin, Praha-Vychod, Czech Republic.

system. An exception to this are the gypsies who somehow or other always find themselves attending special schools and dropping out of education at the age of 15, and hardly ever finding it possible to get any proper vocational or other training. Children in this country no longer have to take part in 'voluntary' work in the fields and, unlike Romania and Albania, they are mostly relatively well-fed, clothed and housed. They generally enjoy a good standard of health care and both vaccination and general education are compulsory and free.

On the other hand, Czechoslovakia is entering the world of the market economy and the economic reforms are extremely ambitious. The problems that accompany such reforms, such as the lack of funds for health and education, could become a serious danger, especially for the youngest generation. The children and young people will have to be given training in economic and legal matters to be able to cope. The trouble is there are very few teachers who are sufficiently knowledgeable and there is hardly any training of this kind available for teachers. A catch-22 situation which is not made any better by the very slow process of ridding ministries and even universities of 'old structures'.

Czechoslovakia is the world's most polluted country in terms of toxic emission per capita and it is the children who suffer most. In this situation the environment will have to cease being merely a matter of protection and the business of green objectives and will have to become a human rights issue. This will require a lot of campaigning and education. With an eye on economic improvement, the country's leaders tend to overlook environmental issues and it took several months for the Federal Parliament to pass the new Environment Act. Environment education is shunned and practically non-existent.

The sudden outburst of freedom and the opening of borders led to an increase in the crime rate, notably among juveniles. A large number of Czechoslovakia's gypsies were up-rooted by the former regime and were brought to live in urban settings in high-rise housing developments and lured to work in industry. The family allowances (the gypsy family has six to eight children on average, as against one to three children in the 'white' family) awarded to the gypsies by the communist regime in the propaganda foray of 'treating ethnic minorities with special care' gave rise to racial unease, later to outward hatred. This hostility was further exaggerated by the stereotypical belief that the crime rate among gypsies is much higher than among the rest of the population. There have been open witch-hunts and street battles between gypsies and skinheads – youngsters fighting for a 'white society'. A public poll in Slovakia in the eastern part of the country showed that 90 per cent of the population would not live in a gypsy neighbourhood. Anti-semitism, on the other hand, was official policy under the communist regime, under the guise of anti-Zionism and friendship with the Arab countries. After the November 1989 revolution, the new government restored diplomatic relations with Israel and there has been a revival of Jewish community life and culture, which has a long tradition, especially in the Czech lands. The response has been violent, especially in

Slovakia, where Jewish graves have been smeared with graffiti and unwanted politicians of Jewish faith all but driven out of the country. This is a very serious matter, one which, luckily, so far does not seem to have affected the youngest generation. (The skinheads are youths roughly between the ages of 16 and 25.) Given our history, bringing together children from different communities within children's parliaments, or children's hearings, or similar activities, will be very difficult but absolutely indispensable. All the more important because children in this country are strongly influenced by parents and grandparents. Skeletons in the cupboard like Jews and gypsies are not discussed. The well intentioned and uninformed statement 'you know, they are simply different from the rest of us, so why should we mix?' from children makes education of the youngest even more important.

The Czech and Slovak family is very autocratic with parents very much dictating to their children what to do, where to go, how to spend their free time, etc. This too is a serious matter. In a country where several generations have been brought up to believe that 'he who does not steal robs his own family', where work morale was (and still is) very low and personal responsibility was an unknown phenomenon, the priorities of parents will often be questionable. Children have been taught that rights go with responsibility, that other people too have rights, that people should stand up for their own and other people's rights.

In this situation, some leading members of the Government are enforcing the institution of an ombudsman. In a country where people still do not know much about democracy and how it works and have very little experience with personal accountability, independent thinking, tolerance and fair play in general, this is beset with problems. The appointment of an ombuds officer in a society without thorough and all-pervading human rights education seems to have the characteristics of building a house from the roof downwards. In addition to this, the bright-eyed young generation should, I believe, first have come to terms with the fact that all that sparkles in the previously banned 'West' does not shine; that even there, one has to work to make money and buy the goodies; that law and order is something to be observed everywhere.

The situation could be greatly helped by the press outside. Yet the free press is something which most journalists, let alone politicians, are still learning to handle. With the press coming under the strains of the market economy and having to 'sell', and television and most radio stations still being state-owned, this is quite difficult.

In this situation, the question of the rights of children, that generation which, after 40 years of totalitarian regime, will in fact be the first to live in a democratic state, is a question of a cautious and well thought out process of empowerment.

CHAPTER FIVE

The Role of the Child Welfare Society of Kenya in Implementing the UN Convention on Rights of the Child

Munene Kahiro

INTRODUCTION

The Child Welfare Society of Kenya is a charitable organisation established in 1955 to protect and promote all children in Kenya, but in particular children living in special and difficult circumstances. The Society operates through its headquarters in Nairobi and 17 active branches which are situated in the length and breadth of Kenya.

PROGRAMMES

The Society runs the following programmes:

Adoption

This is where an unwanted child is legally found adoptive parents and a permanent loving home. The process has to be sanctioned through the court to ensure its legality.

Fostering

Our social workers, after receiving older children who cannot be committed for adoption, look for foster parents to give temporary foster care while solutions to the child's problems are looked into. Fostering is a temporary measure while adoption is a permanent one.

Family rehabilitation

This is where families of very poor children are identified and empowered financially to enable them to run small-scale businesses and thus to assist their children.

Community development

The Society encourages communities to take care of its own children. The intervention area here is through child-based community programmes. Another is through organised women's groups. Women are encouraged to carry out income-generating projects with a view to assisting their children with school fees, clothing and food.

Child Educational Sponsorship Programme

We solicit for education sponsorship for poor children. We have the following sponsorship programmes:

1. Finnish sponsorship – sponsors are from Finland

2. Local sponsorship – sponsors are local Kenyans

3. Bright Girls Scheme – this is also a Finnish sponsorship programme specifically for bright girls who might have passed their exams and have no money to continue with their education. The selection criteria are based on poverty.

Advocacy: rights of the child and HIV/AIDS

Since 1989, the Child Welfare Society of Kenya has been a leading force in advocating and promoting the UN Convention on the Rights of the Child. There is also a new programme introduced in the Society after realising that more and more children are infected with the HIV virus. The children are either abandoned by their mothers or are AIDS orphans. In this programme, we are teaching housemothers in our children's homes how to handle children with AIDS with love, understanding and tolerance. The housemothers are given training by AIDS experts.

Institutional emergency care (children's homes)

This is where we temporarily house children with difficult circumstances while we conduct investigations into the root cause of the problem to enable us to determine the best solution.

Child care training

This is the programme in which we train young girls in child care and domestic work.

EFFORTS TOWARDS IMPLEMENTATION
OF THE UN CONVENTION

Kenya Law, and specifically Cap 141, defines a child as a person below the age of 18 years. A child should be entitled to life, good education, proper health care, shelter and a sound upbringing.

In the African tradition, the responsibility for bringing up a child was an extended family and communal affair, and not solely for its parents.

With the influence of western civilisation, most of our customs which held the extended families and the community together have been eroded. We are in the process of establishing small family units which exclude the extended family. The development of the nuclear (small, independent) families has put the responsibility of the children upon parents. To a certain extent, this has affected the Rights of the Child because the discipline and authority of the community and the extended family is no longer in practice and parents may ignore their duties. Parental laxity in the welfare of the child can lead to its suffering.

In observance of the above and with the good timing relative to the General Assembly of the United Nations adopting, by consensus, the Convention on the Rights of the Child, the Child Welfare Society of Kenya decided to seriously address itself to assisting the Government to ratify and consequently implement the Convention.

On 26 May 1989 the Child Welfare Society of Kenya organised a mini-workshop on advocacy and action for ratification and implementation of the Convention. The workshop brought together representatives of many non-governmental organisations (NGOs) to deliberate on effective ways of harnessing our efforts and channel them profitably towards achieving a common goal. Over 26 non-government organisations dealing with child welfare were represented at the workshop.

After careful examination by these organisations, it was felt that the NGOs' efforts in the area of children's rights were uncoordinated, resulting in each group working independently and being unconcerned with its counterparts. This resulted in considerable duplication of projects and wastage of the meager resources available to the NGO Community, which depends on charity for finances. The need to co-ordinate and harness the efforts of the non-government organisations, the International Government Organisations (IGOs), governmental organisations and other agencies working in the area of children's rights became crucial. With combined efforts, these groups would yield better results. The result of the workshop was that a body should be established to co-ordinate the entire effort in the area of promoting the ratification and implementation of the Convention on the Rights of the Child. This co-ordination would, consequently, minimise duplication. Thus the Child Welfare Society of Kenya was charged with the responsibility of co-ordinating the setting up of the body to be called 'The National Alliance for Advocacy on Children's Rights'.

The following NGOs which were represented at the meeting agreed to be founding members of the Alliance:

- Child Welfare Society of Kenya
- Christian Children Fund (CCF)
- African Network for the Prevention and Protection against Child Abuse and Neglect (ANPPCAN)
- Association of the Physically Disabled of Kenya (ASPDK)
- The Aga Khan Foundation (AF)
- The Christian Health Association of Kenya (CHAK)
- Kanu Maendeleo Ya Wanawake Organisation (KMYWO)
- The Kenya National Council for Social Welfare (KNCSW)
- The Kenya Society of the Mentally Handicapped (KSMH)
- Undugu Society of Kenya (USK).

These were to form the nucleus of the Alliance which was to be open to all groups working in the area of child welfare.

The Constitution states that the National Alliance for Advocacy on Children's Rights (NAACR) is a national, non-profit making entity for co-operation in all matters of child welfare. It is established to advance the interest and overall well-being of children in Kenya regardless of race, colour, sex, language, religion, political or other status and for the promotion of their rights and interest as enshrined in the Convention on the Rights of the Child.

The objectives of the NAACR are mainly to:

- Organise and improve information exchange and co-operation among its members.
- Educate national opinion on the rights, interests and overall well-being of children everywhere.
- Promote and organise conferences, seminars, study groups and other meetings on matters relating to children's rights and welfare.
- Promote and advance the interests and rights of children and, in particular, the implementation of the Convention on the rights of the Child.

The membership of the Alliance is open to all legally-recognised national non-governmental, non-profit entities which directly or indirectly perform work related to the care and welfare of children. The formation of the Alliance was considered necessary for various reasons. The Convention on the Rights of the Child having been adopted by the General Assembly of the United Nations, we, as child workers, needed to play our role in procuring early ratification by as many states as possible.

Kenya has declared its intention not only to ratify the Convention but also to call on other states to do the same. The Alliance's principle role will, therefore, be one of promoting the implementation of the Convention in Kenya. As we approach the 21st Century, we need to co-ordinate our efforts in fostering and promoting the implementation of the Convention. This will require a comprehensive and planned strategy. The Alliance will be further faced with the task of ensuring that the Convention is fully publicised. It will also be called upon to set up an effective and continuous monitoring of its implementation. That is the challenge of the future.

The Alliance will also be required to co-ordinate the varied activities of its members in the enforcement of civil, economic, social and cultural rights spelt out in the Convention. Each member of the Alliance will contribute its special expertise in the field of its activity. The total pool of expertise will be directed to the achievement of the objectives of the Alliance.

The Alliance will be called upon to complement the Government's efforts in publicising the principles and provisions of the Convention. It will be the Alliance's principle activity to make sure that the Convention becomes a household document and does not remain an international treaty binding only states. It should be a document which gives rise to obligations and duties, and which is understood by adults and children alike. To do this, the Alliance will involve itself in activities such as:

- Holding conferences, seminars and workshops and other forums to discuss the Convention and its relationship with domestic law and how the latter can conform to the Convention.

- Carrying out research to establish the status of child rights and to make recommendations.

- Publicising the proceedings of such conferences, seminars and forums and the findings of the research undertaken to as many people as possible.

- Undertaking media educational campaigns and other channels to inform people of the rights of the children and the provisions of the Convention.

- Printing and disseminating the Convention.

- Translating the Convention into local languages including paraphrasing terms to make the text easy for children and other people with limited literacy to understand.

- Preparing video and other media presentations depicting the various rights that the Convention declares and the manner in which they can be enjoyed by our children.

- Documenting and publicising all information that may come to light relating to non-observance or violations of the provisions of the principles of the Convention.

The Alliance will be charged with the duty to monitor and evaluate the implementation and non-observance of the principles and provisions of the Convention within Kenya on a continuous and permanent basis. The Alliance could set up a committee or group and charge it with the responsibility to keep adequate surveillance on the implementation of the Convention. It could also prepare and maintain reports, and periodically convene review meetings of inter-disciplinary groups to appraise those reports. It could, in conjunction with governmental, United Nations and non-governmental organisations work out a joint plan of action aimed at setting up a machinery for enforcement of the provisions of the Convention. Such a group could be charged with the duty to ensure that the contents of the reports to the Committee on the Rights of the Child set up by Article 43 of the Convention are accurate and submitted on time. It could also gather information and data for inclusion in such reports as well as liaise between the Government, the UN agencies and the NGO community.

Since the formation of the National Alliance for the Rights of the Child, the CWSK has spearheaded various programmes aimed at the implementation of the Convention. Some of the programmes are:

- Participating in the translation of the Convention into *Kiswahili* language which is widely read and understood by the majority of Kenyans. The aim has always been to translate the Convention into as many local dialects as possible.

- Seminars and conferences for the youth in schools and other organised youth groups to synthesise for them on rights of the child and, of course, to hear from them how they would like adults to treat them.

- Seminars and conferences on child sexual exploitation.

- A study on the situational analysis of the female child in Kenya.

- Research on forced female circumcision in Kenya, its health, social and psychological effects.

- Research on the sexual exploitation of children with the family and commercial enterprises in Kenya.

The CWSK is now addressing itself to the rights of children in the streets and other working children.

CHALLENGES FACING THE CHILD WELFARE SOCIETY OF KENYA IN THE 1990S

The vision of the CWSK in the 1990s is to establish ways and means of coping with the increasing new challenges facing children in Kenya. Our emphasis is, and has always been, to work with 'children in difficult circumstances'.

Some of the new challenges facing this category of children – apart from poverty, malnutrition and lack of shelter – are:

- Children as orphans of AIDS.
- Children born with AIDS.
- Children displaced due to violence such as civil war or tribal clashes.
- Children of refugees from neighbouring countries.
- Children as victims of drug trafficking and sex tourism.

CONCLUSION

The United Nations Declaration of the Rights of the Child (1959) includes in its statements

> ...mankind owes to the child the best it has to give... The child shall enjoy special protection and shall be given opportunities and facilities by law and by other means to enable him to develop physically, mentally, morally, spiritually and socially in a healthy and normal manner and in conditions of freedom and dignity... The child shall be protected against all forms of neglect, cruelty and exploitation.

CHAPTER SIX

Implementation of the UN Convention on the Rights of the Child in the UK

Gerison Lansdown

The adoption by the UN General Assembly of the Convention on the Rights of the Child in 1989 represented a considerable leap forward in the recognition that children are people who have rights that must be respected. The incorporation for the first time in an international treaty of the recognition of children's civil and political rights makes this Convention particularly significant, and the ratification within four years by 177 countries is further testimony to the importance now attached internationally to promoting children's rights. No other Convention in the history of the UN has achieved that level of support within such a short time scale. However, adoption by the UN and ratification by individual countries, whilst important, will not in themselves create real change in children's lives. That will only happen if Governments look seriously and in detail at the implications of each of the articles it contains and are prepared to take an imaginative and radical approach to the legislative, policy and attitudinal changes that must ensue.

GOVERNMENT COMMITMENT TO THE CONVENTION

In the UK, the Government ratified the Convention in December 1991. When ratifying, a Government is entitled to enter reservations to any part of the Convention indicating its unwillingness to comply with that particular provision or Article. The UK Government have entered a number of reservations including:

- They will not provide any protective employment legislation for 16- to 18-year-olds arguing that this age group are adults in the labour market and not in need of any special protection in respect of their health and safety or against economic exploitation. It is worth noting that the Government is at odds with its European partners on this issue and has opposed a draft European Directive on the Protection of Young People at Work which would introduce many of the measures necessary for full compliance with Article 32 of the Convention, the right to protection at work.

- They will continue to place children and young people in custody together with adults where there is either a lack of alternative suitable accommodation or, indeed, where it is considered beneficial to mix adults with children in custodial accommodation.

- They have reserved the right to apply UK immigration and nationality legislation whether or not it contravenes the principles in the Convention. This reservation has implications, for example, for the articles dealing with children's rights not to be separated from their parents, the right to have their best interests governing decisions which affect them, the right to a nationality, the right not to be discriminated against.

Ratification took place with almost no publicity whatever – merely a prepared parliamentary question which enabled the Government to announce it in the House of Commons. There was no accompanying press release or government spokesperson to address its significance for children in the UK nor to describe what implications ratification would have for law, policy and practice in this country. But the Government are required under the terms of the Convention to promote it. Article 42 obliges States to 'make the principles and provision of the Convention widely known, by appropriate and active means, to adults and children alike'. To date, there has been little governmental progress on this duty. Copies of the Convention have been sent to every local authority and it is available at cost in government bookshops, and a leaflet setting out the main articles it contains has been produced by the Department of Health. Beyond that little has happened. They have failed to either produce or commission the production of any information on the Convention specifically for children.

A further obligation under the terms of the Convention was to report to the UN Committee on the Rights of the Child within two years of ratification on its progress towards the implementation of children's rights. This Committee was established under the terms of the Convention and consists of ten members selected from amongst ratifying states. The members, all experts in the field of children's rights, have the task of interpreting the implications of each of the principles and standards contained in the Convention and monitoring the implementation of the Convention by individual countries.

The Committee have drawn up guidelines for Governments in producing these reports, which address both the process and the structure which should be followed. In respect of the process, the Committee stress that the report should be used as an opportunity for 'conducting a comprehensive review of the various measures undertaken to harmonise national law and policy with the

Convention'. However, there is no evidence to date that the Government have taken heed of this advice during the past year in the passage of new legislation and the development of new policy proposals. For example, the Education Act 1993 offered an ideal opportunity to introduce the principles of participation (Article 12) and the best interests of the child (Article 3) into education legislation but all efforts to achieve this during the passage of the Bill through Parliament were totally rejected by the Government. New proposals for the creation of secure training centres to contain persistent offenders aged 12–14 years run entirely counter to the principle of custody as a measure of last resort and for the shortest possible period of time, required by Article 37, and will mean children being placed at long distances from their homes making family contact difficult to maintain (Article 9). They have been opposed by almost all organisations working in the field of youth justice both because they will potentially breach many of the fundamental principles in the Convention and also because similar approaches to tackling youth crime have demonstrably failed in the past. The proposals in the Bill appear to be more concerned with populist politics than a serious attempt to address a problem in line with respect for the Government's commitments to children under the Convention. Proposals to amend existing homelessness legislation also have profound implications for children within those families. The 1993 consultation document on homelessness, published by the Government, suggests that the right of homeless families to priority consideration for permanent housing should be removed and substituted with limited rights to temporary housing for up to six months. Further, it proposes that families should only be considered as being in priority need of housing when they are actually roofless. There is already well-documented evidence of the significant harm that homelessness can cause to children. These proposed changes can only serve to compound the problems of disruption, lack of adequate health care, loss of education, social isolation and stigma experienced by homeless children. It is difficult to reconcile these proposed changes with a commitment to the promotion of children's rights.

The guidance from the Committee also states that the process of producing the report should be one that 'encourages and facilitates popular support and public scrutiny of government policies'. The response of the Government to this requirement has hardly been enthusiastic. The Department of Health was given the task of co-ordinating the report which was due for consideration by the UN Committee in January 1994. The first draft of the report was received, with a request for comments, by a limited number of organisations shortly before Christmas 1993 with a deadline for comments by the end of that month. The consultation period amounted to little more than eight working days. The report is 130 pages long and at no stage prior to its distribution for comments had anyone outside the relevant government departments had any opportunity to see its contents. As such, the process was clearly not intended to provide any serious attempt to contribute to the report and signifies a lack of enthusiasm on the part of the Government for effective participation and debate on its contents.

It is clear then that the *process* of producing the report has not been undertaken in the spirit of the UN Committee's guidelines. The *content* gives little more cause for optimism in the commitment of the Government to active promotion of the Convention. Their report states in its introduction that the UK Government is not complacent in its approach to children's rights. It comments that accession to the Convention did not require any amendments to legislation but accepts that 'there is a continuing need to take active measures to ensure that the aims of legislation are translated into everyday policy and practice... Ratification of the Convention will help to ensure that the needs and interests of children are given a high profile across government'. However, that said, the report contains no further indication that any change is required to any aspect of children's lives in order to achieve compliance with the principles and standards the Convention contains. There is no acknowledgement of any need for improved resourcing, improved legislation, or changes in attitudes or practices towards children. As such, it does not give a true picture of the state of our children.

The UN Convention on the Rights of the Child provides a challenging and exciting opportunity to open up a wide-ranging debate about the rights of children in our society. The Children's Rights Development Unit has been monitoring the initial reports to the UN Committee from other European countries and it is evident that, unlike the UK, many Governments have attempted an honest appraisal of the state of their children, being prepared to acknowledge problems and engage in a national debate on how to make children's rights a reality. Our Government has so far failed to grasp that opportunity and our children, and indeed the whole of society, are the poorer for that failure.

AN ALTERNATIVE APPROACH TO PROMOTING CHILDREN'S RIGHTS

It was anticipation of this lack of commitment on the part of the Government towards children's rights that led, early in 1990, to a recommendation to be put to the Gulbenkian Foundation that a 'secretariat' should be set up to ensure that, once the Convention was ratified by the Government, it was taken seriously and implemented as fully as possible. After consultations with key organisations, the Foundation appointed a consultant to carry out wider soundings. The response generally favoured a new independent but short-life unit and the Foundation then brought together a steering committee to progress this – forming a company and seeking charitable status and funding. The steering committee grew into the Council of the new unit – named the Children's Rights Development Unit – which began its work in March 1992. Its brief was to promote the fullest possible implementation of the Convention in the UK. The Unit's first task was to evaluate the state of children's rights in the UK. This evaluation, A UK Agenda for Children, provides a detailed analysis of the extent to which law policy and practice in the UK complies with the principles and standards in the Convention. It sets out changes that are needed and identifies gaps in current knowledge which make it impossible to assess whether or not the principles and standards are being met. The Agenda, which was sent to the UN Committee on the Rights of the Child, provides a more critical commentary on the state of the UK's children than that provided by the Government. The methodology for producing the Agenda was as follows:

The Unit compiled a database of interested health authorities and trusts, local authorities, key national voluntary organisations, academics and professional associations willing to participate in a process of consultation. Fourteen policy areas were identified which between them spanned the range of principles and standards embodied in the Convention. In each policy area, three underlying principles are addressed: the requirement that all the rights in the Convention apply to all children without discrimination; (Article 2), the requirement that in all actions affecting them, the best interests of the child must be a primary consideration; (Article 3), the right of children to express views on all matters that affect them and to have them taken seriously (Article 12).

Having established the central themes, initial research was undertaken to explore relevant law, policy and practice in each area and evaluate it against the standards and principles embodied in the Convention. Consultation papers were then produced which identified key areas where there was either an explicit breach of the Convention or where there would need to be changes to legislation, its implementation or levels of resourcing to achieve full compliance. Action necessary to achieve compliance was identified. The draft papers were then sent out for consultation to every organisation or individual who had expressed an interest in that policy area.

There are marked differences in legislation, administration of statutory services and cultural experiences within the four jurisdictions in the UK which needed to be reflected in the UK Agenda. The Unit identified a number of areas where the experience in Scotland and Northern Ireland was of sufficient difference to require a separate paper being produced – for example, youth justice in Scotland and armed conflict in Northern Ireland. Where the differences were more marginal or were quantitative rather than qualitative, such as in issues around poverty, it was agreed to circulate the same paper and rely on the feedback from participants to identify critical regional concerns that needed to be addressed. Separate consultations and seminars were convened for a number of the policy areas in Scotland and Northern Ireland. A close dialogue was established with the Children in Wales organisation, which ensured wide circulation of draft papers in Wales, in order that any specific issues concerning Welsh children were adequately addressed.

The Agenda needed to be informed as fully as possible by the views of children and young people. A short document was drafted to accompany each policy paper which set out the key rights addressed and asked a number of questions about how far those rights were respected in practice. When the policy papers were distributed, every participant was asked to use the document as a basis for discussion with any groups of young people with whom they were in touch and to send the Unit details of any such discussions that were held. Forty-five consultation sessions with children and young people through-out the UK were set up. The participants in these groups ranged in age from 6 to 18 years and sought to reflect the wide disparities in life-experience of children in different circumstances. For example, some discussions were based in schools or youth clubs, others were with young people looked after by local authorities or who were leaving care, others were with young people who were caring for sick or disabled parents or who had been abused or were homeless. The discussions were wide-ranging and produced a wealth of material which was able to inform and strengthen the analysis in the Agenda, and which is reflected by a selection of direct quotes in the text of the reports.

Following the consultation, the Scottish, Welsh and Northern Ireland perspectives were incorporated together with the views and experiences of young people and the comments received. Organisations who had contributed to the process were asked to endorse the report. One hundred and eighty-three national bodies did so. The final document, the UK Agenda for Children, was published and sent to the UN Committee on the Rights of the Child as an alternative report to the one submitted by the Government.

HOW FAR ARE CHILDREN'S RIGHTS RESPECTED IN THE UK?

It became evident in the process of producing the UK Agenda for Children that in some very fundamental ways things are getting worse, not better, for many children. Certainly there are no grounds for complacence. The following paragraphs set out some, but by no means all, of the primary concerns that were identified in the UK Agenda.

The Convention emphasises the right of every child to an 'adequate standard of living' for their proper development. The massive rise in unemployment in recent years together with the rise in numbers of lone parents and changes in the structure of employment, with more workers in part-time and temporary jobs, has contributed to a substantial growth in child poverty during the 1980s and early 1990s. Government figures published in July 1993 reveal clearly that there has been a substantial widening of the gap between rich and poor in the UK (HMSO 1993). There are now 13.5 million people, including 3.9 million children, living in poverty (using the measure of poverty accepted across Europe of less than 50% of average income after housing costs). This compares with 1.4 million children in 1979 and represents one in three of all children. The figures show that children have disproportionately borne the brunt of the increase in poverty in the UK. The number of children living in families wholly dependent on income support also more than trebled between 1979 and 1992. While the Government's own report to the UN Committee suggests that the 'real disposable income of all types of families is now on average appreciably higher than in 1979', it fails to record that the real income of the poorest 10 per cent shows a fall of 14 per cent.

It is evident then that not only are there very substantial numbers of children living in poverty but that the numbers have escalated rapidly in recent years. This pattern contrasts sharply with most of European countries where not only is there less child poverty, but there has been no rise in child poverty during the 1980s. A report produced for UNICEF in 1993 seeks to monitor, over a 20 year period, the social well-being of children in industrial countries through a set of international indicators relating to children's health, education, emotional stress and economic welfare (Miringoff and Opdycke 1993). The report demonstrates that of the 10 countries studied, only in the UK and USA did children end the period with lower levels of social health on every count than they started with. In the UK, charting progress on an index of 0–100, the score was 20 points lower than in 1970. The existence of state benefits and other welfare provision has failed to protect many children and their parents from the worst effects of rapid economic and social changes. As a consequence, not only have we witnessed a growth in child poverty, but, accompanying it, an increase in family homelessness and young people living on the streets. Poverty denies children the right to afford the basic necessities of life, to the best possible health, to education on the basis of equality of opportunity, to opportunities to play, to adequate housing, and perhaps most fundamentally, for many it imposes both a physical and social exclusion from citizenship.

Article 18 stresses that, whilst parents have primary responsibility for the care of their children, the Government must provide help and support to *all* parents in their child rearing duties. It is difficult to reconcile this broad-ranging commitment to a shared approach to provision and services for children with the potentially restrictive implications of the gate-keeping concept of 'in need' which applies in the Children Act. Section 17 of the Children Act 1989 in England and Wales requires local authorities to provide appropriate services for children in need. A child in need is defined in the legislation as any child whose health or development is likely to be impaired without the provision of services, or is unlikely to achieve or maintain a reasonable standard of health and development without the provision of services, or who is disabled. In other words, whereas the Convention describes a responsibility on the part of the state in respect of all children, the Children Act restricts responsibility to those children who are perceived as vulnerable. It was precisely this narrowing of potential entitlement to family support services that united voluntary organisa-tions against the concept during the passage of the Act through Parliament. In practice, the Children Act definition of 'in need' is open to widely different interpretations by local authorities. However, it is already becoming clear that many local authorities are constructing a narrow definition of need which requires individual families to undergo assessment before being able to qualify for access to any services. The Social Services Inspectorate (1992), in their initial research on the Act, comment that one of their most worrying findings is the failure to give high priority to families on income support and family credit, one parent families or unemployed parents. This low rating is of particular concern in view of the known high correlation between material deprivation and the use of accommodation or care. The Children Act Report (DOH and Welsh Office 1992) confirms this pattern with only a quarter of authorities identifying children in low income families as being in need.

Budgets for children in need are resource- rather than needs-led and with local authorities currently experiencing severe constraints on expenditure, there is little provision for any development of family support services. Certainly, research into the implementation of Section 17 of the Act amongst Welsh local authorities confirms that initial concerns that child protection would take the major area of resources with insufficient left over for family support services were well founded. Children suffering from abuse or neglect were receiving the highest priority despite the views of senior managers that putting more resources into family support would reduce the numbers of children at risk (Colton et al. 1995a; 1995b). The NSPCC (1993) have commented that because resources are not available, children need to be deemed to be in need of protection to get help.

An approach to a definition of need which fails to recognise that for many families their problems are rooted in long-term acute structural poverty and not individual pathology will inevitably create a narrow route of access which will deny many families the support services necessary to promote their children's rights.

Day-care provision for children represents a central plank in the range of support services that parents require in bringing up their children. Publicly funded provision for under-fives in the UK is very low compared with most other European countries. The most recent figures on nursery education places Britain eleventh in a league table of European countries with only Portugal providing lower levels. Day-care for under-threes is two per cent as compared with 30 per cent in France and 48 per cent in Denmark. More than 95 per cent of French and Belgian children are in nursery schools from the age of three, as are 85 per cent of Italian and Danish children. In Britain the figure is around 25 per cent with most attending only part-time. There is substantial evidence of the benefits to children of receiving nursery education yet even our current limited provision may be under threat from the Education Act 1993. The amount which will be allowed in the Standard Spending Assessment for nursery education will be devolved down to the individual school rather than held by the local authority. The budget has never been sufficient to fund nursery places at every school, so, inevitably, once the money is distributed in this way, it is unlikely that there will ever be sufficient in any one school budget to provide nursery education. There is, therefore, a serious threat that a service of primary importance for children, already woefully inadequate, may in the future deteriorate much further. These policies demonstrate a clear lack of commitment to the principles embodied in Article 18 of a partnership between parents and the State in the provision of services for children.

Article 12 of the Convention states that 'States parties shall assure to the child who is capable of forming his or her own views the right to express those views freely in all matters affecting the child, the views of the child being given due weight in accordance with the age and maturity of the child' and 'For this purpose, the child shall, in particular, be provided with the opportunity to be heard in all judicial and administrative procedures affecting the child.' This principle is fundamental both to the Convention and to any recognition of children as people with a right to participate in decisions that affect them. The UK is very far from complying fully with it at present.

The Children Act 1989 incorporates the principle, requiring that children's wishes and feelings are considered when decisions which affect them are being made. The recent cases of children applying to court for judgements about where they live and who with are positive examples of the application of this right. But the Children Act only applies to a limited number of children in a limited range of circumstances.

Both from the perspective of the importance of respecting children's basic civil rights and also the value for children of acquiring the skills and understanding necessary to participate in a democratic society, a commitment to a child's right to participation is of vital importance. But, at present, children have no rights in law to be consulted or to be taken account of in any matter concerning their individual rights with regard to educational provision. The education system denies them any formal voice whatever. They have no right to be consulted over school choice, school suspensions or exclusions and special needs. Nor is there any formal requirement to hear the views of an individual child concerning any issue relating to their education or problems such as bullying in school. The extent to which space is created to listen to children and to respond to issues raised is a matter entirely for the individual school head.

Likewise, children have no formal rights to participate in matters of school policy or administration. There is no requirement to involve children in decisions on, for example, school uniform, curriculum, arrangements for school meals, supervision in the playground, discipline, etc. Very few schools have school councils which provide an institutionalised structure within which to consult children and to hear their views or to ensure that they are taken account of in developing policy despite the recommendations of the Elton inquiry 'Discipline in Schools' which stated: 'Headteachers and teachers should recognise the importance of ascertaining pupils' views...encourage active participation of pupils in shaping and reviewing schools behaviour policy... LEAs should regularly evaluate (behaviour) policies in relation to...the perception of...pupils'.

In Sweden, Denmark, Spain and France considerable efforts have been made to facilitate the involvement of children in the management and running of schools. In the UK, by contrast, the limited rights that did exist for pupils to be represented on governing bodies of schools were abolished by the Government in 1988. This principle, however, has not been translated into legislation in this country. Children will, therefore, continue to be substantially excluded from any right to be consulted – either in relation to their individual circumstances or as a group on any matter concerning their education.

Schools are not required to introduce formal complaints procedures. The Government's report to the UN Committee is disingenuous on this issue stating that in the field of education 'there is no obstacle in law to prevent children themselves from making a complaint' about the curriculum or religious education, but fails to mention that children are not informed about this right, no procedures exist to facilitate the making of a complaint and certainly no advocacy or representation is available to help make the opportunity to challenge decisions a reality. Children have no access to a publicised or clearly defined route through which to air any grievance or injustice they have experienced. But the Children Act imposes a statutory requirement on all social service departments to establish complaints procedures to which children have access. Such a provision is integral to any meaningful process of listening to children and giving due consideration to their views. Whilst it is always preferable for decisions to be made through discussion and negotiation, the right to be heard is an empty protection if it is not backed up by the opportunity to challenge any breach of that right. The introduction of a right for children to have their views and feelings considered in the context of their education would also need to be backed up by the provision of statutory complaints procedures. Only by so doing would we achieve any measure of consistency in our recognition of children's rights in the public sector.

In the context of education, it is of particular value that children learn, not only through the curriculum, about human rights and civil responsibilities but through the experience of the way in which they are treated and valued as individuals. Learning that their opinions and feelings are important and that adults want to hear them is one of the most effective means of acquiring a sense of self-worth and learning the value of respect for others. One of the most important aspects of education is the process of learning to participate in a democratic society. A key principle in our society is that, as a democracy, people have an opportunity to express their views – through elections, through the freedom of the press, through the courts, tribunals and complaints procedures and through informal systems which operate in many of our institutions. Children are people too and, as such, should be afforded the same respect for their views as those available to adults. The only means of ensuring that these rights are properly respected is to incorporate them into our legislation. Without this safeguard, there can be no assurance that the right will be upheld and there will be no redress for children whose rights in this respect are ignored.

The right of children of sufficient understanding to make decisions for themselves were enhanced by the 'Gillick' decision in the House of Lords (Gillick 1986) which gave children under 16 years of age an independent right to consent to treatment if they are judged to have sufficient understanding. The original judgement, which made clear that it applied to decision-making on any important matter and not just medical treatment, stated: 'The parental right to determine whether or not their minor child below the age of 16 years will have medical treatment terminates if and when the child achieves a sufficient understanding and intelligence to enable him or her to fully understand what is proposed' (Gillick v West Norfolk and Wisbeach AHA, 3 All ER 402 (1985)). However, a subsequent ruling from the Appeal Court in 1992, in the case of Re W, concerning a young woman suffering from anorexia nervosa, sought to distinguish between consent and refusal to consent to treatment (Re W (A Minor: Consent to medical treatment), 1 FLR 1 (1993)). As a result, a competent child under the age of 18 who refuses treatment which a doctor considers necessary could be required to have that treatment against his or her will if any person with parental responsibility consents to that treatment.

The 'Gillick' judgement was significant in recognising children's rights to growing self-determination and is consistent both with Article 12 and Article 5 which stresses that parents and others with responsibility for children must provide appropriate direction and guidance to children 'in a manner consistent with the evolving capacities of the child'. The 'Re W' ruling, although from a lower court, has placed in question this principle of individual competence by suggesting that those with parental responsibility can overrule the child's refusal to consent. There is, therefore, some confusion at present in respect of the law pertaining to children's right to self-determination which needs clarification.

There is no obligation to take account of the views of children within the family. In Finland, there is a requirement written into their equivalent of the Children Act that parents must consult with their children in reaching any major decision affecting them, subject to the child's age and understanding. Similar provisions exist in Germany, Sweden and Norway. In Scotland, the Scottish Law Commission, in a recent consultation on proposals for family law, found that there was widespread support for comparable provision. However, to date there is no such requirement in law.

The UK has a long way to go before claiming to fulfil the standards required by Article 12. The consultation with children and young people undertaken by the Children's Rights Development Unit during 1993 revealed that concern over lack of respect for their views was the issue that united all the groups. They all described the failure of adults in schools, at home, in politics, in the media and amongst policy makers and service providers to ascertain children's wishes and feelings and to respect those wishes and feelings when making decisions. We do not have a culture of listening to children. Serious application of Article 12 will require that this changes.

Article 3 states that 'In all actions concerning children, whether undertaken by public or private social welfare institutions, courts of law, administrative authorities or legislative bodies, the best interests of the child shall be a primary consideration'. This principle is central to the Children Act in England and Wales, with its requirement that the child's welfare must be the paramount consideration. However, the Children Act and the paramountcy of the child's welfare only applies to courts considering matters about a child's upbringing. Not all courts of law in the UK are subject to such a principle. For example, tribunals hearing immigration and nationality appeals, all the tribunals operating in the education system on school choice, special needs and school exclusions. A case in 1993 of a mother being imprisoned whilst awaiting deportation and her children, all of them British citizens, being taken into care exposes the harsh realities of legislation which takes no account of a child's welfare. Outside the courts too the concept of 'best interests' is notably absent. There is no 'best interests' principle in education law. There is no requirement on schools to take account of either an individual child's welfare when making decisions about that child or children as a whole. This means that decisions to exclude a child, or to withdraw special support services, to close a school, to change the admissions criteria, to refuse children with special needs, to operate their disciplinary procedures, do not have to be made with reference to the child or children's best interests. Other considerations such as economy, parental choice, prestige of the school or efficiency can all take precedence.

Likewise, if we look at planning and environmental issues, children's considerations have a very low priority. If we were to take seriously the duty described in Article 3, it would be necessary to look at the implications for children when a new road was being proposed – what would be the implications for their health in terms of noise pollution, lead pollution, access to play facilities, mobility and the ability to move around within the local environment? How far are children's best interests considered in the housing developments we see around all our cities – with their lack of play facilities, lack of pavements, dangerous road crossings and so on?

Article 19 asserts the right of children to protection against all forms of violence. At present in the UK, children are the only people not protected by law from all assaults. There are detailed regulations forbidding the use of corporal punishment in children's homes and foster care. There is also Department of Health guidance in respect of children in day-care settings stating that physical punishment should not be used in any group day-care setting, including child-minding. This position is reiterated in the Government's report to the UN Committee which states that 'the Government's policy on the physical punishment of children is that it has no place in the child care environment'. However, the status of this Guidance has been thrown into question following a High Court judgement which took the view that the London Borough of Sutton had been too rigorous in its application of the Department of Health guidance when they refused to register a child-minder who declined to agree not to smack children in her care. It is clear that without regulations prohibiting the use of physical punishment, children in such settings will not be adequately protected. However, the Department of Health have since failed to match their earlier commitment to such protection stating that they consider it unnecessary to introduce regulations, and going on to add that, in the light of the court judgement, local authorities should not uphold current guidance so strictly that a child-minder is automatically considered unfit if she uses corporal punishment. There is also no protection against physical punishment in the home and children whose parents pay for them to be educated in private schools can still be subjected to corporal punishment. The legal concept of 'reasonable chastisement' allows both physical and mental violence towards children.

It used to be the case, in this country as in many others, that husbands had the right to beat their wives. Whilst recognising that there is still widespread abuse of women by men, it is no longer reinforced by the law – legal remedies, however inadequate, do exist and the legitimacy of exercising the right to physical integrity is acknowledged. Women were, and are, vulnerable to violent abuse but, as they have fought for recognition of their rights, so social attitudes have began to change and their civil and political rights have been enhanced. Children are less able to challenge prevailing attitudes. They do not have a powerful voice in any of the arenas necessary for creating political or social change. It is, therefore, incumbent on adults to fight the case for providing children with the same rights to physical integrity and freedom from assault as those which exist for adults. The social and legal endorsement of hitting children is one of the most symbolic indications of their low status in our society and until it ceases to be endorsed as legitimate punishment, the UK will continue to violate the Convention and perpetuate children's vulnerability to the abuse of adults.

In many other areas of children's lives, all is far from well – school exclusions are increasing (NUT 1992), possibly as many as two million children under school age are working – many of them in illegal and unregulated employment (Pond and Searle 1992), inequality in health care and life-chances persists with children from poor working class families twice as likely to die in their first year as children from professional and managerial families (Leon 1991) and there are serious concerns about the levels of resourcing in many hospital and community health services for children. There is a reported increase in the incidence of depression, suicide and attempted suicide amongst children as well as increases in eating disorders such as anorexia and obesity (Graham 1986). As many as one in four children and young people suffer from mental health problems (Mental Health Foundation 1993), over 75 per cent of care-leavers leave school with no qualifications whatever (Garnett 1992), and 97 per cent of 16–17-year-olds earn less than the Council of Europe's decency threshold (£5.15 per hour in 1992) (Department of Employment 1992). Obviously not all these problems are capable of easy solution. But the difficulties they represent for children are inconsistent with full implementation of the UN Convention. They need to be acknowledged by the Government as matters of serious concern.

FINDINGS OF THE UN COMMITTEE

In January 1995, the UN Committee on the Rights of the Child, having received both the government and the alternative report from the Children's Rights Development Unit, met with a delegation from the Government to examine the extent to which the principles and standards of the Convention were being complied with. The Government did not emerge from that examination unscathed. Indeed, the findings of the Committee represent a searing indictment of the Government's record in promoting children's rights.

The Committee were concerned about the high, and growing, numbers of children living in poverty, with all the consequent implications for their health and life-chances evidence of the very considerable growth in inequality in the UK between rich and poor – now greater than at any time since the 19th century – and the growing phenomena of young people sleeping and begging on the streets.

The Committee were clearly disturbed by evidence revealing that legislation permitting 'reasonable chastisement' of children allowed levels of violence which were in breach of the Convention. They were not satisfied with the response that the Government considered physical punishment to be a private matter for parents and argued, rather, that the right of children to protection from all forms of physical violence was a fundamental human right from which the Government could not abdicate its responsibility to children in favour of parental choice. Indeed, one member of the UN Committee, during the session in January, observed that 'the UK position represented a vestige of the outdated view that children were in a sense their parents' chattel.'

They were concerned that the right of parents to withdraw children from religious and sex education was not consistent with the obligation to take account of the views and wishes of children. Indeed, they consistently highlighted the failure on the part of the Government to recognise the legislative and policy implications of Article 12 both within the family and in education. The Committee considered that the age of criminal responsibility at 10 years (8 in Scotland) is too low to reflect the spirit of the Convention. But it was the provisions of the Criminal Justice and Public Order Act 1994 which gave greatest cause for concern given that this legislation, which introduces prisons for 12–14-year-olds and extends sentencing for young offenders, so clearly breaches the obligations to use imprisonment only as a measure of last resort and for the shortest appropriate period of time has been brought in since the Government ratified the Convention. They also commented with concern that the principle of the best interests of the child was not reflected in education, health or social security legislation.

It becomes clear then, when reading these and other findings of the Committee, that the UK has a very long way to go before the Government can justify its claim that we lead the world in our treatment of children.

In addition to a number of specific recommendations aimed at more effective implementation of substantive rights in the Convention, the Committee proposed that the Government consider establishing an independent mechanism for monitoring the implementation of the Convention. There is a strong lobby of support in this country for the creation of a statutory Children's Rights Commissioner whose explicit role would be to represent and promote the rights and interests of children in all areas of law, policy and practice affecting them. We have seen, since ratification of the Convention, that we cannot rely on the Government itself to represent children's interests in line with its standards. There are many voluntary organisations, professional bodies and associations bringing public attention to abuses of children's rights, the need for better resourcing, more research and new legislation. But there is a need for more than that. We need a statutory Office with powers to investigate breaches of, and monitor compliance with, the Convention, to monitor children's access to complaints procedures, to develop models for the use of child-impact statements on national and local government policy and to report annually to Parliament on the state of children's rights. We need a Commissioner whose work is informed by the views and experiences of children and young people themselves and who will serve as an independent body to comment on, interpret, and advocate the rights of children.

CONCLUSION

There is a long way to go in order to achieve full implementation of the provisions contained in the UN Convention on the Rights of the Child and improve the status of children in UK society. None of its principles and standards are fully respected for all children. The UK is not a society which places sufficient value on its children. Until there is a willingness to recognise the extent to which those breaches are occurring and until all policy and legislative proposals are scrutinised with a view to considering their implications for children's rights, breaches of the UN Convention will continue and children will continue to be failed.

REFERENCES

Colton, M.J., Drury, C. and Williams, M. (1995a) *Children in Need: Family Support under the Children Act.* Aldershot: Arena.

Colton, M.J., Drury, C. and Williams, M. (1995b) *Staying Togther: Supporting Families under the Children Act.* Aldershot: Avebury.

Department of Employment (1992) *New Earnings Survey.* London: HMSO.

Department of Health and Social Security (1993) *Households Below Average Income: A Statistical Analysis 1979–1990/91.* London: HMSO.

Department of Health and Welsh Office (1994) *Children Act Report.* London: DoH.

Garnett, L. (1992) *Leaving Care and After.* National Children's Bureau.

Gillick v West Norfolk and Wisbeach Area Health Authority, 3 All ER 402 (1985).

Gillick v West Norfolk and Wisbeach Area Health Authority, (1986) AC 112.

Graham, P. (1986) 'Behavioural and intellectual development.' In E. Alberman and C. Peckham (eds) Childhood Epidemiology. *British Medical Journal 42*, 2, 155–62.

Leon, D. (1991) 'Influence on birth weight on differences in infant mortality by social class and legitimacy.' *British Medical Journal 303*, 964–67.

Miringoff, M. and Opdycke, S. (1993) *The Index of Social Health: Monitoring the Social Well-Being of Children in Industrial Countries.* A report for UNICEF. New York: Fordham Institute for Innovation in Social Policy.

National school reporting survey DfE and NUT survey on pupil exclusions: information from LEAS. London: National Union of Teachers.

NSPCC (1993) 'No room for doubt. *Community Care 21 October, 1993.*

Pond, C. and Searle, A. (1992) *The Hidden Army: Children at Work in the 1990s, The National Child Employment Study.* London: Low Pay Unit.

Re W (A Minor: Consent to medical treatment), 1 Family Law Report 1 (1993).

Social Services Inspectorate (1992) *Capitalising on the Act: A Working Party Report on the Implementation of the Children Act 1989 in London.*

Thompson, R. (1993) *Mental Illness: The Fundamental Facts.* London: Mental health Foundation.

PART FOUR

Providing an Education

CHAPTER SEVEN

Equality Assurance,
Children's Rights and Education
A UK Perspective

Andrew Hannan

INTRODUCTION

In April 1991 delegates at a conference on 'Entitlement for All: Race, Gender and the Education Reform Act' held at the University of Warwick decided to set up a working party (under the aegis of The Runnymede Trust) to try and provide the guidance which the National Curriculum Council had failed to produce on the implementation of important aspects of the rhetoric of the Education Reform Act and its various associated papers and statutory orders. The outcome was the publication of *Equality Assurance in Schools: Quality Identity, Society – a handbook for action planning and school effectiveness*, which was launched at follow-up conference at the same venue in April 1993.[1] The writing of that handbook involved numerous meetings of the 24 members of the working group and a series of consultation exercises – the largest of which involved the distribution of over 2000 copies of a draft in April 1992. The re-writing process was still under way when the Children's Rights conference took place that September.

It is not the intention of this chapter to analyse the process of compiling the handbook or to detail the nature of the recommendations for good practice in terms of whole school issues, the wider system and all of the subjects of the basic curriculum at each key stage of the National Curriculum. Instead, the focus will be on the opportunity which now exists for re-examining the nature of the

---

1   Copies of *Equality Assurance* can be obtained from The Runnymede Trust, 11 Princelet Street, London, E1 6QH. Telephone 0171-375 1496 for details of bulk orders, pricing, etc. Individual copies £5.95.

education to which, or so the legislation tells us, all children in England and Wales are now entitled.

KEY TASKS

The handbook (*Equality Assurance*) outlines three inter-related 'key tasks' with which we must engage in order to provide all children with equal rights, consideration and opportunities in our schooling system. These are described as follows (p.11):

- how to ensure high quality education for all pupils (*Quality*)
- how to support the development of cultural and personal identities (*Identity*)
- how to prepare pupils for full participation in society (*Society*).

In terms of *Quality* then:

> differences in average attainment, connected with differences of class, gender and ethnicity, are well known. However, they should not influence expectations of any one particular child. Schools would be wrong to accept the view that inequalities in the outcomes of schooling merely reflect inequalities and differences in wider society, and that there is nothing that education can do to counter them. Both research and practical experience show that schools can and do 'matter' – they really can make significant differences to young people's lives and life-chances, for there are specific measures which they can take to avoid perpetuating inequalities in wider society…governors, teachers and headteachers are rightly concerned with providing and assuring quality, and the highest possible standards of achievement. This necessarily, however, involves attention to issues of equality as well. Quality and equality strengthen and support each other, and neither is complete without the other. A school has to do as much as it reasonably can to ensure that it provides genuine equality of access, opportunity and treatment for all' (pp.11–12).

No one can accuse the authors of this passage of being naïve about the nature of the society in which they make a plea for equal rights, nor are they ignorant of the crucial role played by educational attainment. There is no sacrifice here of quality for equality, no surrender of equal opportunity for cultural relativism. This is neither romantic multiculturalism nor dogmatic egalitarianism.

Identity refers to a process of cultural development in which education has a significant part to play, although there are many complexities involved:

> For each child may have a range of loyalties, allegiances and identities that need to be held in balance. Similarly, society as a whole has to work out a balance between diversity on the one hand and shared values on

the other. Every individual may take part in a range of different cultures and communities. Some of these may be at variance with each other. Many are interrelated and continually exchanging with each other. All are in a state of development, affected both by internal tensions and by external factors often beyond their control. Not all cultures and communities have equal status: the formation of personal identities may therefore take place within contexts of uneven power and influence. Teachers and schools have increasingly complex and difficult tasks in their responsibilities to a wider society, and in the support they give to each child or young person in their care. Each child or young person needs to develop a sense of identity which is:

- confident, strong and self-affirming, as distinct from uncertain, ashamed or insecure

- open to change, choice and development, as distinct from unreflective, doctrinaire and rigid

- receptive and generous towards other identities, and prepared to learn from them, as distinct from wishing to exclude or to be separate.

Each individual's combination of identities and loyalties is unique, and alters over time. At any one stage each has particular priorities, difficulties, needs and opportunities (pp.12–13).

A scheme is outlined which sets out aims in terms of knowledge and understanding, skills and attitudes, which include the following objectives:

- ability to analyse and criticise features of cultural traditions, and to identify instances of prejudice, intolerance and discrimination

- willingness to sustain the positive aspects of one's own traditions, and therefore willingness to be constructively critical when appropriate

- to place emphasis not only on learning about diversity but also on values and concerns which different communities and cultures have in common. (p.13)

No attempt here, then, to advocate the uncritical transmission of cultural traditions seen as unchanging concrete entities. Rather, education is seen as a process of enhancing cultural awareness, of expanding horizons.

Society refers to the process of learning for citizenship and preparing for full participation in society.

These aspects of *Equality Assurance* are defined with reference to the statement on 'human rights in the school curriculum' issued by the Council of Europe (1985), which is reproduced below:

Council of Europe

HUMAN RIGHTS IN THE SCHOOL CURRICULUM

The understanding and experience of human rights is an important element of the preparation of all young people for life in a democratic and pluralistic society. It is part of social and political education, and it involves intercultural and international understanding.

Concepts associated with human rights should be acquired from an early stage. For example, the non-violent resolution of conflict and respect for other people can already be experienced within the life of a pre-school or primary class.

Opportunities to introduce young people to more abstract notions of human rights, such as those involving an understanding of philosophical, political and legal concepts, will occur in the secondary school, in particular in such subjects as history, geography, social studies, moral and religious education, language and literature, current affairs and economics.

Human rights inevitably involve the domain of politics. Teaching about human rights should, therefore, always have international agreements and covenants as a point of reference, and teachers should take care to avoid imposing their personal convictions on their pupils and involving them in ideological struggles.

Skills

The skills associated with understanding and supporting human rights include:

INTELLECTUAL SKILLS, IN PARTICULAR:

- skills associated with written and oral expression, including the ability to listen and discuss, and to defend one's opinions
- skills involving judgement, such as the collection and examination of material from various sources, including the mass media, and the ability to analyse it and to arrive at fair and balanced conclusions, and
- the identification of bias, prejudice, stereotypes and discrimination

SOCIAL SKILLS, IN PARTICULAR:

- recognising and accepting differences
- establishing positive and non-oppressive personal relationships
- resolving conflict in a non-violent way
- taking responsibility
- participating in decisions
- understanding the use of the mechanisms for the protection of human rights at local, regional, European and world levels.

This statement is part of the appendix to the Council of Europe's Recommendation No.R (85) 7 of the Committee of Ministers to Member States on Teaching and Learning about Human Rights in Schools, adopted by the Committee of Ministers on 14 May 1985. A more informal statement of some important aspects of those rights comes from 7–8-year-old children of a primary school in Manchester (p.14):

Charter of rights

EVERY CHILD HAS THE RIGHT:

- not to have to fight
- to expect people to be kind
- not to be made fun of
- not to be made sad
- not to be scared of the teachers
- to have friends
- not to be scared to come to school
- to be safe.

The concept of rights applies here in terms of protection and respect. Overall, education is clearly seen as the very opposite of indoctrination – it is about empowering young people as active citizens, knowledgeable about their society and able to challenge prejudices, stereotypes and injustice.

COMMENTARY

We are entering a new phase in the struggle over what goes on in our schools. Until recently the Government has had things more or less its own way. There have been exceptions to this, such as in Scotland where a united front of parents and teachers prevented the introduction of the system of testing which was required for England and Wales. There has always been strong opposition from some local authorities, teachers and academics to aspects of the Government's reforms but these have previously been dismissed as the bleatings of the education establishment moaning about attacks on their privileges and vested interests – complaints about the bad taste merely confirming the effectiveness of the medicine administered. The retreat from the testing of 7- and 14-year-olds prompted by the teachers' boycott, and the massive changes recommended by Sir Ron Dearing (1993) now accepted by the government, have created the opportunity to put the sorts of 'key tasks' highlighted by *Equality Assurance* at the centre of the process of re-thinking the foundations of the school curriculum in England and Wales.

Schools groaning under the weight of the huge bulk of National Curriculum documents now have the opportunity to put some of the demands of detail to one side. The attitude, which many teachers have adopted, of careful compliance with the minutiae of orders and guidance has been undermined by the amazingly frequent retreats and reversals. All of this creates opportunities for those wishing to pose fundamental questions about the nature of the National Curriculum our schools are supposed to deliver. There has never been a better time to go back to basics; to questions about what education should be like for our children.

This is the biggest contribution of *Equality Assurance*, it articulates fundamental notions about what our schools should be doing. It is important that this is not merely a philosophical exercise which teaches us how to ask the questions but fails to provide any answers. Here we have a publication which unashamedly puts its money where its mouth is, which risks losing its ideological purity because it boldly goes beyond critique and theoretical justification to advocacy and practical recommendations. The underlying principles enshrined in the trinity of *Quality/Identity/Society* are elaborated in terms which relate to, but transcend, the paraphernalia of the National Curriculum; which show how a good education is about ensuring high quality education for all, developing cultural and personal identities and preparing for full participation in society. Here is a chance, then, to step back from the particular and examine the general, to ask how the curriculum delivered in schools meets these basic criteria, to escape from the check list approach, to look at the *why* and not simply the *what*, to place the rights of children and young people at the heart of education.

REFERENCES

Dearing, Sir R. (1993) *The National Curriculum and its Assessment: Interim Report.* London: HMSO.

The Runnymede Trust (1993) *Equality Assurance in Schools: Quality, Identity, Society – a Handbook for Action Planning and School Effectiveness.* Stoke-on-Trent: Trentham Books and London: The Runnymede Trust.

CHAPTER EIGHT

Creating an Adaptable Science Curriculum for Children in Rural Africa[1]

Alan Peacock

OBSTACLES TO ACCESS TO SCIENCE LEARNING

There is a large body of literature relating to constraints on the development of effective primary schooling in Africa which affect the curriculum and learning in general, and which it is not appropriate to review here. This chapter attempts only to highlight some of the features which affect rural children and science learning in particular, notably perceptions of science learning; geographical and resource constraints; centralisation of educational management; and the notion of relevance.

Perceptions of science learning

Traditional African teaching comprised three steps: observation, imitation and explanation. From the vantage point of his mother's back, the traditional African child was able to observe all kinds of objects and activities in his environment. When the child was not on his mother's back, he was either sitting in the shade in the garden, the front yard, or on the hard floor of the house. There, the child was able to manipulate many things that were the object of his curiosity. Once he was a bit older, two years old let us say, the child began to imitate adult activity. His desire to help his mother to weed led her to make him a miniature hoe. It is through observation and imitation that the son of the blacksmith learnt how to forge iron. It is through the same methods that Nyakyusa

---

1   An earlier version of this chapter was first presented at the World Conference on Research and Practice in Children's Rights, University of Exeter, September 1992. In its present form it has since been published in the International Journal of Science Education 17 (2). Taylor and Francis, the Publishers, have kindly granted permission for its inclusion here.

youths were able to build their own huts and establish what were called 'age-villages'. Observation and imitation were so much insisted upon by traditional African education that a child who asked too many questions was frowned upon. As for explanation, it was sparingly provided. Adults gave explanations in response to children's questions, but they refrained from giving unsolicited explanations. (Erny 1981, p.14)

There are important indicators here of traditional pedagogy and curriculum. For whilst the pedagogy is not dissimilar from current 'western' ideas of science learning through skills modelling and adult mediation, the traditional curriculum is perceived differently. In particular, work and education are a unitary whole; separation from real life is avoided, children learn the duties of adults, and schooling is one dimension of education. For boys, this has traditionally meant learning about planting, hunting, house building, keeping flocks; whilst with girls it involves cooking, pottery, fire lighting, child care, hygiene. It also implies that, as Erny points out, children learn with real (if miniature) tools, not toys. Moreover, other authors (Clarfield 1987; Peat 1995) have drawn attention to ways in which traditional world-views in indigenous communities present children with quite different, 'non-scientific' ideas and interpretations of natural phenomena.

Many of these traditional perceptions still hold sway in rural communities where, at present, the majority of parents and elders often have no experience of schooling themselves. Some of the ideas embodied in the traditional curriculum have been adopted in Science texts for primary schools; for example, the 'Beginning Science' series in Kenya (Berluti 1981 onwards) incorporated the study of 'Making work Easier' and required pupils to make a set of tools for evaluation and use in subsequent activities. However, powerful internal and external pressures have radically modified the view of Science curricula in Africa in the last 25 years, as pointed out by Hawes (1979). Internal pressures, after independence, were usually directed towards new national goals and aspirations, the most important of which, for education, were providing the kind of education which they had been denied by the colonial powers (i.e. universal primary education, formal, academic, geared to certification) along with a need for a rapid increase in 'high-level manpower' with technical skills to implement development plans. These pressures often worked in conflict, as discussed below.

They were reinforced at the time, where Science is concerned, by powerful external pressures, namely the massive support in Britain and America for change and expansion in Science curricula to bridge the gap between research and schooling; and the rapid increase in aid to newly independent African states. Thus prophets of change and modernisation abounded at a time when aid was relatively abundant and when the message was exactly the one that their audiences wished to hear. There was clearly a tension between the traditional curricular objectives and those of capitalist, individualistic societies; but, in almost all cases, this tension was ignored or resolved in favour of a 'process approach', in other words, a Science programme designed to help develop the skills and processes of scientific thinking modelled on American and British curriculum development programmes. The African Primary Science Programme (APSP) which, in 1969, was handed over to the African organisation, the Science Education Programme for Africa (SEPA), was a prime example of this, its materials being adapted and adopted in a number of countries including Kenya, Ghana, Ethiopa, Malawi, Nigeria, Sierra Leone and Uganda.

The perception of science learning embodied in this process approach was very different to that understood traditionally by parents, teachers and children alike. This, and the fact that such notions as what is living and non-living differ between traditional and Western cultures, has continually led to ineffective learning of science, as exemplified by Russell (1991) in relation to appropriate Science knowledge, and by Jegede and Okebukola (1991) in the sphere of skills learning. Modification of traditional perceptions has also been slow, and handicapped by the constraints referred to below, so that the present state of affairs in many rural African primary schools is that of teachers attempting to teach a syllabus which they do not understand (and in some cases will never have seen), using methods which imitate the didactic methods of former colonial teachers but which ignore the values inherent in traditional pedagogy at the same time as they fail to conceptualise the process approach of the new science curricula. And yet, in virtually every independent African state, Science is and has always been a compulsory element of the primary curriculum examined formally at the end of the primary phase, which, for most rural children, is the termination of their schooling. Thus there exist great gaps in the perception of Science between traditional ideas of skill learning amongst adults and children in rural areas, the national aspirations and curricula of ministries and training institutions which have adopted largely anglo-american models, and teachers in the classroom who, through inappropriate higher education, are themselves largely marooned in older, pre-independence models of didactic teaching of factual knowledge.

Geographical and resource constraints

The rapid introduction of universal compulsory primary education after independence imposed massive financial commitments on most African states. Newly independent states have typically spent a much higher proportion of their Gross National Product (GNP) on education than most western countries. For example, Botswana from 1980 to 1985 spent, on average, eight per cent of GNP (almost 20% of all Government spending) on education, of which over 50 per cent was spent on primary schooling (WCEFA 1990). Despite this, because of the huge proportion of spending on teachers' salaries, other resources for schools have always been spread thinly. In countries such as Kenya, for example, construction of classrooms and furniture has remained a community responsibility. This in itself has been a handicap to practical Science since desks are still largely constructed from local timber on the old colonial sloping-top model making it difficult to stand apparatus upright. In Botswana, classrooms are built by the state to high quality specification, but this has meant that in most rural schools with expanding populations there are many more classes than rooms, thus requiring lessons to be carried on outside or on a shift system. Lack of storage, sun, wind and dust again create difficult conditions for effective practical work. The capitation allowance for materials is tiny in most countries and, therefore, purchase of Science equipment is largely out of the question. In Kenya this has been turned to advantage by incorporating a philosophy of improvisation into the curriculum through the textbooks available (see, for example, SEPA 1976 and Berluti 1989). In Namibia kits of essential Science resources are beginning to be provided along the lines adopted in many secondary science programmes in other neighbouring states by donor agencies.

But perhaps the major resource constraint in rural schools is difficulty of access to training and materials through inadequate communications and infrastructure. In northern Namibia teachers are invited to aid-agency in-service sessions by local radio. This often means travelling up to 200km without access to public transport, and finding one's own accommodation (Peacock 1992a). Even this leaves many rural teachers beyond the reach of centrally-provided in-service facilities. Botswana has developed an admirable network of Teacher Advisers to provide in-service education to primary teachers, but these well-trained and qualified staff are hampered in their work by lack of transport facilities and poor salaries (Peacock 1992b). In such countries, with low population densities, harsh climates and few metalled roads, travel and distribution of materials is difficult and very costly. The combination of these constraints ensures that working conditions for most rural teachers (many of whom will be posted to schools away from their home area and possibly outside their tribal/language group) are extremely difficult. The situation has been summed up as follows:

> A large number of teachers are unaware that many of the official policy documents exist. They are too busy operating the system to have much time to think about what its objectives are and whether they are suitable. Sometimes the goals are too general, and are not translated into specific policy instructions. Yet even when they are translated into instructions, teachers and administrators do not always follow them. (Bray, Clarke and Stephens 1986, p.145)

In rural schools, therefore, in an area such as Science, where there has been significant recent curriculum change in many countries, lack of access to resources and in-service 'upgrading' are a crucial constraint on pupils' learning.

There has, of course, been considerable assistance from developed countries to provide Science education backup to African states via in-country programmes such as those operated by the Free University Amsterdam in Zimbabwe, Botswana, Lesotho and Namibia, and by means of dedicated masters courses in developed countries, particularly the UK and USA. However, in-country projects have tended to focus on the secondary phase of schooling and on materials production for this phase, often as a consequence of locally determined priorities (INSTANT 1991). Furthermore, study overseas is usually restricted to those with the best academic qualifications, which largely excludes primary teachers.Even in-country courses, such as the B.Ed courses at the University of Botswana or at Kenyatta University, Nairobi, largely recruit from those with no primary teaching experience, graduates being posted mainly to teacher training institutions. The net effect of all the above factors is that few people with higher education experience in Science find their way into primary teaching or in-service work.

Centralisation

A characteristic of nearly all African states since independence has been the national-level control of curriculum, examinations, deployment of teachers and resource allocation in line with the newly created philosophies associated with such unifying concepts as self-help (Kenya), self-reliance (Tanzania), and social harmony (Botswana). In the case of Science curriculum development for primary schools, this has usually been in the hands of expatriate advisers collaborating with local educators in institutes based in capital cities and has resulted in curricula which departed radically from traditional views of learning. But also, and crucially, curricula have also often differed markedly from what would be implied by rural development priorities. Curle (1963) set out, at the beginning of this era of development, the priorities in terms of health, nutrition, employment, housing, sanitation and agricultural development; but it is only in isolated examples that, until recently, primary Science curricula have attempted to reflect these priorities. One reason for this is the tension between the status and credibility of academic qualifications on the one hand, and the drive for vocational relevance on the other. Politicians have often seemed to go along with the latter by supporting substantially-funded international aid programmes in education (for example, the World Bank funded Basic Education Project in Kenya) whilst, in practice, resisting the implementation of such programmes where they conflicted with academic imperatives. In the case of the Basic Education Project, for example, this resulted in non-implementation of the Project's intention to change the language of primary education from English to Kiswahili. Similarly, in Namibia, after independence, an early decision was made to adopt the International GCSE for Science at secondary level, whilst development of a new primary Science curriculum has been seen as a lesser priority, and is still not resolved, making teacher training in Science difficult to plan.

Meanwhile, Science texts for primary schools have often found it difficult to address the implications of vocational and developmental issues for schools in rural areas. The best (for example Berluti *op. cit.* 1981 onwards) deal with such issues as biogas production, solar power, local construction methods and water purification; but other, often more recent texts, still use photographs of largely urban contexts and require purpose-built scientific apparatus such as electric bells, fire extinguishers and syringes (Simuyu, Omar and Muthui 1988). Moreover, I have discussed elsewhere research which reveals the extent to which science texts in English prove to be inaccessible to second-language learners in Africa, partly through difficulties in the language itself and the way it is taught to children and partly as a consequence of a lack of visual literacy (Peacock, 1995).

Another disincentive to effective Science teaching is often provided by centralised recruitment and posting of teachers. Much of the talk amongst primary teachers away from the main centres of population is about insensitivity in posting, promotion, payment (often by cheque, for example, in remote areas!) and whilst this talk can sometimes be put down to generalised frustration, its sheer ubiquity enforces the observer to take it seriously. For example, Kenya has had a policy of mixing tribal groups during teacher training, and posting them regardless of tribal origins, as a deliberate means to promote national unity and reduce tribal tension. However, for many young unattached teachers this means working far away from home and family, teaching children who do not speak the teacher's mother tongue and often feeling unwelcome in the school community. Again, this perceived insensitivity of central planning adds to the disincentive to engage in in-service activity, which is crucial to improving Science teaching and learning.

Relevance

As already mentioned, a characterisic of primary Science in many African states is the discrepancy between traditional ideas of what needs to be taught, official government curricula and what teachers actually do in the classroom. Knamiller (1984) has discussed the many daunting dimensions of the search for relevance in science education in developing countries. For children in remote rural areas, a crucial issue is which of the perceptions of Science is most relevant to the needs of learners. The notion of 'Meeting Basic Learning Needs' has come to prominence in recent years, and has been promoted by the World Charter on Education for All (WCEFA) generated at the World Conference in Thailand in 1990. But prior to this, many countries were acknowledging that, since 'Basic Education' was terminal for the majority, the curriculum had to be such that it provided school leavers with the economic and life skills appropriate to their future in society. As a consequence, both Kenya and Botswana, for example, modified the Basic phase of education from 7 years primary to 8 years Basic (in Kenya) and to 9 years (in Botswana), thus extending the compulsory stage of education in both cases. Changes in curriculum have accompanied this.

What has not changed, however, is the process of selection by examination at the end of this compulsory Basic phase and as long as selection for higher phases of education exists, the examination, and hence to a large extent the teaching in the upper years of the basic phase, will be geared to the needs of the next phase rather than to the needs of those leaving. At the secondary/higher phases in most countries, science curricula are still closely linked to Western models, and a glance at the contents page of any African secondary science text would give few clues to its country (or continent) of origin. Hence a strong pressure on Science learning in rural primary schools, as in their urban counterparts, is the need to teach the testable knowledge dictated by the selection examination and by topics (such as electrolysis) which most rural children are unlikely to encounter or utilise in their daily lives.

The argument for relevance, which will be made later in this chapter, therefore revolves around the need to balance out the conflicting pressures imposed by three main factors, namely:

- the 'minimum entitlement' of a Science curriculum for primary schools, i.e. those elements of science learning which are seen to be essential in all countries and cultures

- the locally relevant science curriculum for children in remote rural areas whose working lives are likely to be dominated by involvement in agriculture, construction, maintenance, retailing, child care and general servicing and supply

- the 'teachable curriculum' or that Science which primary teachers in rural areas are in a position to provide with confidence and competence.

THE POTENTIAL WITHIN EXISTING STRUCTURES

Whilst the constraints described above appear severe, there are indications that potential exists within most systems to promote better Science learning for children in rural areas. Before attempting to reconcile the curricular discrepancies described above, therefore, the potential for improvement will be discussed in three areas, namely changes in examinations, improvisation of materials and parental perceptions.

The nature of Primary Leaving Examinations in Science

As already pointed out, examinations at the end of the primary/basic phase of education have tended to be certification-oriented, testing conceptual knowledge rather than acquisition of higher-order skills, and biased in favour of urban rather than rural contexts (Little 1982). However, some pioneering work has been carried out over the years, for example in Kenya, to expose such bias

(Somerset 1974, 1982) and modifications to eradicate such bias have been introduced with considerable success (Makau and Somerset 1978). For example, questions such as those in Figure 8.1 were found by item analysis to be answered correctly by the majority of candidates from rural schools and nomadic tribes but only by a minority in urban schools. A discussion of this can be found in Githui (1991). Item-writing in-service workshops for teachers in Science have been undertaken in order to foster wider understanding of this contextual dimension. Given the important influence which examinations exert on teaching, there is clearly much more that can be done effectively in this area to influence what and how Science is taught in rural communities. A key question, touched on below, is which parts of the science curriculum need to be examined and which should not.

3. Jane went to fetch water before sunrise, She saw the moon in the form of a thin crescent. Which of the following shapes of the moon did Jane see?

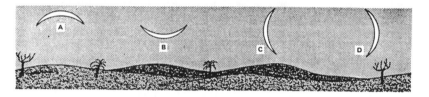

4. In which direction did Jane see the moon?
    A. North.   B. South.   C. East.   D. West.

72. A small fire is made outside on a very still day when there is no wind blowing. Burning small sparks and smoke rise in the air. Which one of the following diagrams **correctly** shows how the smoke and sparks move?

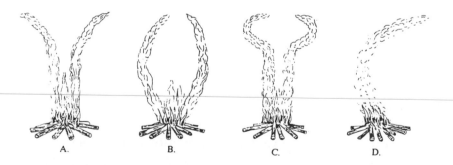

Source: Githui (1991, p.160)

Figure 8.1. Examples of science questions from the Kenyan Certificate of Primary Education (CPE) examination, intended to discriminate in favour of rural and nomadic children

Improvising of materials for science in primary schools

Improvisation is already encouraged by some texts and syllabuses, as already pointed out (SEPA; Berluti, *op. cit.*); and others have testified to the effectiveness and relevance of encouraging students to construct their own scientific apparatus such as working windmills, gardens, aquaria, etc. (Githinji 1992). The key importance of this, however, relates to the use of real tools and materials which have relevance to the traditional skills and demands of community work and life. To allow for this to happen, it is clear that the curriculum has to leave room for adaptations which are locally relevant. For example, basket weaving is a widespread and important craft in rural areas in most countries but the tools, materials, purposes and techniques vary widely from place to place and are closely integrated with other cultural imperatives such as seasons, festivals, rituals, etc. Hence the Science curriculum must be capable of local adaptation to take account of the concepts to do with properties of materials, forces and structures which are directly relevant to local needs, whether these are for winnowing baskets on the one hand or fish traps on the other.

Parental perceptions

Parental support for primary schooling in rural areas is a complex issue, which cannot be dealt with fully here. As already indicated, parents play a powerful role in traditional education through the modelling of adult work roles, although these are usually strongly divided on gender lines after infancy. The notion of the 'ideal man' and 'ideal woman' is a significant factor in education in some societies (Bray, Clarke and Stephens 1986) and practical education, which incorporates much we would see as Science, is often determined by the father's occupation and the mother's role. Age groups, craft guilds, religious centres and secret societies also play a role. Learning about medicine, for example, is a complex process involving different agencies and many rituals. It is difficult to generalise, therefore, about the extent to which primary schooling along Western lines is seen as supplementing, complementing, replacing or frustrating these traditional forms of education. What is emphasised repeatedly in the literature on traditional education, however (see, for example, Erny 1981), is the vital link between knowledge and experience. Thus, if schooling operates in ways which demonstrate that these are inextricably linked for their own children, it will surely be perceived to be of value by parents and have their support.

The 'bookish' and often academic education provided in primary schools has often fallen short of this and appeared to parents as divorced from the life of the community. At best it was seen as providing literacy in the lingua franca of the wider state and thus access to clerical and other paid employment within the public sector, albeit away from the home community. However, in countries where universal primary education was introduced from the late sixties onwards, despite take-up being proportionately less in rural areas, primary enrolments increased over threefold in Kenya, for example, in the 12 years following independence (Government of Kenya 1976). Thus the current generation of primary children is more likely to have parents who themselves went to school and are literate and numerate.

Exactly how this affects perceptions of schooling *vis-à-vis* science has not been the subject of reported research as yet. However, recent evaluation work in language learning in Botswana has shown marked differences in parental support for learning in schools where the majority of parents were themselves educated (e.g. in mining areas such as Jwaneng) compared to those in remote rural schools where few parents had been to school, such as Malatswae (Peacock 1992b). In Britain, our own recent research has shown that, at times of curriculum change in Science such as the past 5 years, parental perceptions of what is taught and how can lag far behind actuality (Peacock 1989), but that parental involvement with the school or the child's work can rapidly update these perceptions, even though teachers are perhaps unaware of this (Peacock and Boulton 1991). Thus it seems likely that parents who have themselves experienced primary schooling will be better placed to bridge the perception gap described above, thus being able to understand and, as occupational role models and members of the community, contribute in key ways to science learning, as discussed below.

Other factors clearly have a bearing on the potential to improve Science learning in rural primary schools, such as the training and deployment of Teacher Advisers and the role played by aid agencies and expatriate expertise. However, these are complex issues which affect schools and learning in a variety of ways and space does not permit a full treatment of all the issues here. This section has merely stressed some areas in which potential for progress clearly exists at present in the exemplar countries. In the context of this potential, and the constraints described above, the next section will set out what seems to be the minimum requirement for Science-based on the common content of primary curricula internationally and what is feasible in rural African schools. This 'Minimum Entitlement', which might be thought of as a core curriculum for primary Science, will then be followed by an example of a possible 'Locally Adapted Science Curriculum', based on a case study analysing rural development needs.

A MINIMUM ENTITLEMENT CURRICULUM FOR PRIMARY SCIENCE

What elements of science learning are essential to all children, wherever they may be? One way to address this question is to look at the common elements of primary Science curricula in a wide range of countries to ascertain if there is a consensus. From a survey of primary science curricula in over 30 countries

(Peacock 1993), it was found that there was a much greater emphasis on the natural world and the environment in African, Asian and Pacific countries and, particularly, on those topics which needed contextualising locally to be relevant – such as weather, living things, habitats, agriculture, nutrition, health and earth-science. However, other topics related to universal concepts (such as energy, forces, electricity, change of state, light, magnets and measurement) which are not necessarily context-dependent, could perhaps be better taught from a standard text, if one were to be made available, which could be appropriate to a wide range of countries and contexts.

From the point of view of teachability, economy and training, this distinction offers considerable advantages. The common core curriculum could well be that which is examined towards the end of primary schooling, whilst the locally contextualised elements concerned with environmental phenomena might not need to be examined at all, particularly as this would be difficult to do in a common national examination. A further factor which aids teachability in rural areas is the minimal dependence of the curriculum on apparatus which cannot be improvised; only magnets, batteries, bulbs and lenses – required in the 'core' element of the curriculum – would be seen as essential items which need to be purchased or otherwise provided in kits. The contextualised dimension could rely for its resources on those available within the local environment.

No doubt the Minimum Entitlement Curriculum as outlined above would need careful definition and refining to be widely acceptable. This would, however, not affect the underlying concept of a spare, concept-focused and relatively context-free core curriculum embodying the key Science concepts which are universally considered to be important for all children during their basic education. This Minimum Entitlement Curriculum for Science could then be adopted as the essential core of Science teaching and learning across a range of African countries, the other elements of the science curriculum being provided through the medium of a Locally Adapted Science Curriculum, as described in the next section.

THE LOCALLY ADAPTED SCIENCE CURRICULUM: MEETING THE NEEDS OF RURAL CONTEXTS AND COMMUNITIES

The purpose of a locally adapted science curriculum

Various authors have discussed the educational priorities for the development of rural communities in developing countries, such as Curle (1963) and Coombs and Ahmed (1974) who have provided examples of learning needs of persons engaged in subsistence agriculture, off-farm commercial activities, general services, etc. These needs are often Science related (e.g. knowledge of and application of new varieties, machines, practices; record keeping; storage, processing, preservation; health and nutritional awareness; child care and family planning; quality control; movement and handling of goods; maintenance of equipment). Equally, they are often specific to local contexts, where, for example, climate, water sources, crops, markets and infrastructure vary enormously. It therefore makes sense to see such knowledge and skills being taught in a local context.

An analysis of Table 8.2 (p.97) shows that these topics are also those which are largely context-dependent in terms of knowledge, skills and relevant applications. Not all of these are necessarily relevant to all children in all communities. Indeed, to try to teach all these supplementary topics on top of the minimum entitlement would recreate exactly the problems of overload, inappropriateness and difficulty of teaching which now exist in primary Science. Two main points are proposed here, namely:

1. that children in rural areas should address only those supplementary topics in Science which are of immediate relevance to local development priorities

2. that parents and other skilled adults in the community should be incorporated into the process of teaching the relevant knowledge and skills to primary children.

If a Locally Adapted Science Curriculum can be developed along these lines, then it should go some way towards eradicating the discrepancies between traditional, Western, and taught curricula described above. This is because the methods and content of teaching will approximate more closely to traditional ideas (modelling adult roles, integration of education and work) and because schools and teachers will not have to rely entirely on their own (often inadequate) knowledge, skills and resources. Such local differentiation of the curriculum is already advocated in other areas. For example, the survey of Science curricula in Asia and the Pacific quoted above (NIER 1986) advocates a core curriculum with regional variations and suggests, amongst its criteria for the latter, that they should be immediately meaningful to children, directly related to their own experiences and should be a systematic way for children to explore their natural and social environment. Also, the WCEFA stresses the need for Supplementary Alternative Programmes to help meet the basic learning needs of children with limited access to learning and recognises that parents, community organisations and others should become involved in sharing their energy, skills and expertise by re-orienting their regular work activities to incorporate this learning dimension. Even in post-National Curriculum Britain, examples are already available of schools developing Science programmes matched to the needs and specialisms of local industry, for example in Sunderland (Nellist 1991).

In order to illustrate how this might work out in practice, an example is given from a recent appraisal of rural development needs in Wollo Province, Ethiopa.

An Example of a Locally Adapted Science Curriculum for Wollo Province, Ethiopia

The International Institute for Environmental Development (IIED), in conjunction with the Ethiopian Red Cross Society, have undertaken rural appraisals for local level planning in various districts of Wollo Province as a means to developing sustainable agriculture programmes. An important dimension of this appraisal is the involvement of villagers themselves in collecting and recording information and in diagnosing needs, as indicated by the examples of their work provided in Figures 8.2, 8.3 and 8.4.

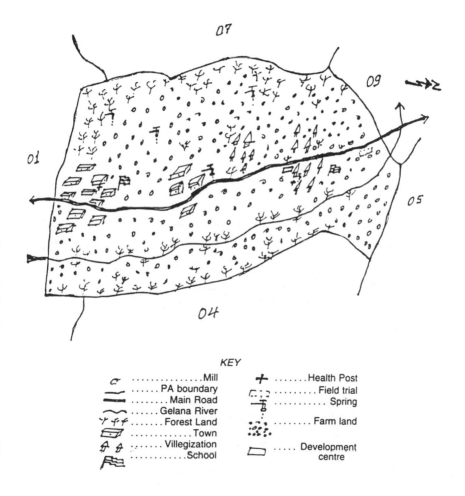

KEY

σ	..............Mill	+	.......Health Post
—	......PA boundary		.........Field trial
■	........Main Road		...........Spring
~~	.....Gelana River		........Farm land
Ψ ΨΨ	.......Forest Land		
	..............Town		..... Development
φ φ	:......Villegization		centre
	............School		

Source: Guijt and Scoones (1991, p.51)

Figure 8.2. Map of Amemo Peasant Association land, produced by villagers as part of Rapid Rural Appraisal Programme

- Before 1928 E.C. The mountain was covered with forests.

- 1929-1930 E.C.   The clearing of forests for the use of farmland.

- 1931-1968   Preparing of farms without terraces.

- 1969-1975   Planting of trees by Ministry of Agr. started.

- 1976-1983   Covered by forest.

Source: Guijt and Scoones (1991, p.64)

Figure 8.3. History of Abalefo Geta (Wollo Province) as told by a 72-year-old community member

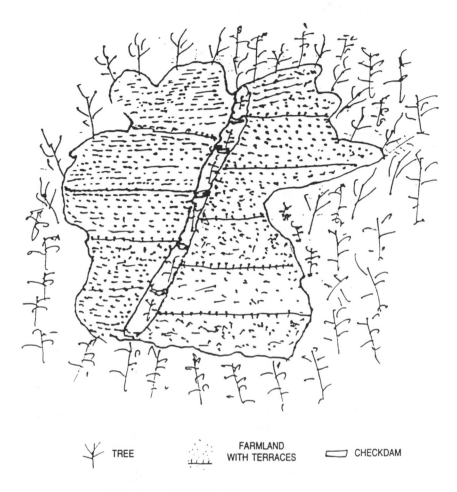

⅄ TREE	FARMLAND WITH TERRACES	⊏⊐ CHECKDAM

Source: Guijt and Scoones (1991, p.66)

Figure 8.4. Area in Amemo to be treated with soil and water conservation measures, as planned by community members

The report of these appraisals (Guijt and Scoones 1991) describes the background and resources in two districts, assesses problems and opportunities, and concludes by proposing a list of 'Best Bets' for each district, these being the initiatives most likely to be practicable and effective. Table 8.1 lists the Best Bets for Amemo District, with a population of 700 households in three villages, lying between 2000m to 2700m above sea level. The soil is clay and agriculture is based on both crop growing and domestic animals. There are a number of natural springs and one river. Land is distributed and managed by the Amemo Peasant Association. A main road runs through the middle of Amemo District.

Table 8.1. Rural development 'best bets' for Amemo district

1.   Tree planting

2.   Improved stoves

3.   Cash crop production

4.   Bee-keeping

5.   Irrigation development

6.   Bamboo and sisal intensification

7.   Clean drinking water

8.   Improved use of seedling nursery

9.   Intercropping with forage

10. Planting fodder crops

11. Improving the service of the Health Post

Source: Guijt and Scoones (1991)

Each of these Best Bets, formulated by the appraisal team in conjunction with villagers and confirmed by them as important, can be seen to have within it implications for Science learning amongst children in the community. Few of the topics relate directly to aspects of the 'core' entitlement curriculum described above. The majority are closely related to those topics not always covered by the existing curriculum, and those most context-dependent. Table 8.2 shows the links between the two by suggesting the basis of a Locally Adapted Science Curriculum for Amemo children.

The implications for science work are clear. The Locally Adapted Curriculum here requires focus on technology skills, observation and investigation, collection and interpretation of data, practical experimentation and application of principles. But these will necessarily be taught and learned in a locally relevant context, where the topics being studied are an integral part of projects being implemented by the whole community, with some expert help from outside. Thus the teaching of this Locally Adapted Science Curriculum need not be left entirely to the school as children will be able to work alongside adults, in a traditional way, whilst learning and will be able to take cognisance of indigenous as well as Western perceptions of such things as health and agricultural practices. Good examples of this process in practice in Kenya are described by Githinji (1992).

Table 8.2. A locally adapted science curriculum for Amemo

1. Energy and motion: design and construction of improved cooking stoves, to decrease fuel-wood demand. Design and construction of irrigation channels from the springs for horticultural purposes.

2. Agriculture (Plant and animal husbandry): development of gardens to grow haricot beans, oil seeds (linseed), fruit trees (guava and gesho). Keeping of bees for marketing of honey and for pollination of crops. Identifying new areas for bamboo and sisal growth to provide materials for local use (furniture, fencing, utensils, rope) and to generate income. Making use of the seedling nursery to full capacity to overcome local shortage of seedlings. Introduction of drought-resistant fodder crops to make best use of available space for cultivation where there is a shortage of grazing land.

3. Environmental conservation: tree planting for fuel-wood and to resist erosion and drought. Intercropping with forage. Introducing piped water from the springs.

4. Personal/community health: supplying piped clean spring water to the villages. Improving the services of the Health Post to provide a more appropriate choice of medicines on a reliable basis.

5. Earth science: irrigation channels, planting of trees/bamboo/forage crops to prevent erosion (as above).

That adults who are not teachers can demonstrate the skills necessary to such learning is evident from the Amemo Project Report referred to earlier. Figures 8.2, 8.3 and 8.4 are examples of data gathering and representation undertaken by community members as a basis for shared learning. In fact, these 'mapping' and other visual representation techniques were deliberately fostered by the appraisal programme as participatory learning tools to overcome barriers of class, culture and language and are clearly appropriate to the learning of (Locally Adapted) Science topics by children alongside adults from the community.

SUMMARY AND CONCLUSIONS

This chapter has described the main obstacles to effective teaching and learning of Science in rural African primary schools in terms of perceptions, geographical and resource constraints, centralisation and relevance. In so doing, it has emphasised the major discrepancies which continue to exist between traditional curricula and pedagogy, nationally-imposed Science curricula and the actual taught curriculum. It has also highlighted some areas of potential for improvement within existing systems, namely successful reform of primary leaving examinations in Science, trends towards improvisation of materials for practical work and the change in parental perception accruing as a result of the spread of universal primary schooling.

Arising out of these situational factors, it is proposed that access to improved Science learning in rural African primary schools would be brought about by a re-structuring of the Science curriculum into a common core or Minimum Entitlement Curriculum, supplemented by a Locally Adapted Science Curriculum. The former would be based on a review of the common elements of Science curricula in a wide range of developing countries. A version of this Minimum Entitlement Curriculum is set out and is seen as being concept-based and largely context-independent. The latter must be adapted to the needs of specific, individual communities and their rural development needs. A summary is provided of a recent appraisal of such needs in Wollo Province, Ethiopa, and an example of a Locally Adapted Science Curriculum for one part of the province (Amemo District) is proposed.

The advantages of this restructuring in terms of access and adaptability are seen as follows:

- The simplifying of the core curriculum, making it relevant to many countries, would allow for common texts to be produced and common forms of examining could be developed, capitalising on reforms and improvements in a number of countries. At the same time, focus on a smaller number of context-independent concepts will make the teaching of the Science curriculum easier for less well qualified and educated teachers in rural areas and should, in the long term, make primary teacher training for Science more effective.

- The idea of a Locally Adapted Science Curriculum should assist in bridging existing gaps between official curricula and local relevance and in recreating the link between curricular knowledge and children's indigenous experience, which has been shown as an essential element of traditional notions of education. It should also make it much easier, as the example from Ethiopa illustrates, to involve the local community in the process of children's Science learning since both groups will be involved in solving the same problems. This in turn reduces the pressure on schools and teachers to be seen as the sole providers of Science expertise. Finally, linking Science learning to community projects obviates the need for specialist Science apparatus in the schools, and allows children and teachers alike to participate in the application of scientific skills and principles using 'real' materials.

REFERENCES

Berluti, A. (1981 onwards) *Beginning Science: A Course for Primary Schools in Kenya (Standards 4–8)*. Nairobi: Macmillan Kenya.

Berluti, A. (1989) *Science 6–14: An Activity and Resource Manual for Teachers*. Nairobi: Macmillan Kenya.

Bray, M., Clarke, P.B. and Stephens, D. (1986) *Education and Society in Africa*. London: Edward Arnold.

Clarfield, G. (1987) *The Rendille Ethnosociology of Persons and Action*. Nairobi: Bureau of Educational Research.

Coombs, P.H. and Ahmed, M. (1974) *Attacking Rural Poverty; how Nonformal Education can Help*. Baltimore: Johns Hopkins University Press.

Curle, A. (1963) *Educational Strategy for Developing Countries*. London: Tavistock.

Erny, P. (1981) *The Child and his Environment in Black Africa*. (translated by Wanjohi,G.J.) Nairobi: Oxford University Press.

Githinji, S. (1992) 'Using the environment for Science teaching; a teacher's view from Kenya.' *Perspectives 45*, 105–123.

Githui, M.K. (1991) 'Primary Science teaching in a developing country; the lesson we can learn.' In A. Peacock (ed) *Science in Primary Schools: the Multicultural Dimension*. Basingstoke: MacMillan Education.

Government of Kenya (1976) *Report of the National Committee on Educational Objectives and Policies* (The Gachathi Report). Nairobi: Government Printer.

Guijt, I. and Scoones, I. (1991) *Rapid Rural Appraisal for Local Level Planning, Wollo Province, Ethiopa*. London: International Institute for Environment and Development.

Hawes, H. (1979) *Curriculum and Reality in African Primary Schools*. London: Longman.

INSTANT (1991) *Planning a Follow-up to the INSTANT Project for 1992–1995*. Windhoek: INSTANT Project.

Jegede, O.J. and Okebukola, P.A. (1991) 'The relationship between African traditional cosmology and students' acquisition of a Science process skill.' *International Journal of Science Education 13*, 1, 37–47.

Knamiller, G. (1984) 'The struggle for relevance in science education in developing countries.' *Studies in Science Education 11*, 60–78.

Little, A. (1982) 'The role of examinations in the promotion of the 'Paper Qualifications Syndrome.' In *Paper Qualification Syndrome (PQS) and Unemployment of School Leavers*. Addis Ababa: International Labour Office.

Makau, B.M. and Somerset, H.C.A. (1978) *Primary School Leaving Examinations, Basic Intellectual Skills, and Equality; some Evidence from Kenya*. Research report no. 3, Examinations Section Research Unit, Ministry of Education. Nairobi: Government Printer.

Nellist, J. (1991) 'Science lessons from industrial processes – Sunderland.' In P. Richmond (ed) *Industrial and Commercial Perspectives in Initial Teacher Education*. Southampton: Bassett Press.

National Institute for Educational Research (1986) *Primary Science Education in Asia and the Pacific.* Tokyo: NIER.

Peacock, A. (1989) 'What parents think about Science in primary schools.' *Primary Science Review 10,* 20–21.

Peacock, A. (1992a) 'If you think you've got problems...developing Science teaching in Namibian primary schools.' *Primary Science Review 24,* 6–9.

Peacock, A. (1992b) *Botswana – Evaluate the 'Breakthrough to Setswana' Programme.* London: British Council, ODA Projects Department.

Peacock, A. and Boulton, A. (1991) 'Parents understanding of Science at key stage 1.' *Education 3–13, 19,* 3, 26–29.

Peacock, A. (1993) 'A global core curriculum for primary science?' *Primary Science Review 28,* 8–10.

Peacock, A. (1995) 'An agenda for research on text material in primary science for second language learners of English in developing countries.' *Journal of Multilingual and Multicultural Development* (in press).

Peat, F.D. (1995) *Blackfoot Physics.* London: Fourth Estate.

Russell, T. (1991) 'Primary Science and the clash of cultures in a developing country.' In A. Peacock (ed) *Science in Primary Schools: the Multicultural Dimension.* Basingstoke: MacMillan Education.

Science Education Programme for Africa (1976) *Source Book for Science Teachers.* Accra: SEPA.

Simuyu, P., Omar, T.S. and Muthui, H. (1988) *Start Finding Out; Pupils Book for Standard 7.* Nairobi: Longman Kenya.

Somerset, H.C.A. (1974) 'Who goes to secondary school? Relevance, reliability and equity in secondary school selection.' In D. Court and D. Ghai (eds) *Education, Society and Development; New Perspectives from Kenya.* Nairobi: Oxford University Press.

Somerset, H.C.A. (1982) *Examination Reform; the Kenya Experience.* Brighton: Institute of Development Studies.

World Charter on Education for all (1990) *Framework for Action to Meet Basic Learning Needs.* New York: WCEFA.

CHAPTER NINE

Tomorrow's Europeans
Human Rights Education in the Primary School

Cathie Holden

Our Extra Rights:

- To be proud of yourself
- To be trusted
- To be able to choose your own friends
- To know what's going on in the world
- To know what's going on in your family

Figure 9.1. Leo illustrates 'the right to know what's going on in your family'

The children had been looking at the United Nations Declaration on the Rights of the Child and felt the adults had missed out some important rights. After discussion, they added their own supplementary rights and Leo, aged nine, poignantly illustrated the last one. He thus demonstrates how a curriculum which embodies human rights education can help children link events in their own lives with the abstract notion of 'rights' for others. The children in his group agreed that the UN should have included the right to knowledge about one's immediate family situation in their list.

RATIONALE

This chapter aims to demonstrate that taking human rights as an underpinning philosophy can help the teacher to foster a democratic classroom, enhance the curriculum and empower children to think about and act towards creating a more just future.

Human rights in this context is taken in its broadest sense. It is taken to mean those values inherent in an education committed to equality, justice, respect and social and environmental responsibility. It takes as its basis the Council of Europe's recommendations (see also Chapter Seven) to member states on teaching and learning about human rights:

> Schools need to reaffirm democratic values in the face of intolerance, and the re-emergence of racist and xenophobic attitudes. Concepts associated with human rights can, and should, be acquired at an early age. For example, the non-violent resolution of conflict and respect for other people can already be experienced within the life of a pre-school or primary class. (Council of Europe 1985 in Stankey 1992, p.22, 23)

There has long been a debate about the appropriateness of teaching young children about human rights and social justice. Those arguing against have voiced two areas of reservation. The first has been that such issues should be left to the secondary school as concepts related to rights, democracy, justice and injustice are too complex to be understood by young children. However, this viewpoint does not take into account the day to day life of young children where they are surrounded by issues of fairness, justice and responsibility. The pre-school child is well acquainted with 'its not fair' and 'he didn't share' and the ethos of the primary school is based on caring, sharing and learning responsibility and respect for others.

The second reservation centres around content. Some teachers question young children's awareness of human rights issues and maintain that childhood is a time of innocence where children are not (and should not be) aware of the injustices of society. However, recent research indicates that children as young as seven are aware of unemployment and homelessness in their community. As they progress through primary school, children are increasingly aware of, and concerned about, issues of social justice. They are anxious about their own future and equally concerned about their local environment, traffic pollution, homelessness, poverty and violence. On a global scale, young children's hopes and fears are less definite (as might be expected) but still indicate a concern with human rights issues of equality and injustice and a commitment to action. By the end of secondary school, pupils are still concerned but more sceptical.

The enthusiasm of the primary school child has given way to the doubting teenager. Whilst the research shows that some school leavers are still committed to creating a better world, many no longer feel that they can have much influence on society. Active citizenship appears to hang in the balance (Hicks and Holden 1995).

The challenge for the teacher, then, is to build on the awareness young children already have of human rights issues and to harness their commitment to creating a better world. Such an approach would ensure that children are given chances for action, be it in the classroom or in the community. It would also involve education for the future where children are helped to understand the power they will have as adults and the choices they will be able to exercise in their role as active citizens. This entails not only information about issues of human rights, but also a democratic teaching methodology where children are treated (and treat each other) in a manner commensurate with respect for human rights. Education for human rights is, therefore, not only knowledge about but also action for, either now or in the future.

HUMAN RIGHTS AS A BASIS FOR THE DEMOCRATIC CLASSROOM

It is argued here that good human rights education starts with children's understanding of rights in their own lives and that this must be reflected in the management style of the classroom. The Council of Europe's Recommendation states:

> Democracy is best learned in a democratic setting where participation is encouraged, where views can be expressed openly and discussed, where there is freedom of expression for pupils and teachers, and where there is fairness and justice. The skills associated with understanding and supporting human rights include:
>
> - intellectual skills, in particular:
>   - skills associated with written and oral expression, including the ability to listen and discuss, and to defend ones opinions
>   - skills involving judgment, such as the collection and examination of material from various sources, including the mass media, and the ability to analyse it and to arrive at fair and balanced conclusions; the identification of bias, prejudice, stereotypes and discrimination
> - social skills, in particular:
>   - recognising and accepting differences
>   - establishing positive and non-oppressive personal relationships

- resolving conflict in a non-violent way
- taking responsibility
- participating in decisions.

(Council of Europe, R(85)7)

The first stage must be to ensure that children have a basic understanding of the concept of rights before starting on building a classroom based on this ethos. The teacher might begin by asking children to look at their own needs and those responsible for providing them. Starting with needs rather than rights avoids the pitfall of children listing a great many material goods which they would like (and may therefore think they have a right to).

Make a list of all your needs and write them down in the left-hand column. Then decide who provides these needs for you and write that in the right-hand column.

My needs are	This is who is responsible for providing each one.
food	farmers
Water	rivers
Oxagon	Trees.
My body	me
Earth	Everybody in the world
groable soil	Earth
Farillys	mumys e daddys

Source: C. Holden modelled on work by UNICEF; Rights of the Child
Figure 9.2. Needs (two boys, aged 9)

The next step would be to ask the class to list those needs which they think are essential rights, applicable to all children but which may be denied to children in some circumstances. In the ensuing discussion it is important to provide examples of children in Britain, as well as in other parts of the world, who are denied basic rights as otherwise stereotypes of deprivation in Third World countries may be reinforced. The UNICEF teaching materials provide good material. Further work, comparing the UN Declaration on Children's Rights with their own list, can consolidate children's understanding.

Once children have a basic understanding of the universality of human rights, this knowledge can be used to facilitate the democratic process. This may take the form of using a rights framework to establish classroom rules, with children deciding which rules are appropriate and how best to protect the interests of all. It can be extended beyond rule making to establish the most productive and fair way of working in the classroom. Teachers and children have used the central tenets of equality and justice to devise ways of sharing access to the teachers' time, the expertise of more able children and scarce resources.

A human rights framework can also be useful for sorting out bullying, name calling or playground squabbles. Rules for the playground can be based on justice and fairness arising from the basic premise of protecting the rights of all.

Children's rights in the playground

1. Every child has the right to play with who they like, as long as it is alright with the other person.

2. Every child has the right to feel safe.

3. Every child has the right not to be bullied in the playground.

4. Every child has the right to be in a quiet place and to be alone.

5. Every child has the right to be free.

6. Every child has the right to have safe play equipment.

7. Every child has the right to do as they like as long as it does not hurt others and it is not destructive.

8. Every male child has the right to play netball.

9. Every female child has the right to play football.

10. Every child has the right to a clean playing environment.

Figure 9.3. Rules for the playground (aged 9)

The Standing Conference of European Ministers of Education (1991) maintained that 'education promoting respect for human rights and human dignity is an essential element of a collective response to racist and xenophobic violence'. The primary school teacher can use children's understanding of rights to facilitate the discussion of prejudice and racism. The right to respect and to be treated equally can be a starting point for such discussions. Children can be given the opportunity to discuss relevant incidents from their own past and can learn about others who have suffered injustice (in this country and abroad). Understanding that holding prejudiced or racist views is a denial of a person's rights may provide a starting point for acquiring a value system based on tolerance and respect.

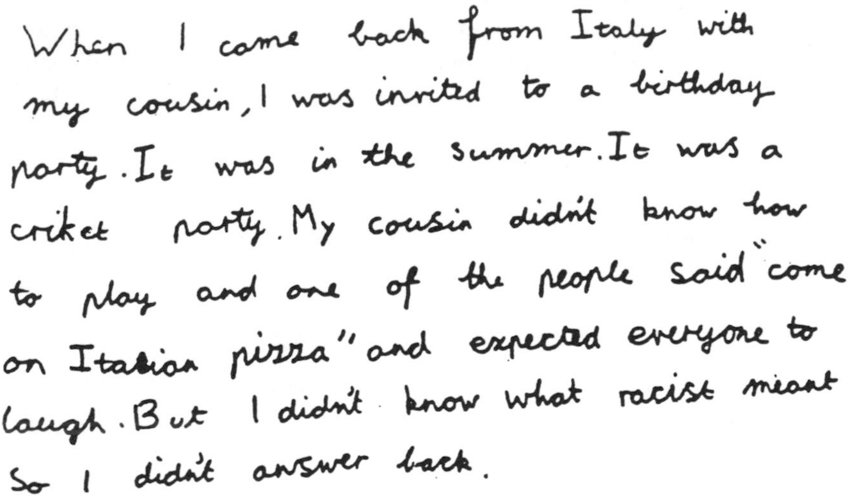

When I came back from Italy with my cousin, I was invited to a birthday party. It was in the summer. It was a cricket party. My cousin didn't know how to play and one of the people said "come on Italian pizza" and expected everyone to laugh. But I didn't know what racist meant So I didn't answer back.

Figure 9.4. Peter's experience (aged 9)

HUMAN RIGHTS IN THE PRIMARY CURRICULUM

The primary curriculum has always included topics which relate to human rights issues but many teachers have either been unaware of this perspective or been unsure as to how best to introduce sensitive or controversial issues. Added to this has been the pressure to cover a fixed body of content, a pressure which has increased since the introduction of the National Curriculum. This has been the case, in particular for history (and to a lesser extent geography), where there is a strong emphasis on teaching a prescribed content. The humanities, however, is the obvious place where such a perspective can be introduced. Antonouris and Wilson's model (1989), where the humanities programme in a school is built around certain key concepts which are revisited, lends itself to human rights education. If the key concepts of power, justice, rights, tolerance and respect are identified, these concepts can be referred to and built upon in each history study unit. The class learning about Ancient Greeks and understanding how they ruled, who had power, who was denied full rights, can transfer this understanding to their next topic, be it Benin or Tudors. Likewise, the geographical study of an economically developing country can encourage children to look at the people of the country: how they live, how they are ruled, with whom the power lies, their rights and access to basic requirements.

Such an approach has advantages for the child's learning in two ways. First, rather than perceiving history as separate boxes of time unrelated to other periods, the child is given a framework of linking concepts to identify common ways of living and governing. Second, he or she can relate history to the present day as comparisons can be made between the people of a given time in the past and the way people live today. The process of creating a democratic classroom can be linked to the study of democracy in Ancient Greece. The rights of girls in Victorian times can be compared to the rights of girls today. Prejudice against the Jews during World War II can be compared to the denial of rights experienced by some minority groups today. A geographical study of a developing country could include mention of those who fought for human rights in the past as well as reference to the issues of justice and equality for that country at the present time.

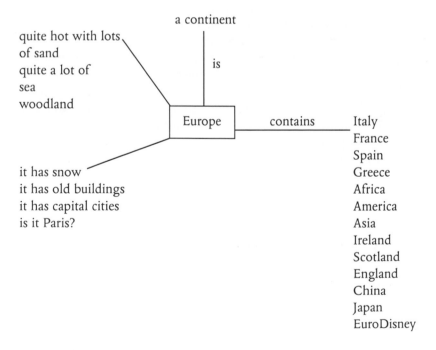

Figure 9.5. What is Europe? Brainstorm by 8-year-olds

Research indicates that student teachers in Britain are less likely to see themselves as European citizens than their counterparts in other European countries. They see themselves first as British citizens, second as global citizens and only then as Europeans (Steiner and Voiels 1995). Coupled with this is evidence that for many children the notion of Europe is extremely hazy and difficult to understand (Holden 1996). This is worrying if we are to educate British children to be active participants in the new Europe. It indicates the need for a European dimension in primary school geography; a dimension which would include information about the structure of Europe and the part played by Strasbourg in human rights issues. If the children of today are to be active participants in a European democracy, exercising their right to vote in European elections, they will need to be educated about such possibilities.

CREATING A MORE JUST FUTURE

Whilst it is important that the teacher does what is possible within the confines of the school to enable children to put rights into action, an equally important dimension is that of the future. As indicated earlier, children are concerned about the future and wish to play an active part in creating a more just society. As they grow older, pupils feel increasingly powerless, suggesting that schools are not producing school leavers who feel themselves to be active citizens. The curriculum needs to take account of children's concerns and ensure that they feel empowered as the decision makers of the future, the voters of the 21st century. Children can be encouraged to think about the kind of future they want and how today's problems might be resolved. One way of approaching this is through work on the local environment.

The local community is often overlooked in work on social justice and rights and yet this is the area of immediate concern to children and one where active citizenship can begin. As noted above, children are concerned about their local area. They hope for better facilities (amenities and housing) but fear that the future will bring an increase in crime, pollution, racial tension and environmental damage. On a practical level, children can discuss these and other current human rights issues in their local community and decide what can be done. They can invite local councillors in to talk about facilities for the elderly, the disabled and for themselves as children. They can take on board environmental issues by finding out about local recycling schemes, campaigning for cycle tracks and finding out about town planning for the near future.

They can also be encouraged to envisage the kind of community they want and the rights of people in that community. How might they, as adults, hope to influence town planners and local politicians? What kind of society do they want and how might this come about? Such activities can introduce children to the nature of controversial issues and the awareness that each solution inevitably brings more dilemmas.

The reason why I have made a boarding house for the homeless and disabled is because it will be to much money to build more houses and too much land to use to build the houses on, so I arailled that situation by building a boarding house and people can come and go when they want.

Figure 9.6. Louisa's house for the homeless and disabled (aged 10)

Louisa thought she had solved the housing problem for the future but it only engendered a fresh debate about the rights of such people to the same resources as others and the right to dignity and privacy. She was not despondent, however, but gratified by the interest in her suggestion and perplexed as to what could be done. It was a lesson for the whole class in the complexity of creating a just society and the responsibility of people who make these decisions which then affect the quality of life of others.

It is harder to involve children in action for a more just society on a national or global level, but not impossible. Again, children can be encouraged to articulate their hopes for the future and their concerns for the present. In so doing they can clarify for themselves the values they hold and have a vision of what could be to hold on to. In articulating their concerns they can debate the possibilities for change and be introduced to people and organisations who are

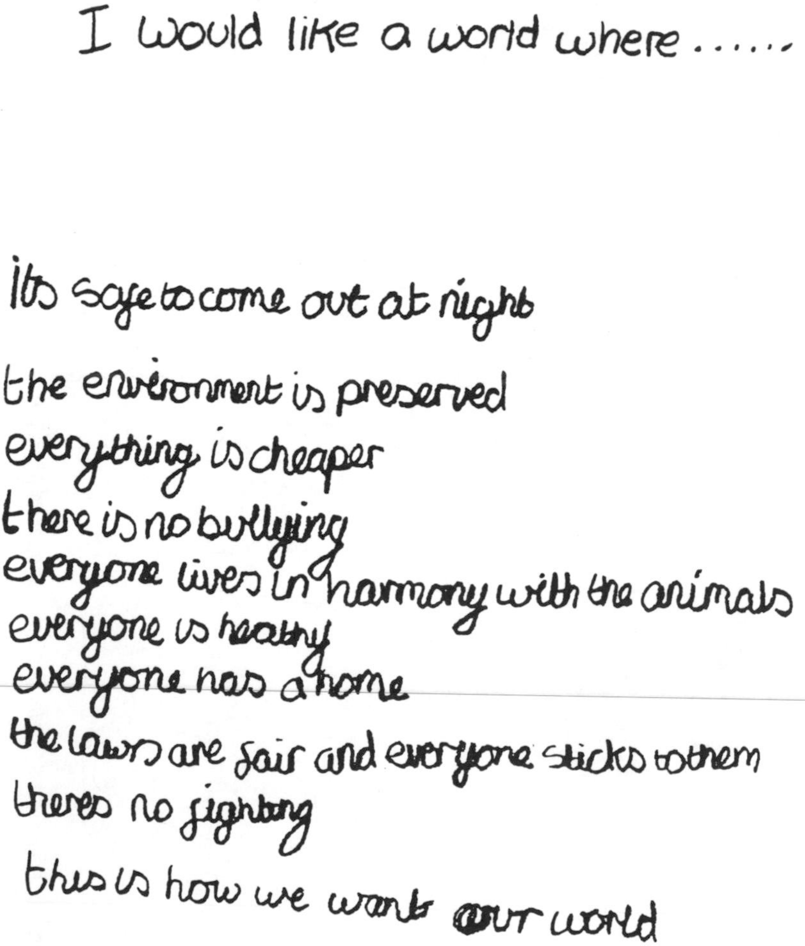

I would like a world where ......

Its safe to come out at night

the environment is preserved

everything is cheaper

there is no bullying

everyone lives in harmony with the animals

everyone is healthy

everyone has a home

the laws are fair and everyone sticks to them

theres no fighting

this is how we want our world

Figure 9.7. A just future (girl aged 10)

working for change in that area. Many such organisations (Oxfam, World Wide Fund for Nature, Amnesty International, Unicef) produce educational materials to support such work. Again, a European dimension can be introduced by ensuring that the work of the Europe Union in areas of human rights and social justice is known.

If schools can promote a classroom ethos where children are listened to and valued, if teachers can adapt the curriculum to include issues of social justice and the rights of people now and in the past, and if children can be encouraged to feel they have a part to play in their own and their community's future, then we will be on our way to helping today's children to be active citizens of the twenty-first century, committed to creating a more just future.

REFERENCES

Antonouris and Wilson (1989) *New Dimensions in Topic Work: Equal Opportunities in Schools.* London: Cassell.

Council of Europe (1985) Recommendation No R (85) 7 of the Committee of Ministers to Member States on Teaching and Learning about Human Rights in Schools. Strasbourg: Council of Europe. In H. Starkey (1991) *The Challenge of Human Rights Education.* London: Cassell.

Council of Europe (1985) Recommendation No R (85) 7 of the Committee of Ministers to Member States on Teaching and Learning about Human Rights in Schools. Strasbourg. Council of Europe. In H. Starkey (1993) *Human Rights Education Activities of the Council of Europe.* Oxford: Westminster College.

Hicks, D. and Holden, C. (1995) *Visions of the Future: Why we need to Teach for Tomorrow.* Stoke-on-Trent: Trentham.

Holden, C. (1996) Making links: The Romans and a European dimension. *Education 3–13* (in press).

Steiner, M. and Voiels, V. (1995) Preparing to teach for citizenship. Paper for Erasmus Symposium: Education for Citizenship in a New Europe. Berlin.

Unicef (1990) *The Rights of the Child.* London SCF/Unicef.

CHAPTER TEN

Realising the Educational Rights of Institutionalised Romanian Children

Margaret Ralph

INTRODUCTION

This chapter briefly reports on the first few years of an ongoing longitudinal study by 'Muzika in Romania', a charity set up in 1990 in response to the plight of Romania's orphans following the revolution in December 1989. Kate Baxter, the co-founder of the organisation with Margaret Ralph, is primarily a musician. As a freelance consultant she has developed an approach which uses music and the creative arts as a tool for calming and establishing contact with children who have mental and/or behavioural disorders (Baxter 1994). These activities are used to develop, where feasible, co-ordination skills, to reinforce memory patterns and to establish routines, all as precursors to other forms of learning. Another important advantage of using music in this project is to surmount the barriers of language. 'Muzika' members are mainly teachers experienced in working with profoundly handicapped children. Others have experience with behavioural disorders, are speech therapists, psychologists and child-centred social workers. All gave up holiday time to work voluntarily in Romania whenever their skills could be useful.

The two founder members went out to Romania in May 1990 to meet officers of the various Ministries who had responsibility for the orphanages and the homes for abandoned children. The intention on this visit was to establish the long-term needs of such children and, if the expertise of the team could be usefully employed, seek permission to set up an initial visit to an institution to explore the feasibility of our proposed method of working with the children and staff.

Establishing the scale of the problem was virtually impossible. Until recently it has been very difficult to get any social statistics at all. These were always considered to be state secrets and were not published. The Ceaucescus, it is believed, wanted the rest of the world to perceive that all social problems had been eliminated. Records are now beginning to be kept, although often in a non-systematic way so co-ordinating appropriate intervention is problematic. On our last visit we spent much time liaising with the authorities responsible for the orphanages. It became apparent that there were no proper records of the names and locations of institutions, especially in remote areas – or of the number of children in them, let alone their ages and sex. We did, however, gain some insight into the institutional structure.

THE INSTITUTIONAL STRUCTURE

The Laegun

The home where all children under three years of age who are orphaned or abandoned would be sent. Around the age of three they will be assessed prior to moving on to the *Prescolare*, or a *Home Hospital*. 'Irrecuperable' is the term used to define those who at the ages of three and/or seven fail the psychological assessment which determines where they will spend the next four years (at age three) or the rest of their lives (at seven). The tests are conducted by a psychologist and involve simple tasks which any normal child of that age should be able to perform. At three this involves an identified level of speech. The tests take no account of what opportunities children have had to acquire these skills, nor how long they have already been institutionalised. The term 'irrecuperable' is used to cover a multitude of major and minor medical and behavioural problems. There was not – and to date still is not – any educational provision for these children. They are deemed to be stateless and therefore without rights. The fact that many of them are potentially bright children with the ability to benefit from a normal education is dismissed as irrelevant.

The Prescolare

The orphanage where those who pass the age three assessment are sent. It broadly follows the curriculum offered to other children in nursery and pre-school systems within the limits of minimal resourcing and staffing. In areas where there is no immediate *Home Hospital* and there are spaces in the *Prescolare*, children who might normally have 'failed' could end up in the *Prescolare* to be re-assessed later. Our experience is that where these children exist, they are regarded as a nuisance and their needs are not well catered for.

The Scoala Ajutatoare

The institution to which the *Prescolare* children will proceed, providing that they pass the assessment at seven. Again the curriculum broadly follows that of an ordinary school until the age of about eleven or twelve. Those children – very few in our experience – who show particular talent might be able to transfer to attending an ordinary primary or secondary school, whilst still living within the orphanage. For the rest, the curriculum is very basic, aiming to teach literacy and numeracy to an acceptable level and skills in crafts (boys) and needlework (girls) which will enable them to earn some sort of a living as adults. The quality of provision varies enormously from school to school.

The Camin Spital (home hospital)

The institution where those who are deemed to have 'failed' the assessment, either at three or at seven plus, will be sent. They can also be sent at any stage after that if they are found abandoned and are assessed as being most appropriately placed there. These homes are the ones which this country saw first in December 1989 on BBC news. They are grossly underfunded and understaffed and are often to be found in accommodation which is in a state of total neglect and disrepair without proper heating and water. Although many have had large injections of relief aid in the form of clothes and medication, and for a few, major rebuilding programmes, there is still a need for long-term staff training and government commitment to rethinking the rationale behind these institutions. In areas where places in the *Prescolare* are scarce, some children will end up in the *Camin Spital*. Since the revolution, pressure has been brought to bear – often by foreign aid workers – to reassess many such youngsters, who are obviously misplaced, and arrange for their transfer to orphanages. Where accommodation is available this is slowly beginning to happen, but there are still signs of discrimination against Gitanes (travellers) who form a significant proportion of those in the *Home Hospitals*.

Assessment centres

These are mostly in large cities and range from units which are heavily guarded and run almost like prisons to much smaller family units where the emphasis is on rehabilitation and careful placement into an appropriate institution. The declared intention is that they should be centres where children remain for no longer than thirty days whilst efforts are made to trace their family, if they have one, and re-unite them. Boys who regularly absconded from institutions by stowing away on trains to Bucharest would often be picked up and sent to this centre. If they would disclose the information they would be returned to the institution from which they came. In Bucharest the Assessment Centre was heavily guarded by half a dozen 'heavies' with large sticks. They were there to control some of the larger boys who had been sent there many times before, had no desire to stay and were involved in various forms of crime but were too young to be put in prison. Children as young as three who had absconded with older brothers and sisters were very much 'at risk' from these older violent youngsters.

SETTING UP THE PROJECT

Conversations with officers at the Ministry established that they were very happy for a team of qualified staff to come and work with their orphan population. They regarded our wish to work with 'irrecuperables' as misplaced, however, because they regarded them as totally without hope of recovery, and because they are parentless and without rights.

After much negotiation visit to the *Camin Spital* at Gradinari was arranged. Meetings with the staff there had been intended to discuss with them the needs of the children and to establish whether 'Muzika' volunteers had the expertise to meet those needs. Staff in charge had little or no concept of needs beyond clothing the children and providing them with basic medical care. In many instances this meant wanting sedatives to maintain docile behaviour in the most disturbed. We found on our first visit there that the provision for these children was unsuitable, inflexible and grossly underfinanced. As a consequence these neglected children were extremely vulnerable to starvation and disease and suffered regular abuse from their peers and their carers. The following describes a situation familiar to many who went out in those early months:

> In the *Home Hospital* situation children too weak to feed themselves simply starve to death. Most terrible of all is the way that lonely and neglected children, unused to contact, are unable to play with, or even look at each other. They have never learnt how to. And because their cries have never been answered they have forgotten how to cry... It became apparent that many of the children who had appeared mentally handicapped are simply in a state of arrested development due to lack of stimulation. Many have never been touched by an adult. They just need to be cuddled. (*The Guardian*, March 1990)

Relatively few did survive so the mortality rate was high. Bitter winters with little bedding or heating increased susceptibility to infection and disease. Poor management and medical attention meant large numbers succumbed. In one *Home Hospital* we visited, 42 out of 126 had died the previous winter. In two others, one had 17 deaths out of approximately 120 children and the other lost a staggering 60 out of 220 in the hard winter. Equally shocking was the fact that there was a whole generation of young adults in these institutions condemned to a life of misery in circumstances which are, at best likely to be totally unsuited to their needs and at worst, of undernourishment, sedation and being unoccupied for the rest of their lives. For example a young man now 32 year of age was taken, at the age of 16, to a *Camin Spital* by his mother who was forced to abandon two of her children because she couldn't afford to feed and clothe them. He was chosen because, like most 16-year-old boys, he ate a great deal. He has with him, to this day, certificates from the craft school saying that he is proficient in various technical skills and suitable for employment. There is nowhere in the *Home Hospital* for him to use these skills. When we met him he had been institutionalised for 16 years and was showing signs of mental stress, not surprising as he had been incarcerated with three schizophrenics and several seriously disturbed young people. He desperately wanted books to read. This, at least, we could assist him with. For him, as for so many others, it was too late to try to rehabilitate him into society as no appropriate facilities existed.

CHANGES IN ROMANIAN FAMILY LIFE

In the years leading up to the demise of the Ceaucescus there was intense pressure to produce large numbers of children who could work for the state. Contraception and abortion were forbidden – the penalties for flouting this rule being imprisonment for long periods and subtler penalties such as family members losing their jobs and being inexplicably unable to obtain other work. Families at large were encouraged to spy on each other, reporting anything which broke party rules.

After World War II, most ordinary families would have lived in a small, rather ramshackle single-story dwelling surrounded by a plot of land to grow food. So, with poultry and the odd cow, they were relatively self-sufficient. In the 1960s, Ceaucescu began his programme of flattening these village communities and moving the villagers into enormous blocks of rapidly-erected flats in the towns where they could so much more easily be watched, and watch each other. The amount of space allocated to families for their living accommodation was regulated by the number in the family. Slightly larger accommodation could be obtained by informing on your neighbours, so temptation was great.

The result of these measures was huge families, mostly living on the poverty line in cramped conditions and many, many hours having to be spent queuing for what little food was available. In order to survive, many resorted to petty crime and, as conditions worsened, families took drastic action to ameliorate their situation. Many, with between six and twelve children, living in two-or three-roomed flats – some with no inside sanitation – could cope no longer. Breaking point for many came when another baby arrived or when the husband lost his job and feeding everyone became impossible. The terrible decision to put one or more children into care would be made. Sometimes this was done 'officially' by taking the children to an orphanage or frequently children would be left somewhere to be found. A mother recounted such an experience and how, after the revolution, when she could manage to have them back with the rest of the family, she had no idea which of the 200 orphanages they were in. She is still searching.

Often the children abandoned would either be the youngest in the family or, because of the additional expense, disabled or sickly. Such children would quickly succumb to the poor standards of food, hygiene and medical care and die or become the institutionalised 'rockers' and 'head bangers' whom we saw so often. Some mothers, in desperation, sought an illegal abortion or attempted to induce a miscarriage. Bungling, unsuccessful attempts sometimes resulted in babies with physical or mental disabilities who were then often abandoned.

The situation of Gitanes (travellers) was also severely affected by Ceaucescu's regime. Gitanes have always had large families. Ceauscescu's destruction of many of their homes on the fringes of villages and moving them into flats in the town forced many to return to their former nomadic life. Traditional wooden caravans cannot cope with more than six occupants so many families were forced to abandon any additional children on the streets or at the doorsteps of the *Camines* or orphanages – sometimes hoping to return when times got better, but this rarely happened.

A CULTURE IN TRANSITION

Since the revolution little has significantly changed. Food is becoming less scarce but queues, although shorter, still persist. The medical situation remains desperate, although teams of doctors and nurses from many countries have come and treated, as a priority, child victims of surgical malpractice. Contraception is theoretically available but financially beyond most women's means.

At times we have felt intense optimism for what might be achieved in time, sometimes near despair as the necessary changes seem almost impossible. Many Romanians seem unmotivated to lift themselves from poverty and outdated systems. Day-to-day survival seems to be the focus. Many of our expectations and assumptions are confounded in encounters with a culture which has had such a very different history to our own. We have begun to appreciate that the population in a post-totalitarian state does not necessarily shake off old attitudes or ways quickly, if at all. Both the political situation and the economy are unstable and swinging changes are likely to occur at any time, without notice. This can result in entire departments being removed/re-organised/re-staffed, overnight. The results of these upheavals work their way down to local institutions where the Director can suddenly be removed to make way for a 'friend' of whoever has just been appointed to a new post further up the hierarchy. He, in turn, will bring his own friends in as staff and the whole system can quickly become totally corrupt.

This happened in Bucharest when the resignation of the Prime Minister in October 1992 led to his replacement with a non-communist successor. This shake-up worked its way down the ministerial hierarchy and the Director of the Assessment Centre, where we are working, was sacked and replaced by a friend of the new Minister of the Handicapped. He is an engineer, a nice enough man but with little or no knowledge of the needs of street children. Several other key personnel whom we had worked with and begun to train were replaced. We have come to expect and accept this as we can do little except to keep emphasising the need for stability and keep notes on the impact that unplanned change has on both staff and children and to feed back such reports the Ministry official with overall responsibility for these institutions.

In a society which is still relatively unstable with an economy showing little signs of steady growth, there is an understandable tendency for Romanians to accept any offers without having an overall strategy or clear long-term goals. The fact that on any flight out to Bucharest there were likely to be aid workers from four or five different organisations, at least three of whom had been given the impression that their particular programme for training would be adopted for the whole of Romania, was an indication of the desperate state within the new ministry and their unwillingness to refuse anything that was offered. It was in an effort to co-ordinate initiatives that, in the UK, the All-Party Select Committee on Aid to Eastern Europe was set up. A similar exercise is now being mounted in Romania to register all groups working there and to receive outline plans of the work they are doing.

CONCEPTUAL BACKGROUND TO THE PROJECT

In planning our project, information was sought from a number of academic, legislative and administrative sources. Legislation and government papers from Romania relating to the provision for the orphaned, abandoned and those with special needs proved almost impossible to obtain. Newspaper and magazine articles published in this country which refer to the conditions prevailing at the time of the revolution have been a helpful source of information. Looking at the international context, the fact that Romania is a signatory to the UN Convention on the Rights of the Child has given us a framework of a stated commitment to improving children's welfare within Romania itself which will hopefully be helpful as a lever in activities to bring about change.

Research on the psychological effects of deprivation of maternal care and institutionalisation upon child development (Clarke and Clarke 1976; Ainsworth 1962) was studied and guided our understanding of what we saw and what could realistically be achieved, informing our hopes that such damage as had occurred could be reversed or ameliorated with appropriate intervention. Relevant literature relating to effecting change within educational settings and within management was also consulted for guidance (Bell 1991; Warwick 1984; Bowers 1984; Gash 1993).

Ideas on the use of music and the creative arts as an appropriate vehicle for focusing our work were further explored. The work we planned was not music therapy in the Nordoff and Robbins sense (Nordoff and Robbins 1985). It does, however, embody much of their philosophy of the power of music to unlock minds and limbs held fast by emotional and/or physical trauma. Our approach has been more eclectic. Romanians who have worked with us have been amazed by the responses to music they have observed in children who have shown little or no response for many years. We were also influenced by Miriam Wood's

(1982) views on the value of structure and repetition in working with handi-capped children. A sense of structure and routine, which we felt was important for a child to feel secure, was built into each session by the pattern of musical activities. In evaluating our work, we were encouraged by Wood's reminder that, for some children who do not communicate, the only visible results will be their pleasure in the sessions or, later, in behaviour which is less disturbed, sleep patterns which are improved and sometimes in a desire to communicate in words for the first time. Experience certainly taught us to recognise those breakthroughs as the possibility of further success. Dobb (1966) emphasises the power of the voice and the tremendous pleasure children gain from singing. We built on his suggestions for developing musical confidence and competency through song and in the stages of 'singing' which do not require words but often lead to a desire to communicate with words. We found materials developed by some of these teachers to be of great use in their universal approach to music making, encouraging simple and very basic response, using the body as a first instrument.

In addition to the substantial amount of research literature that we consulted and sifted for relevance (too extensive to list fully here), other material that informed and shaped our project came from a growing number of 'insider' reports produced by Romanians themselves and by other charities working in Romania assessing the level of success of the many initiatives which have sprung up in the last few years.

On the basis of this research, literature information and our own experience in the field we developed realistic plans and came to understand the Romanian context a little better.

THE ROMANIAN SPECIAL NEEDS CONTEXT

During the period of the Ceaucescu regime in Romania, education legislation made almost no reference to those who were physically and mentally handi-capped. The last special needs teacher was trained in 1978. The system was supposed to be perfect, so its citizens had to be so too. Only those children who could be trained to be useful as workers received any education, and then only if they had parents who would look after them and ensure their regular attendance at the corrective schools. Provision was made in the cities for these children, but the few remaining in rural areas were neglected.

By the middle of 1991 a new Education Act, drafted by Education Ministers, with their regional advisers, was going through the Romanian Parliament. A strong lobby by Professor Paunescu of the Methodological Institute ensuring a commitment to education for all follows:

> This Government believes in the right of every child to an education commensurate with his ability and regardless of handicap... Children without parents, for whatever reason, and wherever they may be placed,

have an equal right to educational provision, either in the place where they reside or at a local school. (Draft clause within provisional Education Bill 1991)

During the progress of the Bill through Parliament there was a change of leadership. A number of those in sympathy with the clause were replaced. The deteriorating economic situation made opponents quick to point out the enormous costs involved. It has not been possible to obtain a copy of the new Act. The Special Education Inspector for Bucharest, who has also not seen it, believes it has been re-worded to make a vague commitment to 'improving provision, over a period of time, for those handicapped children who at present have little access to education'. That improvement has been largely left to the aid organisations working on health and hygiene situations in the worst *Camin Spitals* and hoping in time to include basic skills education. A Romanian working in Bucharest says:

> The Government has been happy to accept everything that was offered, with no thought for the future. These people cannot stay for ever. Their gift of their time and the resources they have brought has been a wonderful gift to our abandoned children. What will happen, though, when they go, as one day they will? There is no provision to maintain support at the same level. This problem must be addressed and resolved unless our people are prepared to allow the horrors of the pre-revolution situation in the Camin Spitals to return. That, we cannot allow. (Rodika Manoliu 1992)

Many who agree have equally grave concerns about the future. Jonathan Eyal (1992) (Romanian by birth) of the 'United Services Institute for Defence Studies' writes:

> The revolution was a revolution of the many, not the few; the trend has been to encourage differentiations, so the dispossessed parts of society – women children and gypsies – are even more dispossessed... When the Government presented its programme after the elections in May, it was all about starting private companies, not about health services. And not an eyebrow was raised. The orphanages will remain as they are because there are no votes in them, and you're not going to change that position with charity. At the same time, the withdrawing of the charity now would be a calamity that the Government would not be able or willing to plug...it is up to the charities to impress upon the government that the commitment cannot be open-ended and that they must start to pick up the task for themselves.

It is easy for us to assume that certain levels of humanitarian behaviour are common to the human species. Chris Jenks reminded us in 1992 at the first 'Romania Aid' Conference in Craiova that '... In Romania there is no history of welfare; it never happened. So, even when we use the word 'needy' it's a Western notion.' Another UK observer, Deletant (1992), amplifies this:

> Romania was a sort of vassal state to the Ottoman Empire, under which there never developed the sort of civic societies that did begin in neighbouring countries under the Hapsburgs. No non-governmental organisations developed... The state of Romania as it emerged in 1859 had no means, record, tradition or model to turn to in order to develop the sort of institutions that developed here and in Western Europe – and this in turn led to an apathy towards social institutions. There is still no unemployment benefit, no DHSS equivalent, no provision for the victims of life.

The result was that when the communist regime emerged there was no voice within the population to articulate the demand for those structures which we accept as an intrinsic part of society. In the absence of these the family took it upon itself to provide the sort of care which, in other countries, would be provided by the state and for those without family there was no social conscience about providing for them.

INSTITUTIONALISATION AND ITS EFFECTS

Research in Britain often concentrated upon the consequences of residential care for children and insufficiently upon what might be done to prevent or reverse these consequences (Prosser 1976). Dinnage and Kellmer Pringle (1967)asked what the aims of enrichment programmes for children should be: 'How can a therapeutic community be created so that children leave residential care emotionally and intellectually strengthened, rather than even more deficient or damaged than when they entered?'. Many such long-standing UK concerns are now being expressed about Romanian provision, including the quality of staff in residential institutions. In both countries political will and financial constraint impede the pace of change.

The work of Bowlby (1969), which had a profound effect in many countries upon practice in the institutionalisation of young children, had no influence on Romanian practices. We saw many of the long-term symptoms of which he and other researchers (Ainsworth *et al.* 1962) speak manifest in the older children in Gradinari Home Hospital. From our observations of the older children, a considerable number of those who survived to adulthood provided some evidence of Bowlby's prognosis that prolonged deprivation in the early years could lead to an affectionless, psychopathic character.

Nevertheless, in conditions one would think would defy normal growth and development of any child, we did find in each institution some children who have not only survived but who appeared reasonably confident and intelligent. Although on our first encounter they had no sense of identity or grasp of language, they responded rapidly and with relative ease to the variety of activities we presented to them. These children speedily acquired language from our interpreters, such was their desire to learn and participate. Staff suggested that the 'immunity' of some children to psychological disorders was due to 'special environmental circumstances' created by, for example, 'the child's attractiveness or personal appeal to one or more institutional workers'. (cf., Prosser 1962). Mead's observations (1954, 1962) about the effects of learned behaviour patterns upon infant survival offer another explanation of the survival of so many abandoned children whom one might have expected to die in the appalling conditions in which we found them. Those in Romania who survive the first three to five years have a remarkable tenacity and overcome the deprivations of food and affection so long as they do not fall prey to specific infection and disease.

It is impossible to summarise our findings briefly as many of the changes were slow, subtle and at a micro level, and the work is still in progress. The following account illustrates clearly the immediate impact which inspired us to go on.

When we first saw Marinela (not her real name) she was a pathetically undernourished baby, or so we thought, lying in a cot with two others. She was unable to sit up without help, covered in sores from constantly being bitten by flies and suffering badly from ringworm. From her size and weight we estimated to be about two years old. She was actually five years and two months. I had spent some time in the room where she was situated singing to and holding the hands of many of these tiny children who looked so emaciated and disturbed. Many of them were rocking or banging themselves against the cot sides. As I came closer to Marinela's cot I was aware that she was trying hard to see where the sound was coming from but could not lift herself up into a position where she could see me. When I finally arrived at her cot and held her hands she struggled to stand, clutching my fingers as a baby would. She was smiling from ear to ear and as I began to sing she rocked with the music and tried to bounce on her urine-sodden mattress. After about five minutes of this behaviour she began to 'join in' the singing. There were no words, but the sounds were clear and in tune with my voice. I was amazed. I tried singing a short phrase (Mi-Re-Doh) and paused. She sang it back to me. It would have caused considerable problems if I had singled her out at that stage but I made a note to find out why she was placed with the 'irrecuperables' when she was clearly far from ineducable. I discovered later that she had failed the three-year-old assessment because she could not walk or stand alone and was, therefore, condemned to a life on her back or propped up with others. A decision was made that Marinela would be targeted for special help when we returned in October.

THE POSSIBILITY OR CHANGE IN PROVISION AND ATTITUDES

It is five years since Romania signed the UN Convention on the Rights of the Child and there is now a core of Ministers and senior education officials who wish to see moves towards establishing the tenets of Articles 19 and 23. In particular:

> Article 19.1: States parties shall take all appropriate legislative, administrative, social and educational measures to protect the child from all forms of physical or mental violence, injury or abuse, neglect or negligent treatment, maltreatment or exploitation, including sexual abuse, while in the care of parents, legal guardians or anyone else who has care of the child

> Article 23.1: States parties recognise that a mentally or physically disabled child should enjoy a full and decent life in conditions which ensure dignity, promote self-reliance and facilitate the child's active participation in the community...

> Article 23.3: ...to ensure that the disabled child has effective access to and receives education, training, health care services, rehabilitation services, preparation for employment and recreation opportunities in a manner conducive to the child achieving the fullest possible social integration and individual development.

Until the revolution, in so far as there was any one system of provision for children with special needs, it excluded those who were abandoned and those who were deemed 'irrecuperable'. The fact that many of them were potentially bright children with the ability to benefit from a normal education was dismissed as irrelevant. Children who failed the assessments at either stage ended up in the 'Home Hospitals' and for them there was no hope.

To meet the terms of the Convention, however, this will have to change substantially. Traian Vrashmash, the Special Needs Inspector from Bucharest, has fought long and hard for recognition for these children. We too have written articles and presented evidence of our success in an endeavour to assist his cause, but so far without success. There will need to be further sustained international pressure before change will be brought about at this level. The resourcing implications are enormous and this factor alone ensures that the proposal never reaches any serious agenda in Parliament.

The hope for Romania seems to lie with the young – those presently in university and training in the professions. They are largely free of communist ideology and see the urgent need for change. As yet they are rarely in a position of power. Students from Bucharest University working with us were determined to continue the fight for equality of rights and opportunity. Although frustrated, they also share Baroness Cox's sentiments:

It is naïve to imagine that an entire society can be changed overnight with the removal of one man. It will take many years for Romania to rid itself of corruption and evil. Without a deep understanding of life under the old regime we can become very demoralised. That level of understanding, however, is virtually impossible without first-hand experience of the harsh realities there. (Cox 1991)

Sadly there are many officials and others who feel that we are wasting our time with the dregs of society. This is an inbuilt attitude which, as a signatory to the UN Convention on the Rights of the Child, Romania has to work towards changing. As Caroline Cox intimates, it is likely to take many years to reverse such conditioned perceptions and to adopt the terms of the Convention into national legislation. Our level of understanding of the obstacles in the way of implementation has certainly been a result of 'first-hand experience of the harsh realities there'.

REFERENCES

Ainsworth, M.D., Andry, R.G., Harlow, R.G., Lebovici, S., Mead, M., Prugh, D.G. and Wootton, B. (1962) *Deprivation of Maternal Care.* Geneva: World Health Organisation.

Baxter, K. (1994) *Fundamental Activities.* Nottingham: Fundamental Activities.

Bell, G.H. and Dennis, S. (1991) Special Needs Development. Networking and Managing for Change. *European Journal of Special Needs Education 6,* 2, 133–146.

Bowers, T. (1984) 'Change in the special school.' In T. Bowers (ed) *Management and the Special School.* London: Croom Helm.

Bowlby, J. (1969) *Attachment and Loss: Volume One: Attachment.* London: Hogarth Press.

Clarke, A.M. and A.D.B. (1976) *Early Experience: Myth and Evidence.* London: Open Books.

Cox, C. (1991) Letter to *The Sunday Times.* January 27, 1991.

Deletant, D. (1992) *Romania Aid Bulletin.* Southampton: Southampton University Press, October.

Dinnage, R. and Kellmer Pringle, M.L. (1967) *Foster Home Care: Facts and Fallacies: A Review and Research in the United States, Western Europe, Israel and Great Britain between 1948 and 1966.* London: Longmans in association with the National Bureau for Co-operation in Child Care.

Dobb, J.P.B. (1966) *The Slow Learner and Music.* Oxford: Oxford University Press.

Eyal, J. (1992) *Vicious Circles: Security in the Balkans.* London: Royal United Services Institute for Defence Studies.

Gash, H.A. (1993) A Constructivist attempt to change attitudes towards children with Special Needs. *European Journal of Special Needs Education 8,* 2, 106–125.

Jenks, C. (1992) First 'Romania Aid' Conference, Craiova, September, 1992 (unpublished).

Manoliu, R. (1992)Report for Romanian Orphanage Trust, May (unpublished).

Mead, M. (1954) 'Some theoretical considerations of the problem of maternal separation.' *American Journal of Orthopsychiatry 24*, 47–83.

Mead, M. (1962) 'A cultural anthropologists' approach to maternal deprivation.' In Ainsworth *et a.* (eds) *Deprivation of Maternal Care: A reassessment of its Effects.* Geneva: World Health Organisation.

Nordoff, P. and Robbins, C. (1985) *Therapy in Music for Handicapped Children.* London: Gollanz.

Prosser, H. (1976) *Perspectives on Residential Child Care.* Windsor: National Foundation for Educational Research.

Warwick, D. (1984) *Management in Schools-Motivating the Staff. The Relevance of the Behavioural Sciences.* London: Education for Industrial Society.

Wood, M. (1982) *Music for Living-Enriching the Lives of Profoundly Mentally Handicapped People.* Kidderminster: British Institute of Mental Handicap.

PART FIVE

Providing for Consultation

CHAPTER ELEVEN

The Voice of Children in Health Education

Use of the *Just a Tick* Method to Consult Children Over Curriculum Content

David Regis

INTRODUCTION

This chapter describes the development and outcome of a method to consult children on the content of the health education curriculum. It is the work of the Director of the Schools Health Education Unit (SHEU), John Balding, and his research team over the last decade and more. A quick word from John:

> The aim, in most aspects of my researches in support of good practice in schools, has been to provide reliable data, in an intelligible form, to help schools make their own decisions. (Balding 1983, p.83)

What can this philosophy do for schools health education? Often in schools the job of sorting out the content of the health education curriculum is given to one or a group of teachers. Their views and expertise may become the deciding factor in determining content when they are not solely responsible for the delivery of the curriculum, nor the only people entitled to view. It seemed to John Balding in the middle 1970s that, rather than have an eyeball-to-eyeball confrontation about the issues, it was better at the outset to consult as widely as possible among colleagues and others about priorities.

DEVELOPMENT OF THE METHOD:
A NATIONAL SURVEY OF SECONDARY TEACHERS

This approach led to the development of the Health Topic Research programme where, between 1975 and 1978, a health topic check-list *Just One Minute* was developed for use in secondary schools. This was taken up by the Health

Education Council (HEC) and the Open University (Open University 1981) and used widely as part of the HEC Schools Health Education Project.

The results from this survey method were very interesting in terms of perceived priorities but there were some other features of the results which were a little disturbing. If you looked at the priorities for the teachers, broken down by subject that they taught (Balding 1983b), you could find amazing things such as:

- the top-rated topic for *Physical Education* teachers was *exercise*
- the top-rated topic for *Home Economics* teachers was *safety in the home*
- the teachers who voted most often for the topic *conservation* were the *Biology* teachers
- the teachers who voted most often for the topic *morality* were the *Religious Education* teachers.

This doesn't disturb you? From the point of view of research, this may be reassuring but from the point of view of moving on the debate on health education, we weren't so sure. If you looked at the results from the same teachers broken down by age and sex you could see readily comprehensible differences:

- younger teachers voting more positively for *contraception* than older colleagues
- older teachers approaching retirement age voting most positively for *use of leisure*
- young women teachers voting more positively for *personal relationships*
- older men losing interest in *sex*.

The point? What this really means, perhaps, is that none of us can look at young people except through the perspective of our own history and position in life; our opinions about what is good for young people are coloured so strongly by our own lives.

As this slightly depressing conclusion was dawning on John, he was approached to develop this consultation method more widely for a national survey of primary[1] schools. The crucial opportunity here was not just to refine the technique of the enquiry but to consult more widely in the community – to ask parents and other adults connected with schools for their views but also to consult the children.

---

1   Schools for children aged 5–11 years (infant/first schools = 5–7-year-olds, junior/middle schools = 7–11-year-olds)

APPROACH IN SCHOOLS

The revised method, called *Just a Tick*, was re-drafted from scratch by John with Teresa Code and Karen Redman supported by a grant from the Health Education Council. Suggestions for inclusion in the topic list numbered 154 at one point (Redman 1983), which was gradually whittled down to a final list of 43 as seen on Table 11.2 (p.134). The other development at this stage was to develop separate versions for teachers, parents, health-care professionals, and children. Only children of nine years old or more were involved in the survey, depending as it did on some level of reading ability (although the procedure in the classroom was highly organised and included the reading and explanation of each topic title to the class).

One important difference between the adult and pupil versions is that the adults were asked to rate the *importance* of each topic for inclusion in the curriculum, whereas the children were asked how *interested* they would be in having lessons on that topic. The detail of the response options can be seen in Table 11.1 (p.132).

Six additional topics were added for a secondary[2] school version: contraception, parenthood and child care, sexually transmitted diseases, control of body weight, violence on TV screen and cancer. Since these questionnaires were devised, they have been further revised including the addition of the issue of child abuse. The pros and cons of the method might include:

Advantages:

- The children (and adults) don't have to come up with ideas or words themselves.
- Data can be collected quickly from a large number of people.
- The groups of people involved welcome being consulted.
- The 'signals' from the different groups can be compared.
- Parents who don't attend meetings, or are not very forceful or articulate when they do, are still represented and their views recorded.

Comments:

- The division between 'health education' and other sorts of important social education is not made here.

---

2   For children 11–16 years of age.

Disadvantages:

- Things left off the list might get ignored in the debate (but that isn't usually true, in our experience, of AIDS or of child abuse).

- The meaning of the phrases might be interpreted differently by different people.

- People may down-grade an important topic because they don't themselves know how it can be taught.

Typically, response rates from parents are very high in primary schools; we know of schools where a questionnaire was returned from every single family who had a pupil at the school. Clearly, parents welcome the opportunity to express their views and many make additional comments on their scripts (a compilation and analysis of parents' comments is to be found in Balding, Code and Redman 1987). Indeed, so positive can be the links created by use of this method, that we have known people in the world of education promote the *Just a Tick* survey in their district to foster better relations between homes and schools! (Balding 1986).

It is, of course, possible for a senior teacher to receive a book of data processed by the Unit, say 'yes, very interesting', and then carry on as before. We are more inclined to see the survey as the first step in a debate with parents, children and others in the community that will lead to a school policy and curriculum which is at least better informed and understood. One common response by schools is to continue the debate with the community it serves by holding a parents' evening to discuss the aggregate results when they are returned to the school. Below, I will go through the method by which we have presented the data to such meetings.

PRESENTATION OF DATA TO GROUPS FOR DISCUSSION

The results for a given topic look might like this:

Table 11.1: Percentages of each group giving each response to topic 1 (example)

	Should be included	Useful if time available	Undecided	Not in this age group	Should be covered at home	Does more harm than good
1. How my body works						
Teachers	81%	13%	3%	3%	0.3%	0%
Parents	74%	20%	3%	2%	1%	0.2%

Table 11.1: Percentages of each group
giving each response to topic 1 (example) (continued)

	Very interested	Quite interested	Not sure	No!
1. How my body works				
Boys	28%	62%	9%	1%
Girls	35%	50%	14%	1%

Source: Schools Health Education Unit, University of Exeter

Clearly, looking at all 43 of such summaries with a group is unfeasibly slow. A device was adopted to get a summary of all the results on one page, which was statistically rather naughty but in practice very fruitful.

First, as can be seen from the example results in Table 11.1, most adults and children were positive towards the topic. In fact, looking across all the results for all the schools, most adults and children were fairly positive towards the majority of the topics. So we examined the percentages of each group giving the *most positive* option, and ranked the topics for each group – for example, the positions of the topics for infant school parents ranked by the percentage saying each topic *should be included* are shown in Table 11.2. We then produced a summary of the ranks for each group, as in Table 11.3.

More parents of infant children voted for *20. Safety in traffic* than any other topic and the topic getting the least votes for definite inclusion in the curriculum was *18. Health and Social Services* (which came 43rd out of 43).

The statistical sins here are several:

- we have ignored the data for all the other responses (although these are less commonly used by respondents)

- we have ranked the data which ignores any possible 'bunching' of results (although we in fact see that the differences between ranks is fairly smooth from first [usually about 90% for the top topic] to last [about 10%])

- we have put responses from pupils and adults together on Table 11.3 even though they answered different questionnaires with different options.

THE RESULTS OF THE NATIONAL PRIMARY SURVEY

Each column in Table 11.3 (pp.136–7) shows the order, from 1st to 43rd, in which the topics were rated by parents (Par), teachers (Tch), Health Care Professionals such as school nurses (HCP), and pupils. The adults indicated that the topic in question *should be included* in the curriculum, while the pupils' results are based on those responding that they would be *very interested* in it. Some topic

Table 11.2. Rank positions among the Just a Tick topics list ordered by percentage of infant school parents from national primary survey responding should be included

Topic	Rank	Topic	Rank
01. How my body works	16	24. Being separated from parents	36
02. Staying well	19	25. Death and bereavement	40
03. Immunisation: injections and drops	31	26. Why people worry	42
04. Illness and recovery	38	27. How boys and girls behave	33
05. Talking with doctors &c	13	28. Differences in growth & development	33
06. Care of hair,teeth,skin	5	29. Getting on with boys & girls the same age as yourself	14
07. Care of eyes	10	30. Understanding people with different coloured skins or religions	9
08. Care of feet	16	31. Feelings (love,hate, anger jealousy)	18
09. How a baby is made	32	32. Bullying	8
10. Menstruation:periods	41	33. Feeling good about yourself	29
11. Food and Health	14	34. Making up our minds	27
12. Drinking Alcohol	39	35. Being honest	3
13. Glue sniffing	28	36. Being responsible	7
14. Smoking	26	37. Spare time activities	29
15. Physical fitness	10	38. Being bored	36
16. Understanding the needs of old people	19	39. Caring for pets	19
17. Understanding the needs of handicapped people	23	40. Vandalism	10
18. Health and Social Services	43	41. Stealing	5
19. Safety at home	4	42. Pollution	33
20. Safety in traffic	1	43. Conservation	25
21. Water Safety	2		
22. First Aid	23		
23. Family life	22		

Source: Schools Health Education Unit, University of Exeter

titles have had to be compressed from the exact wording in the questionnaire: these are shown in square brackets (for actual wording, see Table 11.2 (p.134)).

It is, of course, the original purpose of the questionnaire to collect local data and let local communities run with it; this national collation obscures an enormous amount of variation within and between schools.

Even this greatly simplified data I find enormously rich and I never tire of looking at it and listening to students comment on it. Some obvious highlights are:

- The most topics most often rated as important by all adult groups are the *safety* issues, topic numbers 19–21. These are also fairly highly rated in terms of interest by pupils, together with *First Aid* [22].

- Other topics that most adults think are very important include: moral personal issues like *35. Being honest* and *36. Being responsible; 41. Stealing* and *32. Bullying* also feature among the top ten for adult groups. The biological topics *1. How my body works* and *11. Food and nutrition* are rated highly.

- The most highly rated topic for all groups of pupils is *39. Caring for pets.*

- Other topics very interesting to pupils include: *6. Care of hair, teeth and skin, 15. Physical fitness, 37. Spare time activities, 17. Understanding the needs of handicapped people* and, particularly for the older pupils, *24. Being separated from parents.*

- There is a consensus right across the board about the value of *6. Care of hair, teeth and skin.*

- The biggest mismatches between the ranks of adults and pupils are for the topics *24. Being separated from parents* and *25. Death and bereavement.* This may reflect:
  - adults' reluctance to deal with the issues themselves
  - adults' reluctance to trouble children with these issues
  - a lack of understanding of how these issues might constructively be dealt with in the classroom (a common comment at meetings).

- Two principal ideas that run through many decisions of health education are decision-making and self-esteem. If we look at the ranking of related topics we may discover that decision-making (*34. Making up our minds*) and self-esteem (*33. Feeling good about yourself*) attract no particular support from any group!

- Topic 43.*Conservation* attracts much interest from pupils; we did wonder if this interest was, in part, triggered by the prompt offered as there is a discontinuity between the high votes here and the results from secondary pupils (see Table 11.4, pp.139–40).

Table 11.3: Rank positions among the *Just a Tick* topics list ordered by responses from national primary survey

Topic no. and label	Infant/First Schools			Junior/Middle Schools			Boys by age				Girls by age			
	Par	Tcb	HCP	Par	Tcb	HCP	7–8y	8–9y	9–10y	10–11y	7–8y	8–9y	9–10y	10–11y
01. How my body works	16	24	14	8	6	2	14	12	17	24	16	20	23	26
02. Staying well	19	16	18	30	14	17	26	28	29	27	24	20	20	22
03. [Immunisation:injections]	31	29	33	31	30	27	41	41	41	41	35	36	42	40
04. Illness and recovery	38	30	35	40	38	39	30	30	27	27	26	29	27	28
05. Talking with doctors &c	13	14	9	26	40	23	39	42	43	43	33	33	42	43
06. Care of hair,teeth,skin	5	3	3	8	4	2	13	12	14	16	6	6	6	6
07. Care of eyes	10	17	11	18	11	14	12	9	9	9	12	16	17	19
08. Care of feet	16	18	12	21	15	17	38	38	37	35	29	23	28	32
09. How a baby is made	32	38	40	14	22	13	25	18	13	12	12	12	10	9
10. Menstruation:periods	41	43	42	15	22	6	43	43	42	39	28	25	20	12
11. Food and Health	14	9	7	19	7	9	6	10	10	10	17	17	15	18
12. Drinking Alcohol	39	41	41	26	37	27	32	23	18	20	42	39	38	36
13. Glue sniffing	28	40	37	11	34	23	42	38	33	25	42	39	31	27
14. Smoking	26	37	27	12	22	11	36	28	24	20	35	33	23	24
15. Physical fitness	10	23	20	7	17	16	4	4	2	3	7	7	7	7
16. [Understanding the old]	19	20	31	24	21	36	17	26	33	36	12	14	19	16
17. [Understanding h'cap]	23	20	29	26	22	37	16	16	24	23	7	7	12	11
18. [Health and Social Serv]	43	42	43	43	43	43	26	30	38	39	23	31	37	40
19. Safety at home	4	7	5	12	7	8	5	6	8	7	4	5	5	5
20. Safety in traffic	1	1	1	1	1	1	7	7	7	8	12	10	15	20
21. Water Safety	2	3	2	2	2	5	2	2	4	4	5	4	4	4
22. First Aid	23	36	31	17	31	22	8	7	6	5	3	3	2	2

Adult Groups | pupil Groups

Table 11.3: Rank positions among the *Just a Tick* topics list ordered by responses from national primary survey (continued)

Topic no. and label	Adult Groups						Pupil Groups							
	Infant/First Schools			Junior/Middle Schools			Boys by age				Girls by age			
	Par	Tch	HCP	Par	Tch	HCP	7–8y	8–9y	9–10y	10–11y	7–8y	8–9y	9–10y	10–11y
23. Family life	22	8	16	34	28	25	11	12	18	16	10	10	12	12
24. [Separation from parents]	36	30	25	38	39	39	20	20	14	11	20	17	8	7
25. Death and bereavement	40	34	38	40	41	41	9	12	11	16	10	14	11	16
26. Why people worry	42	38	38	42	41	42	40	40	39	42	35	41	41	40
27. [Boys & girls behaviour]	33	33	33	31	36	29	32	32	35	32	25	25	34	33
28. [Diffs in growth & dev]	33	35	36	23	31	21	23	24	26	27	32	23	26	20
29. [Getting on with others]	14	15	20	22	20	26	26	20	18	20	21	22	22	24
30. [Understanding race etc]	9	13	14	15	9	14	35	36	38	36	33	32	32	30
31. [Feelings:love,hate,etc]	18	11	19	24	19	19	20	18	14	13	18	17	18	15
32. Bullying	8	9	10	8	12	19	19	16	18	15	41	42	38	37
33. [Feeling good about self]	29	19	22	36	27	32	18	20	23	25	21	25	32	29
34. Making up our minds	27	26	29	31	29	38	20	27	31	34	27	29	28	33
35. Being honest	3	2	3	2	3	2	15	11	11	13	9	12	12	12
36. Being responsible	7	6	6	4	5	7	23	32	30	31	29	25	23	23
37. Spare time activities	29	28	23	35	33	30	9	5	3	2	18	9	8	10
38. Being bored	36	32	25	38	35	33	32	32	36	36	40	37	35	33
39. Caring for pets	19	5	13	37	26	34	1	1	1	1	1	1	1	1
40. Vandalism	10	25	17	6	16	12	36	36	27	30	38	43	38	39
41. Stealing	5	12	7	5	10	9	30	32	31	32	29	37	36	37
42. Pollution	33	27	27	26	17	34	29	24	18	16	38	33	28	30
43. Conservation	25	22	24	20	12	31	2	2	4	5	2	2	3	3
Sample sizes	5562	415	219	1036	639	230	621	1438	1744	1831	551	1434	1628	1737

I offer these comments really as a starter for your own reflections – what if these were the results for your school? Would you expect your school's results to be different, and how? Is there more or less consensus between the adults than you expected? Or between boys and girls? Which topics should be included in the curriculum? How should they be taught? And who will decide?

AN ACCUMULATION OF SECONDARY RESULTS

Secondary schools are rather more likely to use our other survey service, the Heath-Related Behaviour Questionnaire. We have performed a similar analysis on the few secondary schools that have used the *Just a Tick* survey method over the last decade.

Each column in this table shows the order, from 1st to 49th, in which the topics were rated by parents (Par), teachers (Tch), and pupils. The adults indicated that the topic in question *should be included* in the curriculum, while the pupils' results are based on those responding that they would be *very interested* in it. Some topic titles have had to be compressed from the exact wording in the questionnaire: these are shown in square brackets (for actual wording, see Table 11.2, p.134).

COMMENTARY ON SECONDARY RESULTS

I should caution that these data have nothing like the stature of the primary survey, being drawn from a smaller collection of schools over a longer period of time. But, as was said before, the point of the surveys is to prompt local discussion and local action. You might begin your reflections by establishing from the table:

- The top topic for parents and teachers is *9. How a baby is made.* Other sex-related topics which get lots of positive votes from adults include *10. Menstruation: periods, 44. Contraception,* and *46. Sexually transmitted diseases.*

- Teachers also see a great important in substance-related topics like *14. Smoking, 12. Drinking alcohol,* and *13. Glue sniffing.* Parents also vote for these topics in large proportions.

- Boys of all ages vote most positively for *15. Physical fitness.* How much of this is a positive vote for sport and how much a shrinking from the more emotional material elsewhere in the list?

- Among the girls there is an intriguing climb from fifth to first for *45. Parenthood and child care.* With the finding above we can be assured that gender stereotyping is working well.

Table 11.4: Rank positions among the *Just a Tick* topics list ordered by responses from all recent secondary schools

Topic no. and label	Adults		Boys					Girls				
	TCH	PAR	Yr 7	Yr 8	Yr 9	Yr 10	Yr 11	Yr 7	Yr 8	Yr 9	Yr 10	Yr 11
01. How my body works	9	2	41	38	14	33	27	38	35	27	32	32
02. Staying well	16	27	31	13	17	11	19	32	31	36	30	18
03. [Immunisation:injections]	40	32	36	41	42	42	33	43	34	35	45	37
04. Illness and recovery	48	45	39	33	30	36	40	41	42	40	43	42
05. Talking with doctors &c	44	40	47	49	47	46	42	45	45	42	42	40
06. Care of hair,teeth,skin	17	25	17	20	23	27	21	21	8	14	10	8
07. Care of eyes	30	33	10	11	8	16	15	29	13	16	12	16
08. Care of feet	35	36	43	42	40	39	43	49	48	46	47	46
09. How a baby is made	1	1	9	3	3	2	2	10	10	10	9	7
10. Menstruation:periods	3	4	49	46	44	45	49	7	12	37	27	29
11. Food and Health	6	13	5	7	4	8	5	26	26	15	11	11
12. Drinking Alcohol	4	14	28	18	12	12	14	33	27	20	24	24
13. Glue sniffing	10	10	25	35	35	26	16	30	24	24	26	22
14. Smoking	2	8	16	31	21	24	10	8	18	12	23	13
15. Physical fitness	8	12	1	1	1	1	1	15	19	17	13	9
16. [Understanding the old]	28	26	42	44	46	47	46	23	28	13	29	30
17. [Understanding h'cap]	32	29	33	37	41	43	41	27	33	19	31	31
18. [Health and Social Serv]	41	42	48	48	48	49	44	48	49	49	44	43
19. Safety at home	26	34	15	19	34	17	23	22	23	34	25	26
20. Safety in traffic	23	21	12	30	25	32	25	35	36	45	40	35
21. Water Safety	31	22	8	12	33	28	18	20	21	38	33	33
22. First Aid	21	11	2	8	7	5	7	6	3	5	6	4
23. Family life	34	37	29	23	31	31	31	13	17	23	16	17
24. [Separation from parents]	39	44	18	16	24	35	37	4	9	11	14	21
25. Death and bereavement	37	41	24	21	19	38	39	17	11	25	19	27
26. Why people worry	45	39	46	45	43	40	47	44	43	33	34	47

Table 11.4: Rank positions among the *Just a Tick* topics list ordered by responses from all recent secondary schools (continued)

Topic no. and label	Adults		Boys					Girls				
	TCH	PAR	Yr 7	Yr 8	Yr 9	Yr 10	Yr 11	Yr 7	Yr 8	Yr 9	Yr 10	Yr 11
27. [Boys & girls behaviour]	38	35	30	39	38	29	29	25	22	21	22	34
28. [Diffs in growth & dev]	18	18	21	10	13	15	12	18	6	26	28	19
29. [Getting on with others]	24	28	23	9	10	7	9	11	7	8	8	10
30. [Understanding race etc]	13	24	44	47	49	48	48	47	47	48	35	41
31. [Feelings:love,hate,etc]	29	30	26	27	22	22	35	16	14	9	7	14
32. Bullying	22	17	38	40	39	41	32	36	40	44	41	45
33. [Feeling good about self]	15	9	35	22	11	9	13	9	15	7	4	6
34. Making up our minds	14	15	32	28	16	14	26	31	30	22	15	20
35. Being honest	12	7	19	26	29	25	34	12	25	28	17	25
36. Being responsible	5	3	34	15	15	18	20	37	29	32	20	23
37. Spare time activities	43	47	27	5	2	4	4	19	38	31	36	28
38. Being bored	47	48	45	43	45	44	45	46	44	43	48	48
39. Caring for pets	49	49	4	4	6	13	8	1	5	6	21	12
40. Vandalism	33	23	14	25	36	21	38	28	37	30	46	39
41. Stealing	27	19	37	34	37	23	30	14	32	29	38	36
42. Pollution	25	20	11	29	26	19	28	39	39	41	39	44
43. Conservation	20	16	13	24	32	30	22	34	41	39	37	38
44. Contraception	7	6	20	32	18	10	11	24	16	4	5	5
45. Parenthood & child care	19	31	7	17	27	34	24	5	4	3	2	1
46. Sex'lly trans'd diseases	11	5	3	2	5	3	3	3	2	1	3	3
47. Control of body weight	36	43	22	36	28	37	36	40	20	18	18	15
48. Violence on TV screen	42	46	40	14	20	20	17	42	46	47	49	49
49. Cancer	46	38	6	6	9	6	6	2	1	2	1	2
Sample sizes	299	461	242	1202	740	1072	1040	278	1198	916	1168	864

- Another top topic for the pupils is *49. Cancer,* which scarcely registers for the adults. Girls are relatively more interested in this than boys: is this because the cancers girls hear about, like breast cancer and cervical cancer, are bound up with their entry into adulthood and the need for self-examination and screening?

- Leisure activities, 37–39, attract little support from adults. Bottom of the adult lists is *39. Caring for pets* which still attracts strong support among pupils, particularly among the younger ones

- Emotional topics like, *24. Separation from parents, 25. Death and bereavement,* and *26. Why people worry* get relatively few votes from adults or children.

- The health educators' two principal ideas of decision-making (*34. Making up our minds*) and self-esteem (*33. Feeling good about yourself*) attract some positive support, particularly *33* among the older girls. (We know from other data that girls often score lower on measures of self-esteem than comparable groups of boys, although that may reflect greater honesty on the part of the girls.)

Again, what if these were the results from your school?

CLOSING NOTE

I resist making any grand conclusions as the purpose of the method is to raise issues that should be dealt with locally. We believe that if schools are to carry out actions they will do so much more convincingly and effectively if they decide on and plan the implementation of those actions themselves. After all, it is too easy to say from our ivory tower that a school should take a particular course of action – it is not our responsibility to assess its feasibility or to make it work. And, undoubtedly, we would get get the blame if it went wrong!

So, simply, we have found in this method a practical and fruitful way for schools to consult with groups of adults and children over these important areas of the curriculum and see it as one way of giving children, among other constituencies, a voice in health education.

REFERENCES

Balding, J.W. (1983) 'Health topics and the parents.' *Education and Health 1*, 5, 83.

Balding, J.W. (1983b) 'Developing the heath related behaviour questionnaire.' *Education and Health 1*, 1, 10.

Balding, J.W. (1986) 'The "Just a Tick" materials and their use in schools.' *Education and Health 4*, 1, 6.

Balding, J.W., Code, T. and Redman, K. (1987) *Parents and Health Education.* Exeter: Exeter University Schools Health Education Unit.

Open University (1981) INSET 'Education for Family Life' P532 SB. Milton Keynes: Open University Press.

Redman, K. (1983) 'Developing the topics checklist.' *Education and Health 1*, 5, 72.

CHAPTER TWELVE

Consulting Children About Play

Viv Hogan

The 'Children Today' demonstration projects were set up by the National Children's Play and Recreation Unit between May 1990 and October 1992. The Unit was given a four-year brief in 1988 by Central Government to plan for 'Children's Play'. One of its main aims has been to identify and promote good practice partnerships with local authorities and the voluntary sector. The way it went about this respects the child's rights to express an opinion and have such an opinion taken into account as embodied in Articles 12 and 13 of the UN Convention on the Rights of the Child. The unit operates in a number of areas including influencing and responding to legislation as it affects children and in education and training backing up, by means of a series of national centres, the framework for the accreditation and training of play workers. The unit also distributes information through its library which provides a rich resource of materials on play and which is open to the public. It therefore holds a watching brief for the play needs of children in this country and provides the structural support to properly recognise the child's right to play as contained in Article 31 of the UN convention which states:

1. States Parties recognise the right of the child to rest and leisure, to engage in play and recreational activities appropriate to the age of the child and to participate freely in cultural life and the Arts.

2. States Parties shall respect and promote the right of the child to participate fully in cultural and artistic life and shall encourage the provision of appropriate and equal opportunities for cultural, artistic, recreational and leisure activity.

In other words, the child has the right to leisure, play and participation in cultural and artistic activities.

Children are affected by a great number of local authority departments. Parks, recreation, education and social services are obvious examples but housing, highways and planning also affect children's lives. 'Children Today' links the work of different departments, increasing their awareness of children and looking at England in the 90s from a child's perspective – working out ways of creating a more child-friendly environment.

It's true that children without toys will improvise and children without play space will find somewhere – however impoverished or unsuitable – but children today feel that that isn't good enough in a complex society that needs to look forward to future generations of well-balanced people, whose life skills may have been nurtured through play. If this basic childhood need is to be fulfilled, adults have to intervene in providing good play opportunities and safe places to play. It's something we have to make priority.

The 'charter' for children's play from the National Voluntary Council for Children's Play defined play as:

> Play is an essential part of every child's life and vital to the processes of human development. It provides the mechanism for children to explore the world around them and the medium through which skills are developed and practised. It is essential for physical, emotional and spiritual growth, intellectual and educational development and acquiring social and behavioural skills.

> Play is a generic term for a variety of activities which are satisfying to the child, creative for the child and freely chosen by the child. The activities may involve equipment or they may not, be boisterous and energetic or quiet and contemplative, be done with other people or on ones own, have an end product or not or be light hearted or very serious.

> Every child needs to play and has a right to play, but opportunities to play are often limited by external factors – discrimination, the effects of disability and special needs, insufficient space and other environmental factors and poverty and other social conditions. Play services are the means by which new opportunities for play are created.

CHILDREN TODAY

Three project teams worked in Devon, Leicestershire and north-west England.

The team in the North-West covered the three metropolitan boroughs of Rochdale, St Helens and Stockport. It put its priorities as raising the profile of play and play work, linking with the voluntary sector and looking at ways of meeting the needs of children with disabilities and those of different ethnic groups.

Co-ordination of play services in a county that has nine districts and includes both rural and urban communities was one of the biggest concerns of the Leicestershire team. Their early consultations with people running adventure playgrounds, out-of-school clubs, youth clubs and playgroups showed up a number of urgent areas of work for the team, including play-worker training, environmental play and looking at links between play and care provision.

The distinctive rural areas of 'Teignbridge and Torridge shaped the agenda for the Devon team, who considered children's isolation and restricted experience by extending play provision and developing play opportunities to suit local needs.

In common with all the projects, the teams drew up contracts with their local partners and encouraged links between different departments and the community. The work was monitored and evaluated by Loughborough University.

Consultation has taken place in both rural and urban settings. The Leicestershire team undertook a survey of street play there aiming to make three urban streets more safe and stimulating for play with a particular emphasis on consultation of residents, especially children, and as a pilot/model for future environmental and traffic calming work.

The survey was carried out in November and December 1991. One street (not one of the three above), Worthington Street (a Woonerf design),[1] was felt to incorporate an understanding of children's play needs – that play is essential to children, that there are a wide variety of play activities which change throughout childhood and that children usually play within reach of home. It seemed sensible, therefore, to look to the Worthington Street experience to see what could be learnt.

No formal or recorded evaluation or monitoring of Worthington Street existed, so Mary Taverner (a Bartholomew Street resident) and Katie Green of 'Children Today' took a brief survey of children's and adult's views about the street (Green, Taverner and Senior 1992).

The children were asked questions, as in the examples which follow, about their feelings about Worthington Street:

Children aged 7–11 (6 girls, 5 boys)

1. What do you like about Worthington Street?

   - Like playing near home.
   - Posts exactly the right width for football goals!
   - We can play football.
   - We can play outside a lot.
   - Lot of my relatives live in my street.

---

1   A street design that gives pedestrians of all ages equal priority to vehicles and recognises residential areas as places where people live – the Dutch government supported over 800 Woonerf experiments

- We can ride bikes – there isn't much traffic as the street is small.
- We play skipping.
- We can play out every day.
- We play more in summer but like snowmen in the winter.
- Like the lampposts. We play outside in the dark sometimes.
- Like jumping over the metal posts.
- Like balancing on the planters.
- Like running up the humps.

2. What don't you like about Worthington Street?

- There's only a little place to play.
- People park anywhere – not enough space.
- Cars pass in front of our ball in the middle of the game and stop it.
- The man at number 13 shouts at us – we hide behind the cars.
- The lady tells us off.
- The houses should be bigger.
- Because two cars can't pass each other on the street, it holds up our games even longer.
- Dog barks at us.

3. What do your parents/adults dislike about Worthington Street?

- My dad doesn't like it. He doesn't like the dog mess.
- They don't like the neighbours shouting.
- The planters smell horrible.
- My aunt got a rash from the plants.
- They don't like next door's bell.

4. What do your parents/adults like about Worthington Street?

- They liked the council putting a leaflet through the door which told people to park in the right place.
- It's quieter.
- They like that we can play.
- They like that they can see us easily when they look out the front door.

5. If you could change anything at all about Worthington Street, what would you change?

- No cars at all.
- No parking at all.
- Tickets for parking wrongly.
- Make swings in the street.
- Make half the street a football pitch.
- Make the street bigger and wider.
- Make the houses bigger.
- Carpet on the street.
- A uniform for the football team in the street.
- Put up a wall in the middle of the street to stop cars.
- Wider street.
- Build a bridge over the street for cars.
- Build a car park.
- Won't need a car park if no cars!
- Build a mosque in the street.
- Make the street the biggest in the world.
- Have a whole county for children only, with another county for adults.
- Build a swimming pool.
- Build a hospital.

[Asked if they thought they might change their minds about cars when they got older they said 'no'. 'I will keep my mind when I get older' said one girl.]

A survey of this kind was not so feasible with the younger children (four boys and three girls aged five to seven years). The original plan had been to use questions similar to those asked of adults and older children but these were soon abandoned as it was clear that the children were still too young to make comprehensive critical comments about their living environment. Partly, they accepted it as a given thing and they were also shy and unused to direct questions on the same theme sustained over a long period. Therefore, the team drew the street and discussed the features of it. It became clear that they:

- played outside quite frequently
- like the humps to run up
- would like more flowers

- were very aware of cars
- found it difficult to play quiet games that they liked because of the noise
- liked riding bikes and tricycles outside
- liked playing ball games
- liked playing 'Kick the Can' (children will play with any loose material in their environment)
- were told not to stand on plants
- like digging in the soil (some children)
- were not interested in the planters – told to get of (some children)
- liked walking with Dad
- liked chasing games
- were used to having people around on the street, especially children.

Katie Green also drew the basic proportions of the street and the children added both the features already there and the ones they would like to see.

In some ways the results speak for themselves, but it is worth emphasising that the children were noticeably aware of lack of space – perhaps because of their physical dependence on the local environment or because they have culturally and economically less control and choice about how the space is used. They were certainly very imaginative and 'multi-disciplinary' about the changes they would like to see.

Because the focus of this 'Street Play' project was on children aged between 5 and 12, the children interviewed were all of primary school age and were approached at the local primary school (Uplands School). Therefore almost all the school age children living in the street were spoken to. In a more formal evaluation it was felt that it would have been useful to get views from children outside as well as inside school, perhaps through a local play project. It was also felt essential in such an evaluation to interview older children and teenagers.

This project did not only involve consulting children about their views on living in the street but also adult residents. This was an important aspect of total community involvement and provided the team with a broader perspective. One resident's replies, however, pointed to the issue of what, in a limited survey of this kind, is meant by 'representative' as he had been one of the resident's representatives when the Woonerf design was implemented yet he, for example, didn't believe children should play in the street and was concerned that the design encourages play. These views have every right to be expressed, but for a truly representative balance of views, women and child residents should also have been given the opportunity to air theirs.

The Leicestershire team felt that this survey had highlighted a number of issues relating to play:

- the importance of evaluation – there is no point in doing something if it has not been established whether or not it works and we can then learn from the mistakes

- the willingness of residents of all ages to share their views – people like to be asked and to give an opinion

- the importance of making sure a wide range of views is sampled. For example, children are seemingly never asked as a matter of course – but they represent one-quarter of the population

- that almost everyone had positive as well as negative comments – there was no 'council-bashing' and criticism was constructive

- that asking people's views is not necessarily a time-wasting and fraught exercise that never works – it can be a productive and enjoyable piece of work.

Unlike its counterparts in Leicestershire and the North-West, Devon did not have a well developed play service. Apart from static playgrounds provided by district councils and a few playschemes supported by social services, there was little in the way of statutory provision. Voluntary provision, on the other hand, was developing to meet a growing demand for out-of-school provision.

As a typically rural county, Devon was chosen as a base for one of the three 'Children Today' projects and was given a warm welcome by Devon County Council. It was agreed that, because it was such a large county, the project would work with the two rural districts of Teignbridge and Torridge. The Devon team were appointed in autumn 1990 and based at Moretonhampstead.

The first task for the team was to establish the level and range of current play provision by consulting individuals and agencies to identify and prioritise local issues and areas of interest. An invitation was sent to key people from these agencies to an initial meeting in September 1990 to discuss the project, with a view to forming a project action/advisory group to ensure that there was involvement and partnership from the beginning.

The meeting was well attended and clearly established the breadth of interest in children's services, evident from the wide range of agencies represented at the meeting. There was thorough and active discussion which resulted in the setting up of a small project action group comprising one representative from Education, Social Services, the Library Service, Teignbridge Recreational Department, Torridge Leisure Services, voluntary youth services, the Community Council of Devon, the Devon Playing Fields Association, and allowing up to three co-options. This project action group has continued to meet twice a year and the support it has given Children Today has been superb.

In November 1990, Children Today officially introduced itself to Devon with an education and training roadshow: *Playwork in Practice – a Profession on the Move.* The response was immense and enthusiastic.

Another area of work which was identified in the early stages of the project was, the development of a county-wide policy for children's services in Devon, but the time available to Children Today was not sufficient to consider this special undertaking. However, a number of events were undertaken to raise the profile of play in Devon and the debate about delivery of services in a rural area. These included: *The Devon County Show* and *Beyond the Hedge*, plus *Living, Working and Playing in Rural Devon*, and *The World Conference on the Rights of the Child* in Exeter.

A consultation process was undertaken through which questionnaires were sent to parish councils, schools, libraries, youth clubs and voluntary groups and interviews were arranged through Teignbridge and Torridge to establish facts and discover views about play in localities, that is, what provision existed, what was good about provision, what were the gaps and what improvements and developments there should be. The main issues identified in this stage of the consultation were as follows (not necessarily in order of importance):

1. lack of play provision/land for play

2. lack of inter-agency, inter-departmental co-ordination/co-operation

3. isolation

4. lack of transport

5. lack of county/district play policy

6. lack of funding

7. lack of community participation

8. lack of recognition of need for provision for 5–15 years age groups

9. lack of information, etc.

10. lack of awareness re play/rural children's needs.

As a result of the issues identified, the team set up five projects in Teignbridge and Torridge. 'Country Play Days' was the title of the project set up to develop play in rural areas and highlighted the importance of consultation with children. The common perception of the countryside as being a 'rural idyll' often bears little resemblance to reality, with a dearth of play opportunities in rural communities as the norm. Country Play Days were set up in seven separate rural venues and relied heavily on local co-ordination and involvement. The play days were well planned and consultation with children was built in to the plans – for instance, Children's Councils were held at the end of each play day.

The Children's views were consistently sought about what was happening and about how and what things should happen in the future. Various methods were employed to gain children's views including using drama, art and craft work and music. Consultation with children was found to be important at every stage but children also need to be given opportunities for exploring new ideas and given new experiences if they are to make informed choices. For instance, in one of the rural areas the children were involved in a project designing model play parks and the resulting designs were dominated by conventional play equipment. This is because they have none at all and aspire only to what they have seen in other villages and Bideford. If children are going to be consulted on designing play facilities they need the opportunity of seeing and using a range of facilities to enable them to make valuable comparisons.

A crucial, very positive element in the work of Children Today has been consulting children themselves. In such consultation we have regarded key messages as follows:

- Consultation should be fun! Consulting with children about their views on play should be made as friendly as possible.
- Consultation should use a variety of methods and approaches which take into account individual needs.
- Consultation should be holistic, i.e. part of the planning, part of the playing and part of the evaluation process.
- Consultation can be enhanced if both children and adults are involved in the process. Even though the format may be different, the dual involvement can legitimise and value the children's contribution.
- Consultation with children can enhance work policy and practice.
- The information gained through consultation with children gives adults a valuable insight into their play.
- Evidence shows that listening to children can be a positive contribution to planning for the future.

The project finished in 1992. The work done, its achievements and lessons for the future, has been recorded in three separate reports plus a national overview.

The Leicester team have also consulted children in relation to plans for traffic calming schemes. This consultation was designed in four parts:

1. an exhibition to start people thinking
2. a survey to identify their ideas
3. models to help residents visualise ideas
4. another exhibition to get feedback on the proposed changes

In a summing up report by Green and Lee (1992) the implications of this consultation are assessed:

> We have not designed the perfect consultation but we have shown that adults and children can be consulted in innovative ways at reasonable cost and in a reasonable time frame. Children should always be consulted when making changes to the streets because they are full of ideas, eager to say what they think, desperate to learn more and relatively easy to

contact via schools or on streets. If nothing else, working with them will restore faith in human creativity and co-operation! (p.9)

REFERENCES

Green, K., Taverner, M. and Senior, L (1992) *Worthington Street Survey. Children Today Play Project.* London: Children Today.

Green, K. and Lee, R. (1992) 'Reclaiming the streets for children's play.' *Transport Review 15, 5.*

FURTHER INFORMATION FROM

National Play and Information Centre, 359–361 Euston Road, London NW1 3AL. Tel: 0171–385 5455. Copies of Children Today and the reports may be obtained from this address.

PART SIX

Providing for Children's Rights in New Technological Advances

CHAPTER THIRTEEN

New Reproductive Technologies
Children's Rights and the Human Fertilisation and Embryology Act 1990

Bob Snowden

INTRODUCTION

Just over 100 years ago the first recorded attempt was made to conceive a human child in the absence of sexual intercourse. This occurred in 1884 in the medical department of Jefferson College situated in Philadelphia, USA. The circumstances surrounding this first case were reported in 1909 in a letter to a medical journal written by a middle-aged doctor named Addison Hard (Gregoire and Mayer 1965). Both the letter and Dr Hard's report of an event which took place 25 years previously appear somewhat bizarre when viewed from our own time, but the issues raised then are still with us today despite the major advances in biology and allied sciences which have taken place during the present century.

Dr Hard's report was a fairly straight forward one. As a medical student in 1884 he had taken part in a class held by the College's Professor of Surgery. During this class Professor Pancoast introduced a medical problem with which he was being confronted that very day and challenged the class to consider how the problem could be resolved. A man and his wife had visited the professor because they desperately wanted to have a child of their own but although they had been trying for many years they had had no success in conceiving a child. After asking a number of questions, Professor Pancoast examined both the wife and her husband to see if he could determine why this particular difficulty was present. He reported to his students that after a careful examination he could find no abnormality in the wife and no apparent problem with her husband. He then asked the husband to provide a specimen of his semen which Professor Pancoast placed under a microscope for closer examination. Professor Pancoast then discovered that the husband was azoospermic – his semen contained no sperm whatsoever.

While the reason for the couple's inability to conceive a child had been found, what to do about this condition was less easy to resolve. It was this problem Professor Pancoast put to the all-male members of his class. After a lengthy discussion it was decided (according to Dr Hard's report) that the best way for the couple to conceive a child was for the 'best looking member of the class' to donate fertile semen and for Professor Pancoast to use this semen to artificially inseminate the wife of the infertile husband. Professor Pancoast did this after placing the childless wife under a general anaesthetic – but without her knowledge or consent and without the knowledge or consent of her husband.

It so happened that the lady in question conceived a child which she and her husband attributed to the medical advice they had received from Professor Pancoast. When Professor Pancoast became aware of the new situation he felt compelled to inform the husband of what he had done. The husband's reaction to this news was to ask if anyone apart from the medical team had been informed and, on being told that his secret was safe, it was agreed that no one – including his wife, the mother of the child – should be informed. A son was born to the couple and Professor Pancoast and the husband kept to their agreement about secrecy throughout the remainder of their lives.

About 25 years after this event, Addison Hard, now Dr Hard, travelled to the home town of the couple who had visited Professor Pancoast all those years before and arranged a meeting. He reports that he did this out of a sense of curiosity and to discover how the family had got on. By this time the husband, like Professor Pancoast, had died but his only son, now a successful young man, had taken over his business and, with his mother, was making a significant contribution to the business and social life of their local community. Dr Hard left mother and son without informing either of them of the strange events in which both of them had unknowingly participated. In his report of this case to the Medical World in 1909, Dr Hard claimed that this use of donated semen from 'the best looking member of the class' in 1884 had resulted in a contented husband, a proud mother and a successful son and that greater use should be made of donated semen where male infertility was diagnosed.

This is the first recorded case of the use of donated gametes in the conception of a human child. The story contains a number of issues surrounding the rights and responsibilities of those directly involved – Professor Pancoast, the mother, her husband, the semen donor, and even members of the class during which the decision to proceed was made. The personal and professional rights and responsibilities relating to these individuals directly and to their relationships with each other, have been used as discussion prompts in medical ethics classes over the years but usually in the context of describing an historical aberration involving well-meaning professionals providing a service at an early stage in its development. Whereas one would expect, 100 years on from the 1884 activity in Jefferson College, that all children conceived by the use of donated gametes would be informed of their different origins, this expectation remains unfulfilled. Indeed, in this reporting of an actual event, no mention was made of the needs or rights of the child who would have been most affected by the activities described; the same lack of awareness may be said to affect most children conceived in a similar way at the present time. Put simply, the child conceived in this way has tended to be treated as a product of a medical procedure and the question of needs and rights beyond those of the individuals directly involved in the treatment procedure has been relatively ignored.

In the United Kingdom there have been many advances in the biological sciences and in technological developments associated with the study of human reproduction and early embryonic development since the American report was published. The proliferation of services specialising in infertility treatment since the 1960s is due mainly to these biological and technical advances taking place at a time when the availability of babies for adoption was greatly reduced. The changing social and legal climate which led to single mothers being enabled to keep their babies, and where abortion was more readily available, meant that the traditional solution for involuntary childlessness, adoption, was no longer available. This stimulated a demand by infertile couples for treatment using the newly available reproductive technologies. The speed of application of these scientific developments (including the freezing of sperm; the establishment of sperm banks; *in-vitro* fertilisation; surrogacy; the ability to 'experiment' on the human embryo at very early stages of gestation, etc.) eventually led to concern being expressed in the community at large (Snowden, Mitchell and Snowden 1983). This expression of concern led to a number of professional and public enquiries and consultations resulting in the enactment of the Human Fertilisation and Embryology Act, 1990 in the U.K.

Addison Hard's report is concerned with *donor insemination*, where sperm is donated by a third party. Until the latter half of the present century this was the only available form of gamete donation. However, during the 1970s, technical advances introduced the possibility of removing eggs from the ovaries of an adult woman, and their external fertilisation – either for further development in her own or in the body of another woman. (This procedure preceded the birth of Louise Brown, the first so-called *test-tube* baby in 1978.) *Gamete donation*, then, describes the provision of eggs or sperm by someone other than the person being treated for infertility. It is important to notice that the use of donated gametes, while dependent on the technological developments associated with the treatment of infertility, represents a significant departure from traditional medical practice. Put briefly, donor insemination 'treatment' does not attempt to cure or treat the male partner's condition of infertility; he remains as infertile at the end of the treatment – even where a child is conceived and born – as he was at the beginning. In this situation a couple's state of childlessness has been circumvented through the provision of treatment procedures directed at the female partner who is medically fit. In other words, the female partner of a couple seeking donor insemination must, if the procedure is to be successful, be capable of conceiving and bearing a child.

Where the gametes used to effect fertilisation are those provided by a man and woman who have a continuing relationship and commitment to each other, the psychological and social implications of achieving a pregnancy in this way are not so much different from those associated with the more usual sexual method adopted by the majority of couples; it is when gametes donated by a third party introduce a discontinuity between biological and social parenthood that difficulties begin to arise. This deliberately planned discontinuity between genetic and social parenting has implications for the relationship between the fertile and the infertile parent, for the identification of family and kinship links, for the identity of the self and, some would argue, for the values which underpin the social structure of society as a whole.

Those concerned about the personal and social implications of the new assisted-conception techniques identify five groups of people requiring consideration and protection: the child born as a result of these techniques, the commissioning parent(s), the gamete donor, the service provider and members of the general public in whose name appropriate regulation should be exercised (Snowden 1990).

Addison Hard's report reminds us that donor insemination – the use of sperm donated by a third party – remains the oldest, and still the most common, of the assisted-conception techniques being used to alleviate childlessness among the 10–16 per cent of couples believed to be suffering from subfertility or infertility (Hull 1986). Like the more sophisticated and complex technique of *in-vitro* fertilisation (whether or not donor gametes are used), donor insemination shares one major feature in common; the ability to conceive a child in the absence of sexual intercourse.

BACKGROUND TO THE HUMAN FERTILISATION AND EMBRYOLOGY ACT

The call for the regulation of research and services associated with assisted conception has a long history which is closely related to developments in donor insemination. The first published account of donor insemination services in the UK appeared in the British Medical Journal in 1945 (Barton, Walker and Weisner 1945). The report initiated a similar reaction to Addison Hard's report three decades earlier in the USA. The topic rapidly became a matter of contention which reached beyond the medical profession. Ethical issues raised by the introduction of a third party into the marital relationship were hotly debated.

The most notable contribution to the early debate was that of the Archbishop of Canterbury who proposed that legislation should be introduced to make the provision of donor insemination a criminal offence. The Government of the time reacted slowly to this suggestion and it was not until 1960 that a report of a committee of inquiry (The Feversham Report) was available (Feversham 1960). While expressing disquiet about the social consequences of donor insemination procedures the report did not recommend the introduction of legislation to discourage or control the provision of such services. The committee members appeared to hope that by refusing to provide a legal framework for the practise of donor insemination, couples would be deterred from recourse to such a controversial and unregulated procedure. The Feversham Committee was wrong in this belief and during the 1960s the demand for donor insemination services increased.

This increased demand for donor insemination services prompted the British Medical Association to set up a working party under the chairmanship of Sir John Peel to study the issue and make recommendations. The working party reported in 1973 (Peel 1973) and recommended that donor insemination should be made available within the NHS. This report did not attract as much public attention as previous reports but the impact within the medical profession was significant. It was this report which, in contrast to previous reports, provided professional respectability to the provision of services using donated gametes.

Another major impetus to the debate about the availability of such services came with the publicity surrounding the birth, in 1978, of the first baby to be born following *in-vitro* fertilisation. Louise Brown's birth led to considerable publicity about all assisted-conception techniques and the scientific work involving experimentation on human embryos associated with them. Following wide media coverage of these developments, a Committee of Inquiry on Human Fertilisation and Embryology was set up by the Government which reported in 1984 (Warncock 1984). Recommendations were made for the regulation of *in-vitro* fertilisation and donor insemination techniques, for the management of surrogacy arrangements and for the control of experiments using human embryos. The Warnock Report acted as the basis for the legislation contained in the Human Fertilisation and Embryology Act 1990.

THE HUMAN FERTILISATION AND EMBRYOLOGY ACT 1990

The Act is a complex piece of legislation and what follows is unavoidably selective, concentrating as it does on the aspects of the Act most directly linked to the needs and rights of the child. Section numbers of the Act are included to provide a guide to a more detailed reading of the Act. The relevant features of the Act are:

- An independent Human Fertilisation and Embryology Authority (the Authority) is created to control and license centres offering treatment using donated sperm or eggs, or involving the creation of human embryos outside the body; storing human sperm, eggs or embryos; or carrying out research on human embryos (S.5–8 and Schedule 1). This control is exercised through powers provided by the Act directly, by regulations to be given by the Secretary of State, directions to be given by the Authority (S.23–24) and through a code of practice the Authority is required to develop (S.25–26).

- In any decision relating to the provision of a regulated service, account must be taken of the welfare of any child who may be born as a result of treatment (including the need of that child for a father) and of any other children who may be affected by the birth. In addition, donors and recipients of donated gametes must be provided with relevant information and be given a suitable opportunity to receive 'proper counselling' before giving written consent to their participation (S.13 and Schedule 3).

- Proper records, including details of the persons donating or receiving gametes/embryos and any child born as a result of the regulated treatment, must be maintained and forwarded to the Authority as directed (S.12).

- The woman who carries the child (and no other woman) is deemed to be the mother of the child (S.27).

- The woman's husband or partner is regarded in all respects as the child's father (with one notable exception relating to inheritance – S.29) unless it is shown he did not consent to his partner's treatment. The semen donor or a male whose sperm is used after his death is not to be treated as the father of the child (S.28).

- A court may make an order for a child to be treated in law as the child of a married couple where the gametes of the husband or wife are used to create an embryo and another woman carries the child through pregnancy, provided: the married couple make an application to the court within six months of the child's birth; are resident in the UK; are over 18 years of age and have the child with them. Evidence of agreement between the parties involved must be presented but the carrying mother cannot give consent until at least six weeks after the birth. No payment must be given or received by any party to the agreement unless this is authorised by the court (S.30).

- The Authority is required to keep a register which links any identifiable person to regulated infertility treatment and to the storage or use of gametes/embryos. A person who is proved to have been born following regulated treatment has a right to receive certain limited information at the age of 18 years (or 16 years in some circumstances) providing an opportunity to receive proper counselling has been given. The content of this information has yet to be fixed by regulation but *the Act specifically prohibits the giving of information which may identify the gamete/embryo donor*. An enquirer will also be informed whether the person whom she/he intends to marry might be related but, again, *no donor identifying information can be made available* at the present time (S.31).

• The courts have power under certain circumstances to make an order requiring the Authority to disclose information kept by the Authority. This could include the identity of the donor. Such an order must be in the interests of justice and disclosure of a donor's name is restricted to proceedings under the Congenital Disabilities Act 1976 which deals with civil liability to a child born disabled (S.35). For example, such a child would need to know the identity of the donor if a claim was to be made for negligence resulting from evidence that the donor was aware at the time of donation that he or she was suffering from a serious medical condition which could be passed on to his/her genetic offspring.

THE AUTHORITY'S CODE OF PRACTICE

Direct guidance relating to the legislative provision in terms of the needs and rights of the child is contained in a 'Code of Practice' the Authority is required to maintain to guide those responsible for providing relevant services (Human Fertilisation and Embryology Authority 1991). This code is linked to, but separate from, the Act and, unlike the Act, is open to relatively rapid amendment and development if this becomes necessary as a result of technological advances or changes in public policy.

While infringement of the code does not of itself constitute an offence under the Act, the granting or renewal of the required licence to provide a service or undertake research (which *are* required under the Act) may be affected. The formulation of this code of practice was a major preoccupation of the Authority during the early years of its existence.

The code was developed by the Authority using the expertise of its founder members and information from reports, comments and enquiries made available since publication of the Warnock Report in 1984 (Kings Fund Centre 1991; Royal College of Obstetricians and Gynaecologists 1992). Publication of this detailed code, together with its supplements and the annual reports of the Authority, demonstrates a continuing interest in the needs and rights of the child born as a result of these 'artificial' reproductive procedures. The term 'artificial' is used here to differentiate these assisted-conception procedures from those normally employed to encourage 'natural' conception and birth. The term 'artificial' in this context should not be understood in a pejorative sense but rather as describing the successful deployment of human skill. These children are among the most planned of any that are born; a claim less easily substantiated where more natural means of conception are employed.

All entries in the code have relevance to the needs (and rights) of the child but some demonstrate a more obvious link than others. The code is presented in eleven sections ranging in content from detailed prescriptions about staffing arrangements and facilities which should be available at treatment centres to requirements for complaint procedures for service users. The sections describing the need to consider the welfare of the child through the assessment and counselling of gamete donors and those seeking to use the regulated services are of more direct relevance to the resulting child:

- Any information obtained from donors or clients *must* be confidential unless disclosure is authorised by law.

- Reasonable steps should be taken to ascertain who would be the legal parent(s) of any child born as a result of the regulated procedures. This includes an assessment of the willingness of the parent and his/her partner to bring up the child.

- The implications for the child(ren) so conceived, and of any other existing child of the family, of the possibility of multiple births must be taken into account at the time of parent assessment.

- Other factors which should be taken into account when assessing the suitability of clients for treatment, include:

  - the child's potential need to know of his/her origins
  - the attitude of other family members
  - the child's likely status in the family.

- The possibility of the gamete donor becoming known to the family.

- A detailed record of how the welfare of the potential child (and other children of the family) was considered has to be kept and this record should reflect the views of those consulted, including the potential parents.

- The maximum number of children born from gametes donated by an individual donor is limited by direction of the Authority (currently the limit is normally 10) or to a lower number at the request of the donor. There is an exception to this maximum number where the donor has already been involved in the creation of 10 children and the parents of one of these children wish for a 'full blood' brother or sister of the existing child. In such cases, and if the donor agrees, the number of children created through the use of the same donors gametes could exceed 10 in number.

The code of practice also contains detailed advice about the selection and screening of potential gamete donors. Throughout the main body of the code repeated reference is made to the statutory duty of those providing relevant services to take into account the welfare of any child born as a result of the service provided. These references sometimes appear among others which seem to be at odds with the underlying principle being expressed. These include:

- Information about any identifiable person associated with the birth of a person resulting from the regulated treatment services can only be disclosed to the Authority or another licensed (treatment) centre but not to the so born, nor to anyone else.

- Gamete donors should be informed that the Act generally permits donors to preserve their anonymity.

In effect, this means that the child born as a result of these new procedures, except in special circumstances associated with disability and donor culpability, has no right to learn of his or her genetic parentage *even where this information is known to be available and held in a register maintained by the Authority*. This requirement is not merely a regulatory provision of the Authority's code of practice but a legally enforceable provision emanating from the Act of Parliament which informs it.

CONCLUSION

While the Act and the code of practice go a long way in supporting the needs of the individuals or couples seeking infertility treatment, the donors, the service providers and, by implication, the general public, there are still those who believe that the needs and rights of the child born following use of donated gametes have not been fully acknowledged. This lack of recognition of the rights of the child is most apparent in relation to the enforced anonymity of donors. The recruitment of donors is essential to the continuance of the infertility services regulated by the Act and it has long been argued that to permit the disclosure of the donor's identity would severely reduce the number of people willing to act as donors. This view has led to a specific requirement in the Act that identifying information, except in a very narrowly defined legal situation, may not be divulged. The enforcement of this prohibition may well lead to distress among people conceived as a result of gamete donation, especially when it is known that this information is recorded and kept by the Authority as required under section 32 of the Human Fertilisation and Embryology Act 1990. This is, perhaps, the most contentious issue relating to the needs and rights of the child in the Act, and appears at odds with the requirement under section 13 (5) of the same Act that account must be taken of the welfare of children conceived using the regulated procedures. What makes this situation so difficult to assess or resolve is the hypothetical nature of its consideration. At the time of infertility treatment the child does not exist and the child, together with his/her needs and rights can only be considered as a potential possibility. This is in marked contrast to the consideration of the rights of an individual occupying a place in definable space and time. Put this way, it is perhaps understandable that the needs and rights of the child's parents, those of the gamete donor and those of the provider of relevant services tend to take precedence over those of the yet-to-be-conceived child. However, children do not always remain merely a possibility or even a child; no doubt in due time donor-conceived children, when adult, will be their own best advocates in pressing for their right to knowledge of their genetic origins. According to Article 7 of the UN Convention on the Rights of the Child, the child 'shall have the right...as far as possible...to know...his parents' and, under Article 8, the state 'undertakes to respect the right of the child to preserve his or her identity including...family relations as recognised by law without lawful interference' The emphasis in Article 8 is on what knowledge in relation to the child's identity is currently available to him or her by law. As things stand in the United Kingdom at present, there is no breach of the child's rights as regards identity as outlined in the Convention. However, a situation in which legislation is introduced to protect the interests of children by regulating the special circumstances of their conception and by reducing secrecy about gamete donation, but which also maintains donor anonymity, creates a contradiction which, before too long, will require resolution.

REFERENCES

Barton M., Walker K. and Weisner B.P. (1945) 'Artificial insemination.' *British Medical Journal 1*, 40–43.

Feversham, Lord (Chairperson) (1960) *Report of the Departmental Committee on Human Artificial Insemination.* London: HMSO.

Gregoire, A.T. and Mayer, A.C. (1965) 'The impregnators.' *Fertility and Sterility 16*, 130–134.

Hull, M.G.R. (1986) 'Infertility: nature and extent of the problem.' In *Human Embryo Research: Yes or No?* London: Tavistock Publications.

Human Fertilisation and Embryology Act 1990. London: HMSO.

Human Fertilisation and Embryology Authority (1991) *Code of Practice.* London: HFEA.

King's Fund Centre Report (1991) *Counselling for Regulated Infertility Treatments.* London: Kings Fund Centre.

Peel, Sir J. (Chairperson) (1973) Report of the Panel on Human Artificial Insemination. *British Medical Journal 2*, Supplement Appendix V,3.

Royal College of Obstetricians and Gynaecologists (1992) *Infertility: Guidelines for Practice.* London: RCOG Press.

Snowden, R. (1990) 'The family and artificial reproduction.' In D.R. Bromham (ed) *Philosophical Ethics in Reproductive Medicine.* Manchester: Manchester University Press.

Snowden, R., Mitchell, G.D. and Snowden, E.M. (1983) *Artificial Reproduction: A Social Investigation.* London: George Allen and Unwin.

Warnock, M. (Chairperson) (1984) *Report of an Inquiry into Human Fertilisation and Embryology.* London: HMSO.

For a more detailed treatment of this topic see Snowden, R. (in press) *The Sociology of Reproduction.* Cambridge: Polity Press.

CHAPTER FOURTEEN

Using Computer Mediated Communications to Enhance Teaching and Learning

Niki Davis

INTRODUCTION

Computer mediated communications have the potential to revolutionise education and training. They could put the learner in touch with virtually any information or experience that might be of value. Commerce and industry now make extensive use of electronic networks in various forms such as electronic mail and computer, video or phone conferencing. However, the current situation in the UK and most countries is that the use of communications is restricted to a few students in a few institutions. This chapter looks at the application of electronic communication and the issues to be addressed to encourage wider adoption. Children and other learners' access to information is frequently mediated by teachers and parents, so they need professional development to become 'drivers' on the Information Superhighway.

A DESCRIPTION OF CURRENT USE

In the USA there is widespread use of electronic communications in some States. Hunter (1991, p.7) describes a wide range of applications. These support the students in the classroom, practising teachers and the students training to be teachers. For example:

- electronic publication of students' products. (Associated Student News Network, University of Alaska: American Telegraph and Telepone (AT&T) Long Distance Learning Network)
- students' collaborating scientific investigations (Kids' Network, USA National Science Foundation (NSF); Technology Education regional Consortium (TERC) Global Change Network, (NSF))

- students' and teachers' access to scientific expertise (InSite, Indiana, NSF private sector partnership; TeleApprenticeships, University of Illinois, NSF)

- students' and teachers' access to libraries, databases and computing resources. (National Geographic Weather Machine; NASA Spacelink; Superquest, NSF; and Blue Sky Telegraph, Montana)

- teacher education and enhancement. (Teacher Link, University of Virginia; Beginning teacher Network, Harvard; NSF; and Educational Network for American Natives, University of New Mexico).

The range of projects within and across Europe is described in Veen *et al.* (1994) such as:

- short projects across many European schools using simple questionnaires on topics such as eating habits or environmental issues

- a Danish tenth form project collaborating with a Greek class over a four week period on the topic 'Young in the thirties – Old in the Nineties'

- students in ten or more Spanish schools developing literacy skills through electronic discussions, including an academic specialist on the topic of discussion, over four to eight weeks.

A review of telecommunications in teacher education around the world is provided in Davis (1995). It describes the following projects in which student teachers, their mentors in schools and university staff use telecommunications to increase reflection on the practice of teaching. Electronic mail and discussion groups are becoming widespread. Also evolving is the use of multimedia and video-conferencing. For example, student teachers observing a classroom some distance away via wider band telecommunications and discussing practice with the teacher.

The use of electronic communication to support those with special educational needs has been particularly impressive. One charitable project, Chatback, permits disabled students to communicate and develop their interests together. Students with special educational needs can gain access to information and camaraderie in this way without many of the drawbacks that their special need imposes upon them. New styles of teaching and learning which encourage flexible learning in which learner autonomy is encouraged can be supported with electronic communications. For example, students with exceptional potential may be encouraged to take on additional activities through this medium and they can gain the support of experts in the necessary fields – for example, in France the Teletel videotex system has a forum for schools where an expert will answer questions from pupils in a two-hour forum using Minitel terminals.

Telecommunications have proved valuable in education and training, but access to them remains a matter of chance and, in percentage terms, few students have access.

ISSUES RESTRICTING ACCESS

Cost

During the first World Conference on Children's Rights, I led an international face-to-face and distributed debate on the proposition: 'Public communication carriers of every nation should make a special case for the education of their children and enable them to access computer mediated communication world-wide.'

Educational discounts are available on most goods, yet most countries do not have educational rates for telephone calls and a number are prohibited from doing so by law. Countries with free local calls have shown it increases participation.

This proposal was debated 'live' in the University and using ISDN2 Desk top Conferencing with school students in Saint Thomas' High School. Contributions were also received via Campus 2000, the Joint Academic Network (JANET) and the Internet from many countries around the world.

Participants generally supported the proposition. A number mentioned the value of communication for multicultural education and defusing ethnic tensions that arise. For example, John Dally in the UK said:

> Our planet has at present many problems. At present one of them is fear and suspicion of the intentions and actions of different nations and, within nations, different ethnic groups. If the young can learn that there is only one human race, whatever skin colour, language, creed or culture then this should go a long way to removing this problem. Electronic communications between young people of all nations is an ideal way to help do this. To this end young people of all nations should have access to computer mediated communications networks world wide.

However, Wigo Skraam in Norway emphasised the need for integration within the curriculum which teachers value:

The Goal

> Our opinion is that email must be made part of the daily routine at a school and that teachers must find that email is a help to improve teaching standards in every meaning of the word before they start using it as an educational tool. As a result of such a process a meaningful contact between students might develop and be a great help in, among other things, defusing the 'hate-all-foreigners' bomb that seems to be placed under our continent. The educational notes proposed could be an

important factor in consolidating educational computer mediated communications.

Wigo also notes that electronic mail is an expensive resource and is obviously not the most important priority for children's rights:

> Children's rights? The most important rights are the right to a stable family life, the right to a decent place to live and proper food every day. When all children in Europe have these rights, we might start talking about your 'email toy'.

From Sydney, Australia several computer pals agreed that global understanding is enhanced by electronic mail. They noted the need for networks to be compatible but they did have two additional points:

> We would prefer the word 'privilege' to 'right'. Rights engenders hostile reactions for a number of reasons... The world does not owe any person, including children, a living... Obviously as many children as possible should be given access, but not at the expense of the older generation with their accumulated experience.

In Exeter, the delegates took issue with the concept of 'privilege'. They felt that education should not be considered a privilege to be earned and that telecommunications should be part of today's education. Telecommunications is akin to published information, to which the library service provides free access.

From Portugal we received this message from young people which emphasises the variety of needs that children have:

Every child has the right to:

> ...five minutes to peacefully wake up, even if everyone at home is already rushing;

> ...warm words at long breakfast, even if that means that mammy can't do the makeup;

> ...unhurried good-bye at school door, even if daddy's friends must wait for him;

> ...understanding of a bad mood because he wants his mammy, even if the school teacher had already heard that a thousand times;

> ...television OFF at dinner time, even if there is an important program to see;

> ...affection and love before she sleeps, even if the time is short for everything that must yet be done.

> ...BECAUSE, after all, that's only thirty minutes of LOVE in one day between everything else that is not as important. ALTINA RAMOS

All those present at Exeter agreed with these sentiments, but the potential of the medium of electronic communications should not be ignored. A right to telecommunications does not reduce the call for other more fundamental rights. Indeed, it increases the voice children have in the world.

John Meadows, who was mailing from the University of Oldenburg in Germany, gave a balanced view and indicated that support is available for some projects. British Telecom also provides support in this way:

> While I firmly believe in the value of international co-operations, I also think there are problems with the medium, especially since few developing countries can afford such luxuries at the present time. Yet the potential for furthering international understanding, multi-cultural perspectives and issues of citizenship, etc., is enormous.

He passed on to the views of Canadians Gregory Staple and Hugo Dixon, that a telegeography has emerged. The world is not composed of one 'global electronic village' but that telecom traffic patterns are three interrelated networks centred on USA, Germany and Japan. The same could be said of educational networking.

Anne Lockhart, educational adviser to the Chatback Project, reminded the debate of the value of the medium for all abilities:

> The less able are encouraged and interested by the idea of writing to children overseas and the replies they receive. The gifted find an outlet for their talents in being able to communicate with a wider audience and in being able to discover information for themselves at their own pace. The disabled use it as an invaluable extension of their horizons and contacts.
>
> It is important that this work is given every encouragement and financial assistance.

Hardware and software

A second issue relates to hardware and software. Individuals will need access to a microcomputer, prefereably in a comfortable study area of their own. The messages will need to be stored and forwarded by a computer with a large file store. The UK school communication systems have been centralised, requiring a Modem and phone to link the students' microcomputer to the central machine. A more recent alternative is a network of computers linked by a variety of interfaces into the global 'Internet' (an inter-connected network of computers around the world). Such a network can be viewed as a web of documents, including pictures and sound. Today it is called the 'World-Wide Web' and, in the future, further developments will result in the 'Information Superhighway'. Thus some structural developments are reducing issues of cost. The adoption of common standards permits transfer of information, despite the different software and screen displays on a range of participant's terminal microcomputers. They also permit customisation to local standards of communication and other software, because the local node may provide support for these and refine the terminal and other software for use in communication. This enhances student progression with skills in computing and communication.

Professional development

Lack of familiarity and access to the computer terminal have been shown to decrease use (Somekh 1989). Clearly, professional development for teachers is a major factor restricting the development of this resource. One way round the problem is to introduce student teachers to the facility in the course of their training. In this way the students realise the potential of the system for education and training and they also gain skill in its use. The Computer Conferencing Project at Exeter has the aim of making this facility available.

Another aspect is the support that electronic networks can provide for professional development of teachers (Davis 1995). Classroom research, frequently known as 'action research' may also be supported. The networks decrease the isolation of the subject teachers in their own classroom, permitting them to share ideas and materials with teachers of their own discipline. They can also give them access to resources and professional support for this work (Hunter 1991).

The success and failure of networks

It would be fallacious to believe that networks develop naturally given the appropriate hardware and software. There is a growing body of research to indicate that many factors affect success. Not surprisingly they relate to the people, their need to communicate and their commitment. Riel and Levin (1990) discuss these issues in terms of: organisation of the group, task organisation, response opportunities, response obligations and evaluation. Critical factors appear to be: existence of a group with a need and a shared goal, easy, efficient and regular access to electronic communication with home as an important location and, finally, a person who will facilitate group planning and work. Data was drawn from a range of educational applications, namely from university researchers, teacher networks, student networks. This is supported by a more theoretical view by Vaske and Grantham (1990). They suggest that communication networks have many structures but electronic communication tends to cut across these structures to:

- reduce the feedback to the 'speaker'
- reduce social influence so status becomes more equal
- reduce or make less predictable the social norms in operation.

Let me illustrate this further using the notion of interpersonal relationships. People's perceptions of interpersonal relationships can be classified into four underlying dimensions: co-operative/competitive, equal/unequal, intense/superficial and formal task/informal. Computer mediated communications appear as co-operative, equal, intense and task-oriented. This reduction of social feedback can make it difficult to co-ordinate communications and projects and additional efforts are required to overcome the deficit.

Individual differences

Experience and attitudes to computers is one dimension of individual differences. Possibly more important is the individual's confidence with the written versus the oral word. Computer conferencing is commonly applied to perform some of the tasks of small group seminars in which a proportion of students never feel confident enough to voice their opinions. However, given the relative anonymity of the computer conference with plenty of time to respond, some courses in higher education have shown a higher participation rate than for face-to-face seminars.

Other individual differences are brought to light when we consider issues relating to social psychology. The relative lack of cues and the anonymity of computer mediated communication needs to be researched. It has been suggested that anonymity can lift the restrictions imposed by face-to-face situations such that behaviour becomes uninhibited. This could have unfortunate consequences. However, recent work suggests that it is important to uncover the stereotype or group which the student perceive they are communicating with (Vaske and Grantham 1990). There is so little information that the student may assume they belong to a very special group in which any sort of behaviour is acceptable. When cues are provided regarding sensible behaviour, which is rewarding to all participants, then deviant behaviour is curtailed.

Differences may obstruct the use of electronic communications for individuals who prefer to be in control of precise communication. They may become alienated by a medium which provides incomplete information on their audience. In contrast, individuals who wish to reach a wider audience may be encouraged. Where the individual's terminal view is locally designed, and so more familiar, this may be less of a problem. A second point is the loss of the non-verbal aspects of communication. The adaptation of the message to include personalised 'headings' and body language comments such as a smile, can compensate to a small extent but it is also useful to note that this sort of information can also be misleading across cultures. The anonymity can be used to good effect to empower the shy or low status members of the group and increase autonomy.

Cognitive anthropology research is studying the way in which the use of metaphors, chunking of information and mental maps vary with the group. For example, I use the metaphor of a restaurant waiter in the TV programme 'Fawlty Towers' with my students to explain a local area computer network. I hope it provides a stimulating mental model which they will not over-generalise because of the comedy. I do this to make them aware that there the file server can only do one thing at a time for its many network stations and that it can be slow and unreliable. Although the TV comedy of Fawlty Towers has been shared across many countries, care needs to be taken with analogies. Chunking of information is also a psychological concept where facts are grouped and partially processed to assist the memory. This grouping is determined to a large extent by previous experience and, therefore, will vary with the culture and the individual. It may be more difficult to communicate and share curricula and research experiences if assumptions about the knowledge implied by a few statements mean they belong to different 'chunks' of information for different users. We already have this problem in agreeing small modules for common science education across schools in Europe. The background of the individuals communicating, and of the communications network itself, will be important to assist collaboration across institutions and countries. For example, sharing information to ensure adequate quality in co-operative groupwork will depend to a large extent on sharing tasks and a strong element of co-ordination. This can only be done consistently if the social issues described above are addressed alongside the technical and access issues.

THE FUTURE

There is a move in Europe, North America and elsewhere to develop a global Information Superhighway. Simplistic views see the links to such an electronic network of information as the solution to many of the issues related to education and training for all. Certainly access to information is part of education and a way to become part of the global community. However, communication also needs to come from individuals into this network. The issues discussed in this chapter will apply to the future Information Superhighway, just as they have applied to computer mediated communication in the past.

REFERENCES

Davis, N.E. (1995) 'Telecommunications for teacher education; preparing for the global information superhighway.' Special issue of the *Journal of Information Technology for Teacher Education 4, 2*.

Hunter, B. (1991) *Grand Challenges: Roles of Computer-Based Communications in Helping to Shape the Future of Education*. Draft paper prepared for Conference on Prospects for Educational Telecommunications, Cambridge, Massachusetts, April 1991.

Riel, M.M. and Levin, J.A. (1990) 'Building electronic communities: success and failure in computer networking.' *Instructional Science 19*, 145–169.

Somekh, B. (1989) 'The human interface: hidden issues in CMC affecting use in schools.' In R. Mason and A.R. Kaye (eds) *Mindweave*. Oxford: Pergamon.

Vaske, J.J. and Grantham, C.E. (1990) *Socialising the Human-computer Environment.* New Jersey: Ablex Publishing Corporation.

Veen, W., Collis, B., de Vries, P. and Vogelgang, F. (eds) (1994) *Telematics in Education: The European Case.* De Lier, The Netherlands: Academic Book Centre.

PART SEVEN

Providing Support for Children

CHAPTER FIFTEEN

Researching Children's Rights Officers

Rosemary Rae

In 1992 I had just embarked on a research project looking at the establishment and development of Children's Rights Officers (hereafter referred to as CROs) in the UK. The purpose was to analyse this policy development over a period of three years; to look at what initiative had led to the establishment of the posts; what influenced the posts over this period; and how, if at all, did the posts influence policy and, in particular, policy as regards young people. It was envisaged that the research would highlight the process of policy implementation enabling us to test existing theories of policy development as well as informing the largely theoretical debate concerning children's rights. The establishment of CROs provided a unique opportunity to do this because they were a new policy initiative – ideologically different from previous initiatives in child welfare.

The end of the study period coincides with the publication of the Exeter Conference and although the process of writing up is at an early stage (and therefore findings are still being tested), the data is suggestive of certain themes, which are outlined below. Four posts were considered in depth, which involved seven post-holders. For methodological reasons only three posts are likely to be written up as case studies, whilst the fourth will join the volume of supporting data. The Children's Rights Officers Association was also observed for part of the research period and data gained from the source informs the study also.

METHODOLOGY

A case study approach was chosen as the most viable method of inquiry. Any attempt to systematically sample CROs would have been misleading because the posts were arbitrarily scattered over various parts of the UK. In addition, I was informed that job descriptions for these posts varied considerably. It was therefore decided to consider four posts as detailed case studies whilst using other posts as supplementary data when appropriate. The purpose of the study was to provide descriptive as well as analytical data. Descriptive data was particularly important because it wasn't clear what CROs were able to achieve, or for whom and therefore any attempt to systematically measure outcomes would have been fundamentally flawed. As Edwards and Talbot (1994) point out:

> Case studies can be used in evaluation studies to allow an examination of the process of change; an evaluation of an intervention which relies on survey data from before and after the intervention can be considerably enhanced by the inclusion of some case studies of the intervention process which examine what the intervention actually meant in the lives of the participants as it occurred. (p.45)

The distinction between statistical and analytical generalisation needs to be highlighted here. Having pointed out the methodological problems with obtaining statistical data, it needs to be reiterated that this was a qualitative research project and as such did not seek empirical data on which to make 'scientific' generalisations about CROs. There is an assumption that statistical data is superior for research purposes but in relation to child welfare policy this is not necessarily the case (see Hallett and Birchall 1992; Parton 1989). A children's rights perspective in part developed because of the dissatisfaction with existing child welfare policy and practice (Harding 1991), and the relationship between research, policy and child welfare practice is, at the very least, problematic (Parton 1989).

Data was collected by interviewing post-holders at regular intervals, interviewing significant people involved with the establishment of each post and collecting relevant written material. Although every attempt was made to be objective and this was reviewed along with the methodology throughout the study period, the findings are interpreted by the author and are not meant to represent the views of CROs or the organisations they represent. In order to protect informants, individuals and organisations are not named in the study although it was recognised and stated during the research period that these posts might be recognisable.

Four posts were chosen as case studies, to be studied concurrently over a three-year period which coincided (interestingly) with the time gap between presenting my original paper outlining the research to the Conference held in Exeter and the publication of that Conference.

BACKGROUND

The 1970s and 1980s witnessed certain key developments which may be seen as laying the foundations for the development of Children's Rights Officers in the UK. In particular:

1. The establishment of self-advocacy groups such as National Association for Young People in Care (NAYPIC), concerned with increasing the power of young people in Local Authority Care (which no longer exists).

2. The establishment of the Children's Legal Centre and the subsequent organisation of two conferences on children and their rights.

3. The establishment, by the National Children's Bureau, of the Child Policy Review Group.

4. In Parliament, the attempts to raise the idea of a Children's Ombudsperson during the passage of the 1989 Children Act, and also of Educational Ombudspeople during the passage of the 1988 Education Reform Act.

5. A proposal for a Children's Rights Commissioner.

6. The UN Convention on the Rights of the Child.

Other related developments can be seen as creating a climate favourable to, and accelerating the establishment of, CROs.

First, there was a growing and critical lobby regarding existing child protection policy embracing politicians, voluntary organisations, parents rights groups, the media and academics (see Franklin 1986 and 1995). Second, it has been argued (Parton 1991) that there was a shift in emphasis from trying to define child abuse to developing a more effective response to child protection. Third, the 1989 Children Act consistently puts the wishes of the child at the forefront of decision making in both public and private proceedings which can be interpreted as some movement away from the more paternalistic 'best interest of the child' principle that had dominated previous policy regarding children. In addition, the statutory duty placed on Local Authorities to establish representation and complaints procedures with an independent and informative element (DoH 1991c) applies to young people also.

Children's rights became an acceptable framework within which to explore the position of children in their communities and rights generally returned to the political agenda with the Conservative Government introducing the 'Citizens Charter'. The rights of the individual were taken up by the Rt Hon Dame Elizabeth Butler-Sloss when she made her now famous comment that children should be seen as people, not objects of professional concern.

In addition, numerous other organisations had shown an interest in the above developments/proposals (see Rosenbaum and Newell 1991) and even more had submitted contributions to the 1989 Children Act (DHSS 1985).

Underpinning some of the above developments was the concern, taken up by the press, about the abuse of some young people by their carers in residential accommodation. This was accompanied by a similarly publicised spate of enquiries into the handling of child abuse queries into young people who had subsequently died.

It is against this background the CROs emerged. There were 16 posts in existence at the time of the Exeter Conference in September 1992 – there are now nearly 30. They are employed in a variety of settings with varying job descriptions all over the UK.

FINDINGS

Most Children's Rights Officers work either with children in care, or deemed to be in need under the 1989 Children Act. In addition, at least over the period under study, most recipients of the service were those young people living in residential accommodation. This means, in effect, that the majority of young people are excluded from this service. In addition, 'children's rights' in the operational sense only apply to those young people who come into contact with child welfare services. This is an issue that CROs themselves acknowledge as a problem and one that the ones I have spoken to are unhappy about.

The Act did play a significant part in the posts being established. One post at least was funded by monies provided to implement the Act. However, there is no duty to establish CROs under the Act and many local authorities and non-statutory child care organisations do not have one. In addition, posts have been established in Scotland where the 1989 Act does not apply. The Act was one of several catalysts. Individuals in positions of power who were sympathetic to a children's rights perspective were also important. Voluntary sector initiatives to increase consumer involvement in decision making were another. Also significant was the public dissatisfaction with child welfare services outlined previously. The establishment of the first post in Leicestershire, and the subsequent publicity and promotion of the work by Mike Lindsay their first CRO, was also a factor.

As already stated the research is in the process of being written up but the data is suggestive of certain points which can be indicated here.

Developing a complaints procedure for young people in the care of specific organisations was commonly held in job descriptions initially, as was dealing with complaints from young people. However, this work was perceived as being ineffective by post-holders were they not also allowed access to the policy making process. Developing a children's rights perspective was seen to be a fundamental part of being a CRO by those people appointed to the posts. Similarly, it was felt that being overly concerned with complaints was a reactive and rather negative attitude to developing a rights service for young people – developing an advocacy service was more pro-active. Where possible post-holders developed their work to accommodate policy involvement and advocacy services either formally or informally.

Independence was sought at the establishment stage of all the posts. Two of the Organisations sought independence by negotiating what was termed a 'partnership' with a voluntary organisation who managed the project. The third was managed by a separate section within the same organisation. In practice the funding organisation had power over the post-holders for two reasons. First, they controlled the finances and second, they controlled the organisation the post-holder was working within. All three post-holders, in varying degrees, had moments when they felt their 'independence' was problematic. It was important, therefore, that the organisations managing the post as well as those funding the posts had some commitment to a children's rights philosophy.

Isolation was a feature of some posts, not just in terms of the individual workers, but also the service. An independent service can also become an isolated (and powerless) one. In addition, the task of supporting complaints is not one that endears popularity within organisations; the very organisations that affect financial and professional status. Future employment and career development can be affected detrimentally by the very nature of the work CROs are employed to do. One worker described an incident where they were criticised by someone outside their organisation for not pushing 'rights' more. They replied that in their opinion at that moment in time the feeling amongst workers in that organisation was such that if 'rights' were pushed more strongly, they were likely to be out of a job and the service was likely to be closed down.

Organisations which are supportive to a Children's Rights Service can change for a variety of reasons. One is the public perception of the issues at any given point in time. Another is that supportive senior managers can leave (or be transferred) and be replaced by less supportive ones.

CONCLUSION

It was not feasible to sample young people in the case study areas, as originally envisaged, for reasons outlined above. To sample those young people who benefit from the service would be to exclude the experiences of the vast majority who do not receive a service.

One should not conclude from this that CROs did not work predominately with young people. Most post-holders spent the majority of their time advocating for and advising young people who needed a service. In addition they provided support and were involved in developing policies which aimed at increasing the rights of consumers, albeit in child welfare services. They also assisted in staff training and visited care staff with a view to involving them rather than alienating them. In this sense most have impacted child welfare services and improved the quality of the service when they were allowed to. All worked over their contracted hours in order to achieve this.

From a conceptual point of view they enable us to understand the pre-requisites for establishing a children's rights service in the 1990s. In a way they can be compared to the Equal Opportunity Posts which developed during the 1970s and 1980s in the UK. One cannot assume that one worker within an organisation can change entrenched attitudes and practices but, by documenting as far as possible what they can achieve and how, we may increase an awareness to enable us to further operationalise children's rights.

REFERENCES

Department of Health (1991c) The Children Act Guidance and Regulations, Vol. 3. Comparative Policy and Practice. London: Department of Health.

Edwards and Talbot (1994) *The Hard-Pressed Researcher.* New York: Longman.

Franklin, B. (ed) (1986) *The Rights of Children.* Oxford: Basil Blackwell.

Franklin, B. (ed) (1995) *The Handbook of Children's Rights.* London: Routledge.

Hallett, C. and Birchall, E. (1992) *Co-ordination and Child Protection: A Review of the Literature.* London: HMSO.

Harding, L. (1991) *Perspectives in Child Care Policy.* Harlow, Essex: Longman.

Department of Health and Social Security (1985) Review of Child Care Law: Report to Ministers of an Inter-Departmental Working Party. London: HMSO.

Department of Health and Social Security (1988) Report of the Inquiry into Child Abuse in Cleveland, 1987 (Cm 412). London: HMSO.

Parton (1989) 'Child abuse.' In G. Kahan (ed) *Child Care Research, Policy and Practice.* London: Hodder and Stoughton.

Parton (1991) *Governing the Family: Child Care, Child Protection and the State.* London: Macmillan.

Rosenbaum, M. and Newell, P. (1991) *Taking Children Seriously – A Proposal for a Children's Rights Commissioner.* London: Calouste Gulbenkian Foundation.

CHAPTER SIXTEEN

Minors on The Run
The Work of the Ombuds Office, Vienna

Michael Singer

INTRODUCTION

The major task for the Ombuds Office in Vienna is to represent the interests of children and juveniles, especially those who are in need for support. This, as you can imagine, involves a variety of issues ranging from simple legal questions to getting complaints from children who have left their home, are in disagreement with school or the Youth Welfare or court decisions, maltreated, abused and neglected children and, lately, refugee children. Since 1990, when we were set up, we have made an attempt to develop a method to deal with this wide range of problems.

The basis of our work is always the personal contact with the child or juvenile and/or his parents if the problem cannot be solved individually (by giving information, advice or by delegation to someone who can help). We move on to a background analysis of the legal, social and psychological situation. This we can do by getting expert advice and, of course, by talking to the people involved and by scientific research. The next step is to present suggestions to the politicans and other decision making bodies. The proper and selective use of the media can help to emphasise and assist in enforcing various kinds of intervention.

This method has also proved useful in our work with refugee children. Among those children, we soon found out that refugees who are minor were in need of special support in the double sense of the word:

1. Being underage – juveniles between 14 and 18 years old who have left home unaccompanied.

2. Minors in the sense that their treatment is second-rate in comparison with other Austrian young people.

Since there was hardly any information available in Austria about the fate of these minors we suggested that an analysis should be carried out concerning the legal, social and psychological situation of underaged refugees seeking asylum. Before we consider the results let me first outline the background of our work with refugees.

Since the beginning of the war in 1990 in former Yugoslavia, Austria, as its immediate neighbour, has become the focus of international attention as regards its refugee policy. Out of approximately 19 million refugees world-wide, half of which are children, 1.9 million come from former Yugoslavia. As a country which is prepared to take in refugees, Austria was in 1992, for the fifth time since World War II, confronted with a wave of refugees.

After World War II, Austria took in 1.6 million war refugees. In 1956 – responding to the Hungarian revolution – it opened its borders to 180,000 Hungarians. In 1968 – following the upheavals in Czechoslovakia – 162,000 Czechs were admitted and in 1981, 150,000 Poles fled to Austria. Since the violence started in Yugoslavia, Austria has admitted over 50,000 refugees.

Even though 50,000 is a relatively low number in relation to the total number of 1.9 million, and even less so in relation to the number of people Austria has taken in during the last 50 years, the question of how many should be admitted and under what circumstances they should be granted asylum is currently fiercely discussed – discussions which are characterised by great differences of opinions.

As a Children and Youth Commissioner it is not my role to analyse the political backgrounds forcing children, whether with or without their parents, to leave their home country. To understand the reasons is very difficult for anybody, let alone children. One thing is certain though: in contrast to adults, and above all, politicians, these children are not guilty of the war. Together with women they are, however, the real victims since this war is primarily aimed against the civilian population – it destroys their homes, kills them or drives them away and, because of it they, end up in refugee camps. Thousands of children have been forced to leave their families and homes in order to find protection from persecution. Among the countries where an especially high number of children have been forced to leave on their own are Vietnam, Cambodia, Ethiopia, Sudan, Turkey and, since the break up of the Eastern block, Romania, Bulgaria and the war savaged regions of former Yugoslavia.

Such children and, even more so, the teenage refugees are widely overlooked by the media. On the news we see reports about shootings, war atrocities and endless political discussions but hardly ever do we hear about the fate of these unfortunate youngsters. In 1991, over a period of eight months, we screened 950 newspaper articles on asylum seekers and refugees with a special focus on the mention of children. In most cases children were used to make a story more dramatic. It is remarkable that, out of 950 articles, only one referred to the situation of minors fleeing their countries on their own. We found this incredible since we knew that, according to the United Nations High Commissioner for Refugees in Vienna, from January 1990 to May 1992, 1800 minors had crossed the border into Austria and applied for asylum. The majority were between the ages of 16 and 18.

As I have mentioned, after having proposed a study on the life situation of minor refugees a report was issued. The results of this study, plus our own experience with individual refugees and knowledge we obtained from professionals working with refugees, gave a picture of the circumstances under which they lived. Instead of going through this information in detail, I present a typical case which illustrates this information. It is not a real case but is a composite story of what we have heard so far through talking to young refugees and from the other sources that have been alluded to. This case will, I hope, shed some light on the general background problem.

RIDVAN: A MINOR ON THE RUN

Ridvan is 17 years old and comes from Kosovo, a small province in the southern part of Yugoslavia. Kosovo is under Serbian rule but the majority of the population are Albanians who are seeking independence from the Serbian military regime.

One day there is a knock on the door. The Militia wants to draft Ridvan for the army. Ridvan, who by chance is not at home at the time, hides in his uncle's house. He knows what it means to fight as an Albanian in the Serbo-Croatian war on the Serbian side. Not only would he have to shoot at his own people but he would be used as canon fodder by the Serbs. For some time now he has seen frequent street searches by the Serbs. One deserter was shot on the streets.

His parents are both out of work. They have very little money to give him but they advise him to try and make his way to Austria. They tell him it is a rich country and people are friendly to foreigners. They think he has a chance of finding work there and he might even go to school. No doubt Austria would recognize his need, realize the danger he was in, and grant him asylum.

'Asylum' is the magic word, it is the key to all doors in Austria. By being granted asylum he can stay in Austria and apply for a work permit which might one day relieve him from the pressing poverty he and his family are in. His uncle knows someone who could help Ridvan get away to Austria for 200 Marks. That's all the money the family has left. He decides to flee.

The journey

Ridvan is driven north along the backroads. Soon he no longer knows where he is. Slowly they overtake a long line of refugees. Ridvan asks the driver where these people are going and the driver tells him that they are going to a safe place. To his question of where this place could be the driver replies: 'God only knows'. When, a little later, they come through a deserted village with a lot of destroyed buildings, the driver starts to swear terribly at the Serbs. Ridvan's opinion about the Serbs is not only negative as many of his playmates and friends at school were Serbs. Before the war it did not matter much whether somebody was Serbian, Croatian, Muslim, Christian or Albanian. But now he also hates the Serbs for leading an aggressive war, forcing him to leave his country.

As they approach the Austrian border the driver repeatedly reminds him of how to behave in case he gets caught by the border guards. Ridvan asks him why they couldn't just drive across the border together since he has his passport on him and a good reason to flee. He would just tell them his story and for sure they would let him in. The driver tries to explain to him that, in the eyes of the border officials, being drafted is no reason to escape. If he tried to cross the border legally they would lock him up and send him right back. And again Ridvan doesn't understand. Didn't his parents tell him that a person in want should receive help? But now the driver confuses him even more. He says that, according to Austrian law, on his way to the border Ridvan has already passed through safe regions where he could have also asked for help. Ridvan thinks: 'But the villages they passed through were destroyed. How could I ask for help from people who had nothing left themselves?'

Crossing the border

The driver lets Ridvan out at the edge of a forest and tells him to cross to the other side where he would wait for him. If he gets caught he should just repeat the word 'Asylum'. Ridvan is terribly frightened about being caught although the driver reassures him again and again that the Austrian border patrols will not shoot at him. Ridvan, after having witnessed the cruelties of war, doesn't trust his words. But then again, what difference does it make if he is shot now or later in the war should he be sent back to the Serbian army?

Ridvan passes the border unnoticed. Suddenly all around him he can see luxury and clean houses. People really look like he has seen them on TV at home. Ridvan notices for the first time how different he looks with his black hair and shabby clothes and he feels inferior. A child discovers him and calls her father. The man starts yelling at him. He calls him a dirty foreigner, for sure he is a refugee and why doesn't he go right back where he belongs since there is no need for him here. Ridvan jumps up and hurries to the car where the driver tries to calm him. He tells him that not all of them are like this, that there are families who will give him a home if he is a war refugee. But, since he is a deserter, or rather someone who refuses to be drafted, he has to make sure that he will be entitled to asylum. This, the driver continues to explain, is only done if the reason for flight is for individual reasons of a political, racial or religious nature.

But, since armed service is a duty for all citizens, it is for this very reason Ridvan might not be granted asylum. Ridvan disagrees. He is indeed leaving for political reasons. His life is in danger because of the Serbian military policy. Furthermore, he has racial reasons because the Serbs in the Kosovo want to get rid of all the Albanians so they can say the country is now Serbian and belongs to them. But now the driver becomes impatient and doesn't want to talk any longer. He says that now he is here, they are going to a place called Traiskirchen – a camp where he will be interrogated and everything else will be seen afterwards. Silently they drive through beautiful and wealthy Austria and Ridvan regains his hope. He likes this country. He would like to live here with these nice people the driver mentioned and he would like to work with them.

The first interrogation

Traiskirchen is a big camp which can take in up to 2000 people. Ridvan is taken to a big building called 'Hilton' where he shares a large room full of bunk beds with people he doesn't know. There is an African, a Romanian, a couple from Iran and also an old man from Albania who speaks German. Ridvan is lucky because this man can prepare him for his first interrogation. He tells him they would have to accept his application for asylum and it would take a long time before a decision on whether he could stay or not would be reached. Ridvan wants to know who 'they' are. The old Albanian tells him that there is an official in uniform who will ask the questions and an interpreter who will translate everything. There also should be a person in charge of him there – his legal representative or case advocate.

Ridvan is unsure about what he should say. The old man reassures him that it is always the same routine – they always ask the same questions. They will want to know his name, whether he has a passport or other documents, where and how he got across the border, whether he has a criminal record, whether he wants to stay in Austria, what school he used to go to, what languages he speaks and, finally, where he last lived and what happened about his military service. That's where he has to tell his story. Then the old man adds something important which Ridvan overhears: he says that no matter what he says he will be denied asylum in the first instance – he will have to appeal again after some time.

The interrogation happens as the old man said. Ridvan goes over the entire process in 40 minutes. Afterwards he feels totally empty.

Life in the camp

Ridvan is taken into Federal care, which means that the state pays for his accommodation and food and even gives him a tiny allowance of ten pounds a month. But he has to be careful because this assistance will be taken from him immediately if he stays away from the camp without previous notice or if it becomes known that he is working. In fact, if there is the slightest suspicion that he is seeking work, he will be denied any further assistance. He even hears of cases where young people were denied further federal assistance just for bad behaviour.

There is one thing Ridvan doesn't quite understand. There are several young refugees from Romania and Turkey in the camp who had left their home countries for similar reasons and who don't receive federal assistance at all. All this he hears from a nice man – his care advocate – who everybody calls Mr Vatter and who runs a care unit at the camp where the young kids can play table football and have a drink and where he can go and talk to other youngsters. But this is about the only nice thing about the camp. All this waiting around makes him quite miserable. Often he has time to think of his parents and his brothers and sisters and how he longs to get away from the dreadful camp and go back to his familiar surroundings. He wants to go home and wonders if he will ever see the Kosovo again. His inability to speak and the fact that he is surrounded by so many people reinforce his fears and insecurities. He wonders how his parents are feeling and thinks he is to blame for everything. For the first time in his life he sleeps badly and has terrible dreams about the war and being killed. But most of all, he is worried about what will happen to him. Often he just hangs out and wants to do something, but doesn't know what. He realises he wants to be a child again, and then he doesn't care about anything anymore.

Ridvan needs help. He goes back to Mr Vatter. Mr Vatter tells him that the employment office would pay for him to attend a German course. Ridvan agrees to do the course and is very enthusiastic. At last he has something to do. For the following six months he studies German which, under his circumstances, turns out to be quite hard. He finds the language very difficult.

At the same time, he becomes acquainted with a group of young refugees. They go to Vienna from time to time but, since they have no money, they try to persuade Ridvan to join them to go with older men and entertain them at their flats.

One day, about six months later, he receives a blue letter. It says that he will no longer receive Federal assistance and that he owes the Federal Care 250 pounds. The reason given is that he was not allowed to claim full federal assistance and do a German course at the same time. How should he ever be able to make so much money? The temptation to join his friends to make some easy money is great.

But one misfortune is usually followed by another. His application for asylum is denied. Nobody remembered to appeal in time. All of a sudden Ridvan has become illegal. He has no money, no place to stay and, on top of it all, he has debts. His friends tell him that if he gets caught by the immigration police he would be put in jail immediately and eventually be deported. For several days he joins his friends and spends the nights with a man who wants to touch him but leaves him alone when he realizes that Ridvan is in a very bad state and full of fear.

Mr Vatter takes him to a home belonging to the Caritas. Although by now he should actually be leaving the country, they are willing to take him in and, if need be, hide him from the police. Again he comes across a lot of different people from Turkey and Africa but also a young man who speaks Albanian. Ridvan spends a lot of time talking to him. Again and again he asks why he couldn't stay in Austria, why he has to hide like a criminal. What did he do? Is he too ugly or simply not worth as much as other young people here? Ridvan's new friend starts to whisper, as if he was ashamed of the Austrians. A lot of them think we are taking their jobs away and some think that the refugees only come to steal and resell their loot for big money back home.

Then he tells him of a favourite saying often used in Austria: 'The boat is full'. Ridvan grows pale and silent. He looks across the road into a full shop window and wonders what he will do once he is hungry. But then, the Caritas give him food. Mr Vatter tells him that, in the long run, it would be difficult to keep him. According to the immigration police, Ridvan had been denied the right to stay in Austria and the council, as well the Youth Welfare Office, had agreed to his deportation.

One day a social worker comes to the home. She tells Ridvan that her duty is to help young people who, for example, have no parents left. She talks to them and tries to find a place in school or an apprenticeship for them. Ridvan wants to know whether she does it for all young people who have no parents left? The social worker says 'yes' and points out that her office is in charge of all of them. Ridvan gets all excited because he thinks this would also apply to him. But now she tells him that in his case she couldn't help, although she would really like to. Ridvan is a refugee without asylum and should therefore be deported. 'So it doesn't apply for all', Ridvan says. 'No, not for all', the social worker answers helplessly.

Contact with the Ombuds Office

Seeing that she has few or no other possibilities, she may call the Ombuds Office. So, according to our approach, we will first talk with the refugee. We will have to point out the limitations and possibilities and get as much information as possible from other persons involved in the case. Then we address a 'round-letter' with suggestions to the decision making bodies such as the welfare office, district court, ministry of Interior.

The general point would be that, since Ridvan has lost Mr Vatter as case advocate, he would get a new one, stay in Austria legally and find a permanent home and school. The argument would be that the Youth Welfare Office should not create a difference between an Austrian and a young refugee and, of course, Article 22 – which grants special protection to children who are refugees and defines the obligation of the state to co-operate with organisations providing such protection.

Based on the experience of work with these young refugees, we give the following recommendations:

- There should be full implementation of the relevant articles of the UN Convention on the Rights of the Child – specifically Articles 3, 10, 12, 20, 22 and 39.

- Unaccompanied children arriving without proper documentation should never be returned at the border.

- Apart from legal representation, they should have appropriate counselling during their stay in Austria.

- They should, under no circumstances, be detained for the purpose of return.

- Child refugees should be treated the same as indigenous children under youth welfare legislation.

- They should always be informed about official decisions in their mother tongue.

- Attempts should be made to get in contact with their families.

- Accurate and complete statistics should be available to the public – in particular the number and length of stay of the young refugees, their legal status and the final outcome of each case.

CHAPTER SEVENTEEN

Divorce, Mediation and the Rights of the Child

Monica Cockett and John Tripp

The child has a right to live with his or her parents unless this is deemed to be incompatible with the child's best interests.

The child also has the right to maintain contact with both parents if separated from one or both.

The United Nations Charter on the Rights of the Child, Article 9, adopted 20 November 1989.

When families separate, research has shown that parents are often so over-burdened by their own emotional needs and practical difficulties that the views and needs of their children can be over-looked. Research has also shown that parenting 'quality' can be reduced for as much as two years while the resident parent and the non-resident parent get their lives back on course (see Hetherington *et al.* 1992; Wallerstein and Kelly 1980; Wadsworth 1991). As marriage is a legal contract, it requires a legal dissolution and, under the present system, parents seek separation by individual legal representation – often incurring large legal fees – and may necessitate the production of 'harmful affidavits' thus alienating each other as parents.

DEMOGRAPHY

During the past 30 years there has been a six-fold increase in the annual rate of divorce. At present one in three marriages ends in divorce (Office of Population Censuses and Surveys 1990). A worrying feature of this current trend is that marriages now end earlier, affecting children at a younger age and reducing their chances of making a good and lasting relationship with the parent who leaves the home. The socio-economic consequences mean that children will be exposed to financial hardship, particularly as most children will remain for at least a part of their childhood in a single parent household –

usually headed by their mother. Single parent households are known to be amongst the poorest in this country (Bradshaw and Millar 1991).

THE CHILDREN ACT 1989

The Children Act 1989 underlines the importance of parental responsibility and, even when parents no longer live together, assumes the continued responsibility of both parents. Orders which 'impose' settlements will only be necessary where parents are unable to agree on plans for their children's future.

Children Act – October 1989

- Parental responsibility – not rights
- No order to be made unless making an order would be better than no order
- Views of the child to be taken into account

MEDIATION

> Mediation, unlike politics, is the art of the impossible. (Haynes and Haynes 1981, p.1)

Mediation services for divorcing parents have been available in this country since 1979, following on from the Finer Committee's Report in that same year which highlighted the effects of conflictual divorce settlements on children's outcomes. Initially organised as an 'in court' precursor of the welfare report and provided by the Court Welfare Officer, the first 'out of court' service was introduced in 1979 at Bristol by Probation Officers and other interested family professionals. This was quickly followed by the development of other services in different parts of the country (Parkinson 1986).

Ground Rules for Mediation

- Focus on the future
- Speak for yourself, not for your partner
- Mediator responsible for the process
- The participants responsible for the outcomes
- Neutrality
- Non-judgemental approach to the problems presented
- Attention to power and gender imbalances

AIMS OF MEDIATION

Mediation aims to encourage parents to sit down together with a professional trained in family dispute resolution to try to put aside their partnership conflicts and concentrate on parenting issues. It allows parents time to discuss options and ways forward that can be explored and rejected if neither parent can agree. Such negotiation can be painful and stressful, but the presence of a third party allows for the bitterness, power, and gender imbalances to be recognised and addressed. The basic aim is to recognise the need of each parent to continue to provide loving support for their children in the new structure of their separated lives. Constant emphasis and 'bringing back' to the fundamental principle of shared parental responsibility helps to focus on this shared task and the importance of its outcome for children (Walker 1989).

AVAILABILITY: NATIONAL FAMILY MEDIATION

Mediation services have always been organised by voluntary groups under the umbrella organisation of what is now called the Family Mediators Association. Funding has been provided by Social Services, Probation Departments and client contribution (minimal) but was primarily charity supported. This has meant that most services have struggled and have been unable to expand adequately to provide a professional and nationally available service for families. The RELATE Marriage Guidance Council and some church organisations have also provided support for services in the past.

Divorce

Private grief   Public issue

Because marriage is a legal contract it has to be dissolved

Mediation/Conciliation

Mediation/Conciliation is a way:
- of encouraging parents to sit down together
- to discuss the future for themselves and for their children
- to make their own plans
- of not handing over control to solicitors or to the courts

FAMILY MEDIATORS ASSOCIATION

In 1989 the Family Mediators Association was begun in London to provide a service by lawyers co-mediating with a non-lawyer mediator, working together to provide comprehensive mediation. One of the difficulties associated with voluntary organisations was that their training and selection allowed them to provide mediation only on child-based issues. It was clear from the experiences of these services that couples needed help for a wide variety of problems including financial and property settlements. The Family Mediators Association provided training for lawyers to co-work with other disciplines in order to provide this comprehensive service for parents. From the beginning the FMA was set up as an independent agency with clients paying for the service.

DEVELOPMENTS IN MEDIATION

Mediation was naturally limited to those clients who could afford to pay. However, in various parts of the country sponsored schemes have been set up to enable parents with lesser means to take advantage of the service. The aim of all mediation services, provided in whatever form, has been to assist the dissolution of the 'partnership relationship' and encourage the continuation of the 'parenting relationship' as underlined by the Children Act and to provide the child with 'Rights' as laid out in the United Nations Convention on the Rights of the Child.

Rights of the Children

Where do the children stand?
↓
What are the children's rights?
↓
What are their needs?
↓
Should they be involved in mediation?
↓
What are the best interests of the children?
↓
The wishes and feelings of the children must be ascertained.

When parents separate, children face a fundamental re-organisation of their lives which can include lessened, or loss of, contact with one parent, financial difficulties, social re-location including school changes, lessened parental support and the re-partnering of either of their parents (Kalter *et al.* 1989). Research shows that children are ill-prepared for these changes and many, even in the face of parental conflict, had not expected their parents to separate (Mitchell 1985). Children are rarely consulted about contact arrangements or long-term plans for the family.

Some children's views:

- I felt very let down when I was younger because Dad forgot us
- There are no happy marriages in my family or in my friends
- When Dad left, Mum didn't know what she was going to do
- I liked him before he left us, but I like him less now because he went away and doesn't do anything for us, not like a real Dad

---

THE EXETER FAMILY STUDY

A study was carried out by the University of Exeter, Department of Child Health, for the Joseph Rowntree Foundation, which looked at the effects of divorce on parents and children. The preliminary findings of this study suggested that children valued:

- Explanation from both parents at an early stage.
- A chance to express their views.
- The opportunity to see both parents freely.
- Flexible contact arrangements.
- Planned introductions to new partners and children of new partners.

Children expressed concerns about:

- Unreliable contact.
- 'Boring' contact.
- The non-resident parent being 'alone'.
- Not being able to mention one parent to another.

Research

- Children do best when they can have loving relationships with both parents
- Unresolved conflict can lead to poor outcomes for children
- Divorce/separation usually means conflict that can go on for the whole childhood

---

CHILDREN AND MEDIATION

The Children Act 1989 emphasises that children have a right to be heard and consulted. In the situation of family breakdown, children also need to be protected from feeling responsible for the relationship breakdown of their parents. The 'best interests of the child' may not be seen by those who have the decision-making power to be best served by following the wishes expressed by the child. Children will almost always wish that their parents had stayed together (Hetherington, Cox and Cox 1981). Part of the process of encouraging children to adapt is to accept the inevitability of their parents' decision. Parents themselves are best placed to do this by continually reinforcing the child's concerns that the child will continue to see both parents as much as possible.

SUMMARY

In summary, the needs of children and their parents often conflict at the time of separation and divorce. Mediation services, while able to address these issues, are not well-developed, not freely available and do not always cover all the issues parents must address in order to end their marriages in a 'civilised' way. Where mediation is available, parents can devote their energies towards continuing the parental role and plans for their children's lives can be made in a more effective manner.

Children can sometimes be part of the mediation process and their views and wishes can be sought, but children need to be reassured that, although it is important that everyone concerned knows their views, the decision-making responsibility is not placed upon their shoulders. Children say that they value a chance to be able to say how they feel and have discussion time with their parents so that they know what to expect about how their lives will be organised. Mediation can enable parents to offer better support for their children.

The Exeter Family Study was completed and published in November 1994 (Cockett and Tripp 1994) and further analysis of the data confirmed that although not all children suffer adverse effects following parental separation, at least not in the long-term, children's outcomes overall were negatively affected by parental separation. One-quarter of the children had lost contact with the non-resident parent and only half had frequent and regular reliable contact. Non-resident parents interviewed felt that they were not well-represented legally, or otherwise, and forfeited their rights to have a significant influence on their children's lives once the marriage was over. Resident parents found family lawyers, family doctors and their children's schools supportive but not always able to assist in 'problem solving'. Conflict remained a part of family separation, influencing and affecting children's lives negatively in the long-term.

Study Group

Separated/Divorced	76%
Children aware of rows	97%
Experienced domestic violence	29%
Removed to women's refuge	4%

Contact

Some contact with non-residential parent	71%
Frequent contact	43%
No contact	22%

Maintenance Orders

Maintenance orders made	63%
Payments made now	27%

Custody Orders

Joint custody	25%
Father only	1%
Mother only	73%

The White Paper published in April 1995 (Lord Chancellor's Department 1995) contains recommendations to remove the 'fault based ground' for divorce, allows for reflection on the decision to separate and demands that the person seeking divorce attend an information-giving session. Emphasis is placed on mediation rather than separate legal representation becoming the more usual route along which parents will end their marriage. Funding for mediation will be provided through the Legal Aid Board but the usual constraints will apply. In order to develop services to meet the demand, extra funding will have to be found to provide a professional, adequate service for parents.

REFERENCES

Bradshaw, J. and Millar, J. (1991) *Lone Parent Families in the UK. Department of Social Security Report 6.* London: HMSO.

Cockett, M. and Tripp, J.H. (1994) *The Exeter Family Study: Family Breakdown and its Impact on Children.* Exeter: Exeter University Press.

Haynes, M. and Haynes, G. (1989) *Mediating Divorce.* San Francisco: Jossey Bass.

Hetherington, E.M., Cox, M. and Cox, R. (1981) 'Effects of divorce on parents and children.' In M. Lamb (ed) *Non-traditional Families.* Hillsdale, NJ: Lawrence Erlbaum.

Hetherington, E.M., Clingempeel, W.G. (1992) 'Coping with marital transitions. Family systems perspective.' *Monograph of the Society for Research in Child Development. Serial No. 227,* 57.

Kalter, N., Kloner, A., Schreier, S. and Okla, K. (1989) 'Predictors of children's post divorce adjustment.' *American Journal of Orthopsychiatry 59,* 605–620.

Lord Chancellor's Department (1995) *The White Paper – Looking to the Future. Mediation and the Ground for Divorce.* London: HMSO.

Mitchell, A. (1985) *Children in the Middle. Living Through Divorce.* London: Tavistock.

Office of Population Censuses and Surveys (1990) *Marriage and Divorce Statistics 1837–1983.* London: HMSO.

Parkinson, L. (1986) *Conciliation in Separation and Divorce.* London: Croom Helm.

Wadsworth, M.E.J. (1991) *The Imprint of Time. Childhood History and Adult Life.* Oxford: Clarendon Press.

Walker (1989) *Report to the Lord Chancellor on The Cost and Effectiveness of Conciliation in England and Wales.* University of Newcastle Upon Tyne.

Wallerstein, J.S. and Kelly, J.B. (1980) *Surviving the Breakup: How Children and Parents Cope with Divorce.* London: Grant McIntyre.

PART EIGHT

Providing for the Future

CHAPTER EIGHTEEN

New Powers for Old

Transforming Power Relationships

Rhys Griffith

In making comparative assessments of children's rights to educational resources in different countries and continents, national educational infrastructures are sometimes perceived as a compilation of resources such as facilities, texts, technology, personnel. The cost in each of these areas is added together and then divided by the number of children who comprise the school population to give a per capita figure for annual educational expenditure. Educational provision is seen as a service provided by the state, and the quality of that service is indicated by economic markers.

However, education can also be viewed, not as a composite of material and adult human resources, but as a conceptual resource for the individual child to access, utilise and ultimately control. From this viewpoint – of the child's right to the resource of education as an agency of personal empowerment – economic statistics are likely to be less useful indicators of the quality of educational opportunity provided by the state than examples of typical practice within the school system, as experienced at a personal level by the pupils. The perceived gap between educational provision in the global north and south, often based upon financial expenditure, may be less wide when viewed from a concept of education as a personally empowering resource.

EMPOWERMENT AND THE GLOBAL CITIZEN

The rhetoric of empowerment abounds. International examples are the ratification of the UN Convention on the Rights of The Child (1991) and the Council of Europe Recommendation on Education (1985). Some progress, however patronising, has been made, for example the Children's Hearings at the UN Conference of the Environment held at Rio de Janeiro in 1993. More than lip-service has been paid to the involvement of children in the Norwegian

Voice of the Children project and the 1992 International Conference on the Rights of The Child at Exeter University. National examples, within the United Kingdom, are the Speaker's Commission on Citizenship (1990), and the Great Education Reform Act statement that education should develop the spiritual, physical, moral and intellectual well-being of the pupil (1988). However, the work of such researchers as Hart (1992) and Franklin (1992) indicates that there is still a gulf between the international and national rhetoric, and the reality of practice in educational institutions at regional levels.

The extension of the political franchise to include young people has been addressed by Franklin (1992). His suggestions have obvious implications for schooling. He records that 'children in all societies are still denied rights to make decisions about their affairs which as adults we take for granted'. A critical area of denial is 'children's involvement in their education' and 'the right to a voice in deciding educational curriculum at school'. Franklin advocates the democratisation of schools so that pupils have influence over organisation and curriculum:

> I am convinced that the way to achieve rights for children does not lie in the adoption of any specific group of reforms, so much as acknowledging and supporting the general principle that wherever possible children should be encouraged to make decisions for themselves and act on their own behalf. (p.107)

Freeman (1988), commenting on the Gillick case, suggested that children, acknowledged in law as mature enough to make decisions about contraception, could no longer continue to be denied the right to make other important decisions central to their lives, including upon educational matters. Ronald Davie (1989), in the evidence submitted by the National Children's Bureau that contributed to the Elton Report, also advocated that pupils' opinions should influence their curriculum: 'One specific course of action which we would urge is the encouragement to schools to find ways of listening to and heeding the views of pupils in relation to school procedures, policies and curricula'.

Roger Hart in *Children's Participation: from Tokenism to Citizenship* (1992) argues forcefully for education based upon participation, 'the fundamental right of citizenship'. For Hart, participation requires pupils, teachers and other adults to work together to resolve real community problems. The highest rung on his model of participation is 'child-initiated, shared decisions with adults'. The main object of this approach, which synthesises the child's education and her development as a citizen, is to develop the skills of critical reflection and the comparison of perspectives. Hart claims that the benefit is two-fold: 'to the self-realisation of the child and the democratisation of society'. Notwithstanding these demonstrable advantages (he cites examples of genuine participation-programmes that he has witnessed throughout the world), Hart maintains that there is no nation where the practice of democratic participation has been broadly adapted as a model for state-maintained education: 'Many western nations think of themselves as having achieved democracy fully, though they teach the principles of democracy in a pedantic way in classrooms which are themselves models of autocracy.' (Hart 1992, p.5)

John reiterates Hart's view that conventional educational practices do little to develop a child's self-realisation. Like Hart, she also sees it as a duty of an educational system to develop in the child the shared attributes of the pupil and the citizen. For John, self-realisation, or personal autonomy, is a fundamental educational right. Referring specifically to the UK, she writes that children are presently being denied 'the learning experiences which are central to the development of a sense of personal autonomy and in that way are being denied their rights to education in its most significant and fundamental form' (1995, p.122).

It is clear that such writers regard empowerment as much more than an academic training leading to success in public examinations. Empowerment is seen as the developing ability of the child to control what Giddens refers to as 'the reflexive project of the self'. Gray (1983) and Raz (1986) claim that the ability to reflect critically on the society of high modernity is essential, not only for personal well-being but for the development of society. Post-war writers such as Kandel (1949), McCluhan (1968) and, more recently, White (1991) and Giddens (1991, 1994) point out that a global citizenship to which we all *must belong* is being created as we reach the millennium: '...the level of time-space distanciation introduced by high modernity is so extensive that, for the first time in human history, "self" and "society" are interrelated in a global milieu' (Giddens 1991, p.32).

Such global citizenship is characterised by various kinds of freedoms that are claimed by citizens as their rights: freedom of action (of expression, of the press, of assembly, of demonstration, of employment, of travel), freedom of thought (intellect, conscience, censorship, belief) and freedom from discrimination (ethnicity, gender, language, class, religion, sexual orientation, physique).

'Freedom', writes Mulgan, 'doesn't give any clues as to how to behave to others; how to share; how to think; or how to feel. It tells us nothing about judgment, about right or wrong' (1991, p.42). The freedom of global citizenship is not the self-centred liberty of Rousseau's *Emile* (1762), Neill's *Summerhill* (1926) or Steutel's 'animal freedom' (1991). Concomitant with individual freedom is corporate responsibility, which manifests itself in a moral concern for social justice. It is a concern for responsible action that, for Shotter (1984), is the essence of being human, of 'personhood'. This duality of freedom and responsibility typifies the citizens of the third millennium, Harre's 'bearers of honour and agentive power' (1983, p.271).

Harre (ibid) and Shotter (ibid) draw attention to the active nature of citizenship. The notion of action, of agency, can be traced back to the 1779

Declaration of the Rights of Man and The Citizen in which a right is defined by Creniere as 'the effect of an agreement through which one acts.'

Thus, global citizenship that is based on rights, responsibility and action – the rights to certain freedoms, the responsibility not to abuse these rights and to act with fairness and moral concern, or what Bruner (1990) calls openmindedness, 'the keystone of what we call a democratic culture' (p.30). This moral pressure, of Kohlberg's 'social contract orientation' (1971), is mentioned by Rene Cassin (1991) in expressing doubt that moral authority can be solely entrusted to the legislative and judicial domain: 'Legal force of itself is only a secondary safety valve'; it is the awareness of people of 'their dignity and their duties as citizens and as human beings' (p.15) that is of greatest importance.

The sense of dignity in action is underlined in the claim made by Marie (1985) that all rights are essentially derived from the notion of human dignity. Shiman argues that education for human rights should be impelled by the intention to 'encourage their [students'] *action* rooted in a humane conception of justice and human dignity' (1991, p.189).

Global citizenship is dynamic, action underpinned with moral imprimatur. Such citizenship is more complex than independence or autonomy. To be autonomous, it is true, one has to have the capacity for distanced reflection on society, but autonomy, as defined by Raz and Gray (ibid) (and originally John Locke (see Langford 1985)), does not presuppose and include in its definition the second strand of global citizenship, moral or altruistic action (although White (ibid) argues that it should). Harre (ibid) goes so far as to argue that an autonomous action is necessarily one that violates the legal or moral code of a society. The commitment to moral action is regarded as central, as a duty of the citizen; and it is this duty that signifies and dignifies the citizen as a human being.

A picture then, of the global citizen:

> Not merely aware of her rights but able and desirous to act upon them; of an autonomous and inquiring critical disposition; but her decisions and actions tempered by a moral concern for social justice and the dignity of humankind; therefore able, through her actions, to control and enhance 'the trajectory of self' through life whilst contributing to the common weal, the public welfare, with a sense of civic duty to replenish society.

It is this sense of citizenship that is being referred to when writers such as Hart, Franklin and John address the nature of education as an empowering process.

PRINCESSES AND PRINCES VERSUS DRUDGES AND FROGS

That all pupils in a late twentieth century liberal democracy do have a full entitlement to a free state education intended to empower them as adult citizens, is ostensibly accepted without question. Yet, in the United Kingdom, the extension of a universal educational franchise is a continuing and uncompleted process rather than a concluded series of historical events. For many pupils, educational empowerment has always been, and continues to be, unrealised rhetoric.

Only 30 years ago, until CSE examinations were introduced in 1965, around 60–80 per cent of pupils were disenfranchised, from the age of 11, from any form of terminal 16+ examinations and thus the opportunity of a higher education. It was nearly another ten years (1974) before the Raising of the School Leaving Age (ROSLA) Act ensured that all pupils would stay at school until they had had the chance to take public examinations at 16. It was not until 1979 that gender distinction in pupils' choice of post-14 CSE and GCE courses was made illegal. It was merely seven years ago (1988) that the odious class distinction between CSE and GCE 16+ examinations was resolved with the introduction of the GCSE examination. It is only during the present decade of the 1990s that the integration of pupils with a handicap into mainstream education has really developed.

There is evidence to suggest that these legislative changes may have had a formal rather than a substantive effect upon providing equalising and empowering educational opportunities for all pupils. In 1994 the present government connived to defeat its own parliamentary bill originally intended to equalise the opportunities of the handicapped, significant clauses of which concerned educational entitlement. Many ethnic minority pupils are still disadvantaged by a monolinguistic state examination system that insists that, in England and Northern Ireland, all lessons other than Modern Languages must be taught in English and that all examination papers must be written and answered in English. On May 13 1994, Plymouth MP Gary Streeter, speaking in Parliament, suggested that 'People who live in this country should make an effort to learn *the* language'. (This, in a country with 142 indigenous languages.) In 1995, the ideal of a comprehensive state educational system – equal educational opportunities to create a more equal society – is far from realised. Nearly a third of the local education authorities in England and Wales have retained grammar and secondary modern schools; private schools for the children of fee-paying parents allow a privileged section of society to circumvent the National Curriculum; via grant-maintained status, some state schools are effectively moving into the independent sector and operating their own selection processes for 11-year-old pupils. A recent survey (Corrigan 1990) showed that the statistical probability of C3 working-class boys moving through the educational system to take up A1 professional qualifications has decreased since the 1970s. The research of Measor and Sikes (1992) and Herbert (1992) reveals that girls in many schools do not enjoy equality of opportunity with boys, nor do they feel parity of status.

During the last seven years in the UK (from around the time of the Great Educational Reform Act of 1988) two recurring and increasingly refined visual images have emerged to characterise the educational folklore of national politics, the popular media and, hence, the public consciousness, as 'good things in education'. These two images have had a powerful influence on the construction and presentation of the National Curriculum in state schools in England and Wales.

One image, which can be dubbed 'Princesses and Princes', depicts the *ends of education* and is of a small group of smiling and confident school-leavers: reflexive, adaptable, resourceful pupils about to claim their place as participants, the decision-takers and policy-makers, in the era and culture of high modernity. Autonomous but morally aware, these young people will be the citizens of the next century. Words that might be found in the accompanying caption to this optimistic picture are: capability, empowerment, enfranchisement, social concern, co-operation, investigation, entitlement.

The second, equally recognisable – and perceived, by a significant section of the public, as equally positive – image, portrays the *means of education*, the ways in which pupils learn the content of the curriculum that they study. This picture, which can be titled 'Drudges and Frogs', is characterised by a nostalgic view of schooling that has more to do with the last, rather than the next, century: of neatly and uniformly dressed pupils sitting attentively in orderly rows, listening obediently to the didactic presentation of a clearly defined area of factual knowledge, given by an authoritarian, albeit benign, teacher. Words and phrases that might be found in the caption to this image are: standards, rigour, discipline, healthy competition, traditions, back-to-basics, testing.

Photographic epitomes of both of these contrasting educational images, each commissioned by the UK government in 1992, can be found in the Parents' Charter (Princesses and Princes) and in the national press full-page advertisements intended to recruit Department for Education (DFE) school inspectors (Drudges and Frogs). The underlying message of these before-and-after snapshots seems to be – to continue the analogy from children's literature, and such a transmogrification is exactly in the spirit of fairy tales – that the best life-preparation for an adult role in a culture of responsibility is for Princess Cinderella and Prince Bountiful to spend their formative years in a culture of repression and passivity.

What is the reality underpinning the rhetoric within a pupil's weekly timetable if the school managers wish to include photographs of both these images in their illustrated handbook to parents? How do schools resolve these two disparate views of the educational process? The philosophical dichotomy and resulting pedagogical tension between these two popularly-held images (one of the twenty-first century, one of the nineteenth century, one of the aims of education, one of the means of achieving these aims) was the focus of a five-year research study undertaken by the author of this chapter in one local education authority in the UK (Griffith 1996). Non-intervention (illuminative evaluation) and intervention (intentional interaction) research was undertaken in 97 primary, secondary, tertiary and special schools between 1988 and 1993. The purpose of the research was to make some assessment of the typical curriculum and timetable of 11–16-year-old pupils; and to see what opportunities were offered for personal empowerment.

Research in the study LEA demonstrates that parents want their children to use new technology, to be involved in active learning, to develop the social skills that collaborative and co-operative working encourages. The Government claims that it wants to create an adaptable work-force capable of working in teams, solving problems, negotiating between groups, flexible enough to re-train and re-tool as circumstances change. Industry clamours for confident, articulate managers, creators and planners literate in reading electronic text and in the use of information technology. Society as a whole sees a new need for its citizens to celebrate cultural diversity, at the same time expressing a sincere feeling of responsibility for the common weal of humankind and a concern for its shared global environment. The educational system itself rings with metalinguistic catch-phrases such as entitlement, empowerment, enfranchisement. In short, society sees a need for the Princesses and Princes image of school-leavers. And yet, by and large, the shared perception of all these factions as to what constitutes a good teacher (and hence an effective pedagogy) has hardly shifted from the 1950s archetype of a fair but formal Miss or Sir, authoritative, didactic and certain. Similarly, the shared perception of what constitutes a good education is to do with a knowledge-based rather than a social-skills-based (citizenship) curriculum. The Joseph Priestley-driven view (1778) that education should be knowledge-based rather than experiential has, during 125 years of state education in the UK, developed and consolidated its own concomitant pedagogy: a didactic class presentation of factual information that should be committed to memory.

It is this content-based notion of education – with its most economic style of presentation (the passive class lesson) and its simplistic forms of assessment (written tests of memory) – that underpins the National Curriculum and thus dominates state education in the UK. The National Curriculum itself is little more than ten long, but fairly arbitrary, lists of things for pupils to learn off by heart. Its assessment procedures reinforce this: short, sharp tests, timed essays, the distrust and consequent reduction of coursework, national tests to be taken by all pupils repeatedly between the ages of 7 and 16. What few opportunities there are for pupils to express an opinion are sullied by a concern for the proprieties of Standard English and Received Pronunciation and a view of literacy that is obsessed with the mechanics of handwriting and spelling. In short, society sees a need for the Drudges and Frogs image of school pupils. Such an educational system offers virtually no opportunity for the child to use her education as a resource for personal empowerment.

There appears to be an illogical dichotomy between what British society wants for its children and about how it wants that to happen. These two desires are incompatible if not irreconcilable. It seems that what people are either actively seeking, or passively accepting, is a brace of educational opposites: a knowledge-based curriculum which is at odds with the type of education that parents want their children to have and that the rhetoric claims pupils are getting and a didactic pupil-management system at odds with the way parents want their children to learn that curriculum.

To reiterate the point made above, there is a belief that a Drudges and Frogs education will produce Princesses and Princes citizens. But the social alchemy required to turn Drudges into Princesses and Frogs into Princes requires a fairy-tale formula: these things don't happen in real life. There is an atmosphere of confusion that pervades educational planning as the close of the century approaches. The principal agencies responsible for the education of young people do not have a clear and shared view of what constitutes an education appropriate for the era of high modernity; nor of the most suitable style of classroom presentation of its curriculum. The expectations held for the outcomes of the 5–16 educational system are dissonant with its curriculum and its pedagogy.

In a survey of the study LEA's 31 secondary school prospectuses in 1993, inconsistencies between rhetoric and reality are evident. All of them made claims consistent with the Princesses and Princes image of the ends of secondary schooling with mission statements or school aims, such as the following three examples, taken at random from the 31 prospectuses: '...pupils have the opportunity to develop and display their own individual personality...'; 'Pupils are encouraged to think for themselves and work independently, as well as to work collaboratively with others as part of a team.'; 'To ensure that pupils develop their individual intellectual skills to the highest level of which they are capable, by providing a lively and enthusiastic atmosphere in which a love of learning and a questioning approach to life may be stimulated.'

Yet all the prospectuses, to varying degrees, also promoted a Drudges and Frogs view of the means of achieving these aims. Every prospectus, despite its claims to nourish individuality, had a section dealing with the obligatory uniformity of a school dress code. The intended audience for each prospectus was invariably the prospective parent; not one prospectus was written to the prospective pupil. There were also many inconsistencies between a promise to promote a faculty for critical reflection on society and a commitment to assimilation into the existing order. The following quotes come from the same three prospectuses as the quotes above: 'It is our aim to encourage all pupils to appreciate the values society respects and to develop a sound character.'; 'The school sees it as a principal duty to ensure that pupils achieve the maximum possible success in public examinations. This is achieved within a framework of firm discipline and an ordered working environment in which we insist on the highest standards of work and behaviour.'; 'The behaviour of pupils in uniform but out of school reflects directly on the School as much as the pupils themselves. The staff take a serious view of any pupil bringing the name of the School into disrepute'; 'Earrings and jewellery are unsuitable for school wear and must not be worn. We ask parents to co-operate by discouraging their children from wearing these items.'

Thus, a tortuous balancing act between a Princesses and Princes vision of the citizen-pupil and a Drudges and Frogs vision of the serf-pupil institutional climate intended to achieve this development.

A further tectonic friction between the grinding plates of rhetoric and reality was seen in the public and private areas of all the schools visited (100% of the secondary schools and 20% of the primary schools). The following cosmetic touches, intended for the adult visitor, were noted: new school logos, visitors' parking spaces, a carpeted reception area; soft chairs and furnishings in waiting areas; potted plants; coffee percolators; attractive display stands featuring photographs of pupils' excursions and activities (theatre trips, school camps, cultural exchanges, all depicting happy pupils collaborating in active harmony); the executive suite of secretarial staff and headteacher's office; the power-dressed headteacher, the body-contact of handshakes. This can be contrasted with a pupil-eye view: uniform, a register of attendance taken every 50 minutes throughout the day, pupils locked out of classrooms apart from lesson times, no-go areas during break times, different entrances and exits for pupils and members of the public. There were also examples of how teachers are victims of the institutional pecking-order: teachers locked out of the photocopying room, better classroom facilities for heads of department than other teachers, the headteacher's use of first names but staff referring to her by title or surname, the insistence on ties for male teachers, named car parking spaces for senior staff. The hierarchy of school-workers other than pupils was also plain: different staff rooms for teachers and catering and caretaking employees, cleaning staff referred to by first names but responding by surnames to teaching staff, only teachers included in group photographs of the staff or invited to end-of-term cheese and wine parties.

To see more clearly what lay beneath the adult rhetoric of educational entitlement as evidenced in international declarations, government publications, LEA policy documents, school prospectuses and carefully controlled school tours for prospective parents, lessons were observed in 31 (100%) of the secondary schools and 45 (20%) of the primary schools between April 1990 and April 1993. The purpose of these observations, conducted in each of the four Keystages of the National Curriculum, was to gather evidence as to how, and to what extent, the Princesses and Princes aims of a school, as promoted in its prospectus, were explicitly pursued through the curriculum. What was the rhetoric, what was the reality?

Research to date has shown that, in the secondary sector, whatever the well-intentioned aims expressed in the school prospectus, the predominant teaching style was a didactic presentation of factual information. There was very little collaborative groupwork and what there were poorly structured. There was little or no active research. 'Discussion' was invariably teacher-led question-and-answer on a right or wrong basis. Pupils did not design their own tasks and were not involved in the assessment of their own work. Lesson content was hardly ever related to the experience or interests of the class, to the wider social world or to knowledge in other subjects: it existed without external relevance. There was little or no community interaction or movement from the classroom to the surrounding environment. The purpose of pupils' work was never intrinsic, but only preparation for public examination. To this end, the audience for all work was always negatively critical: teacher or examiner as marker.

The tracking of pupils during a curricular week corroborated earlier findings that practices likely to develop personal empowerment and the characteristics of global citizenship are not common in the secondary sector. During the 3,000 minutes of tracking time which were observed at Keystages 3 and 4, only six per cent of the time involved collaborative groupwork; for 68 per cent of lesson time, pupils worked individually on comprehension exercises or note-making; only during two per cent of lesson time were pupils asked to conduct their own research. Lesson structures appeared to discriminate against the equal involvement of girls in discussion, with boys three times more likely to speak voluntarily or be asked to speak by the teacher (In one lesson, the most extreme example, boys spoke 67 times, girls four times). Discussion was exclusively limited to information verification rather than social or moral debate. In 274 minutes of 'class discussion', one of the tracked pupils (a girl) only contributed for five seconds. Continuity between lessons, either of the same or different subjects, was not evident. After note-making, the largest body of time was spent moving from one lesson to the next – 22 per cent of curriculum time. There was no evidence that any of the aims of the schools, as advertised in their prospectuses, were planned into lessons. When asked, not one teacher or pupil could quote any of the school aims.

Starkey's (1991) belief that 'The school is no longer the information-rich, action-poor, isolated institution that Torsten Husen described' (p.16) is not borne out by the research to date. The visited schools were not social microcosms of liberal democracy. They were structured as totalitarian regimes and Havel's (1986) comment on such regimes is directly pertinent:

> Between the aims of the system and the aims of life is a yawning abyss: while life, in its essence, moves towards plurality, diversity, independent self-constitution and self-organisation, in short towards the fulfilment of its own freedom, the system demands conformity, uniformity and discipline. (pp.43–44)

It was concluded that the factors regarded as most detrimental to the development of a school committed to personal empowerment were the factors most typical of the LEA's secondary schools:

- The notion of learning based on content knowledge rather than the promotion of critical faculties which results in the division of the curriculum into discrete subjects; and therefore the division of the daily timetable into short, uniform periods. This compartmentalisation effectively prevents any possibility of an holistic education.

- A view of the pupil population as a number of individuals that are best isolated from each other: by grouping systems, by a hierarchical view of knowledge appropriate to different groupings, by the attempt to impose silence during lessons, by the denigration of collaborative groupwork as either an easy option or a form of cheating, by a system that frequently imposes timed, individual examinations and by a sense of individual competition rather than group co-operation.

- By a pedagogy that has a lesson content unrelated to the communities and environments of the real world, a reliance on teacher-disseminated texts (blackboard notes, videos, books, worksheets, software) as the source of authority of knowledge rather than pupil research, no sense of audience for the work, and an almost exclusive reliance on traditional manuscripts as the sole means of presentation.

The isolation of the pupil from her peers, aggrandised by her institutional powerlessness, is detrimental to the development either of social relationships or any sense of a holistic learning experience. The system casts the individual into a void where making fulfilling connections with other people or between various aspects of the curriculum is almost impossible. It is a Kafkaesque climate, not of education, but of alienation.

The findings of the illuminative evaluation fieldwork research (pupil tracking at Keystages 3 and 4) suggest that the conventional curriculum and timetable offer few, if any, opportunities for personal empowerment – despite the claims of some schools, in their stated aims, that attributes of empowerment are encouraged. The normal classroom style that was observed was characterised by pupils working individually on short micro-activities that were specified by the teacher. This teaching and learning style was not universally approved by teachers, but was commonly adopted as it was regarded as an expedient means of presenting the National Curriculum. A high majority of the teachers interviewed over the five years of the study expressed strong ideological and pragmatic reservations about the contemporary constitution of a liberal education. Indeed, teachers were keen to experiment and libertarian classroom projects were undertaken in all of the 31 secondary schools between 1989 and 1993. Each of these projects lasted between 6 and 12 weeks, during which time pupils worked in small collaborative groups of their own choice to research a topic of the group's choosing. The research was active and pupils spent much time outside the classroom, often moving into the local environment and community. A range of computer and audio-visual technology was used by the pupils and live presentations of groups' work were made to community audiences. Pupils decided whether any assessment should be made of their work, who should make an assessment and upon what criteria assessment should be based. Essentially, pupils aged 11–16 were encouraged to take the responsibility to do whatever they wanted, however they wanted, with whoever they wanted, for periods of up to a whole term, within particular subjects or lessons.

These projects were overtly intended to promote a learning atmosphere and environment in which individual children could empower themselves along the lines suggested by the above definition of the global citizen. It was hoped that a 'moral concern for social justice and the dignity of humankind' may be engendered as pupils worked together in small teams yet were aware of a responsibility both to the larger society of the class within which they operated (and by extension, to the larger societies in which the school was located), and to the self. Similarly, that the development of 'an autonomous and inquiring critical disposition' may be fostered in these citizens of the classroom as they became decision-takers and policy-makers by designing their own tasks, undertaking their own active research, having some control over the time and pace of their work, and being involved in any assessment of the worth of their labour. Through presenting their research and opinions in facsimiles of the way in which news and opinions about the world are presented to them (via television programmes, newspapers, magazines, public meetings), they might learn how the media always has a point of bias. Thus, by creating their own media artifacts, they could learn 'to read the world' (Jones 1990). These citizens were encouraged to realise that their actions have a wider consequence and relevance by placing their work in the context of the real communities and environments (whether local, national or global) within which they lived. In presenting their work to a wider audience, they were encouraged to see that groups within society can inform others with a view to bring about change. A variety of styles of presentation allowed the efforts of all pupils to be communicated to a wider audience and to be seen as having intrinsic value, thus promoting self-worth and a desire to participate. A capacity for self-critical reflection, an attribute of the post-modern citizen, as identified in Giddens' phrase 'the reflexive project of the self', was encouraged by devolving the responsibility for project planning, execution and assessment to the pupils.

Data were collected in a variety of ways from a variety of sources within the research community. The vast majority of those involved in what became known as 'independent learning' projects, and those who observed them, found them to be stimulating and educationally effective in the domains of cognitive and affective development. The opportunities enjoyed by pupils for the development of a critical disposition, for personal autonomy within a vision of community, for the opportunity to discuss their own involvement in topical social and moral issues, and to advance the reflexive project of the self, indicate that independent learning is a convincing pedagogy for the promotion of personal empowerment and preparation for citizenship in the third millennium.

The four principal findings of the five years of action research (46 half- or full-term projects in all the 31 secondary schools in the study LEA) are:

1. Independent learning projects (despite the rhetoric of international, national, local and parochial publications which suggest that the style of independent learning is the pedagogical norm) were a great novelty to staff and pupils.

2. Both staff and pupils responded enthusiastically and enjoyed working in this way.

3. They found the projects fulfilling because they were demanding.

4. They would like to repeat the experience.

Many data were gathered. Some dominant themes are the difficulties and rewards of collaborative groupwork, problems of time management, the personal engagement that pupils felt with the topic they chose to study, the technological literacy, dexterity and creativity pupils displayed in presenting their work via video, audio and computer technology, and the ingenuity that pupils showed in active research within the environment and working with members of the community (a group of 14-year-olds at one school arranged for their class to be flown around the coastline in an RAF aeroplane so that they could video-record sewage outflows before a tour of a local sewage works and a meeting with the Chair of the District Council and representatives of the regional water company). One of the most impressive findings was that, given a free choice of topic, the majority of collaborative groups – at any Keystage – chose to investigate a social issue.

Analysis of the pupils' end-of-project evaluations and responses to open-ended questionnaires clearly shows that they felt that they had developed qualities of global citizenship. Teachers too, expressed enthusiasm for independent learning as a means of cultivating personal and social skills, but some had reservations as to the amount of mandatory syllabus content that could be covered in this way. A large majority (94%) of pupils felt that they had worked more industriously than in other lessons and that the work had been demanding and stimulating. This was a view shared by most teachers. Many commented that the quality of the work produced by pupils was of a higher standard than usual.

Common to successful independent learning projects was an appropriate level of support for teachers and pupils after they had accepted the responsibility in undertaking an independent learning project. By the end of the control phase of the intervention research, it was clear that the greatest support to teachers and pupils was an understanding of the purpose of independent learning in relation to personal empowerment and global citizenship. This support was considerably strengthened when that understanding was shared with, and approved by, a school's senior management team, parents, governors and LEA officials. Independent learning projects offered an agreed framework for the negotiation of changes to the normal power structure of the classroom so that, during the transition from a didactic to a libertarian style of learning, both teachers and pupils felt supported, confident and proactive. In effect, the projects acted to bridge the divide between an invested and a divested system of power.

THE NATURE OF INVESTED POWER

An invested power system is hierarchical, linear and competitive. All traditional institutions conform to this model: from the armed forces, to commerce and industry, to economic trading and banking, to education, to the processes of Parliamentary government itself. It is a system that rewards individual success, the rewards being social prestige and economic status. Examples of social prestige are type of job and promotion within its structure, membership of certain clubs and forms of public recognition such as the honours system. Economic status is evinced in salary, bonuses, overtime, share options and the attendant conspicuous consumption associated with large amounts of personal money: type and number of cars, clothing, holidays, houses owned, private education and health care. These two markers are not distinct; for instance, a partnership, a directorship or becoming a shareholder all suggest both social prestige and economic status.

The membership processes of invested power are steeped in ritual: initiation ceremonies, arcane rules, curious dress-codes, terms of address. This is true of the child's first day of school, her confirmation within a range of world religions, her becoming a teenager, entering university, taking a position in a firm. It is a membership process that believes in apprenticeship: it seeks to absorb the next generation into its monolithic structure from an early age. Examples of this apprenticeship aspect of invested power are often seen in operation in schools: School Councils, Head Girls and Head Boys, Team Captains, Prefects, monitors of various kinds, pupil librarians, pupils helping in the tuck shop. An extension of invested power is offered to the selected neophytes of the next generation who are considered most likely to consolidate the status quo. Essentially, schools with an invested power structure have an autarchic view of the socialisation role of education (Steutel 1991).

Invested power has a form of language of its own, a language that obscures processes, that sanitises, that depersonalises: citizens are not killed, there is collateral damage; lies are not told, there is economy of the truth; people's jobs are not sacrificed to a political ideology of privatisation but are subject to the exciting challenge of market forces. Children are referred to as the point-of-delivery consumer in the educational process. It is a language of suave intimidation impelled by a determination to protect its power. To this end it derides the language of others and seeks to deny them their own voice by insisting on monolinguism, by promoting Standard English and Received Pronunciation as the spoken code of power, by deriding accent as a class indicator or a source of belittling ethnic or regional humour, by simply not allowing people such as pupils to talk at all. In these ways the silenced are prevented from finding their own forms of voicing.

The holders of invested power are loathe to experiment in the transfer of power, for the way in which these stakeholders define the success of their selves is inextricably bound up with the amount of invested power that they maintain. To share is to diminish the power. The attraction of invested power, and its main characteristic, is that it is exclusive to an elite minority. Invested power obeys the law of centrifugal force: it draws to the centre.

Even when there is an undeniable and successful transfer of power (for example change of government via national elections, the appointment of a new headteacher, the rites of passage of the maturational process that progressively bestows increased responsibilities upon the child as she metamorphosises to young adult), it is only the balance rather than the nature of invested power itself that is changed: there may sometimes be new holders of the old power, but the system of invested power is not compromised; in fact, it is protected and perpetuated.

The stakeholders of invested power in the UK are the Conservative Government, the right wing establishment and the upper and middle white classes.

THE NATURE OF DIVESTED POWER

Divested power is characterised by being corporate and distributive in that it diffuses and gives to the periphery with an organic, regenerative and dynamic view of society that regards change as constant and celebrates diversity. It is the form of power that fits most closely with the definition of the global citizen, with personal empowerment, and the actual practice shown in successful independent learning projects.

Divested power is predicated upon an ethical rather than an economic democracy; it is non-hierarchical and believes in equality of status based upon participation in citizenship. Its citizens envisage society as changing, adapting, growing and transforming and are excited, not threatened by this flux. Its membership processes are wide, encouraging the expression of an individual's multi-faceted personality: it encourages openness. It sees society as having an infinite number of interdependent and interactive collaborative and co-operative communities. Its membership processes show no discrimination.

The language of divested power is human rather than technocratic. Emphasising a shared and supported responsibility, it is non-adversarial – conversation and discussion rather than point-scoring and argument. It is a language that has no absolutism of right and wrong, good and bad. It has no tone of culpability; it strives to understand the other person's point of view. It is a language rich in the expression and promotion of its dialects and accents. It is the language of voicing.

The stakeholders of divested power are every citizen, including the holders of invested power, for the transformation, rather than the transfer of power, frees them as much as anybody else. The transformation of power changes the nature, not just the balance, of power. The nature of the power is transformed from invested to divested power but the old holders of invested power are not disenfranchised: they are sharers in divested power. A topical example of this is the situation in South Africa. President Mandela wanted not merely a transfer of the invested power from the National Party, but a transformation of that power so that no socio-political faction, including the white minority, would feel dispossessed. When the final election results showed that the ANC had taken 62.7 per cent of the vote, Mandela expressed his gladness that he had *not* won the extra 4 per cent that would have given his party the power to rewrite the Constitution alone. Now all the other parties must be involved. Mandela clearly wanted not merely a transfer of the National Party's invested power, but a transformation of the nature of that power to the harmony of divested power. This transformation can be compared with the first-past-the-post electoral system of the UK in which, for most of this century, the two principal political parties have simply transferred, temporarily, the invested power between them, rather than consider the possibilities of transformation that proportional voting and coalition might afford.

DEVELOPING EMPOWERING EDUCATIONAL INSTITUTIONS

As the development of global citizenship will require a change from an invested power system to a divested power system, so independent learning projects, intended as microcosms of the macrocosm, necessitated a change from the invested power system of the typical classroom to the divested power system of collaborative and co-operative working. This change was not a crude matter of 'letting the kids do whatever they wanted'. This would have meant a direct transfer of invested power from teacher to pupils – the simple libertarianism of Summerhill or the ill-fated free schools of the 1960s and 1970s. Early and unsophisticated attempts at independent learning during the circumspection phase of the research spiral, and an analysis during the literature search of the reasons for the failure of libertarian experiments in the free and state schools, led to certain tentative conclusions about such a transfer of invested power.

First, it is virtually impossible for a teacher within the state system to transfer her invested power to a class and then support the pupils as they adapt to the change. The whole style and structure of state education precludes this. But, even if it were attempted, it seems unlikely that it could be achieved because the nature of invested power is based upon a hierarchy in which the many obey a singular representative of invested authority. The chain of command may be long (a constitutional monarchy in which, theoretically, every member of the state is ultimately subject to royal decree) or direct (class to teacher), but the principle of the singular authority of invested power invariably applies. There-fore, the teacher, in simply abandoning her power, is attempting to distribute among the many something that is indivisible. For an effective transfer of invested power it would need one pupil to take on the teacher's role, but research observation suggested that in practical terms this does not happen – for the hierarchical essence of invested power is no longer in place: the pupil does not have the singular authority required to impose an invested power system upon her peers. Classroom observation revealed a common tendency, when a teacher attempted a transfer of invested power from herself to her class, for each pupil to become the leader of a community of one: herself. It was concluded that the attempted transfer of invested power from a hierarchy to a group of peers is likely to lead to anarchy (a point recognised and regarded positively by teachers and pupils involved in libertarian educational experiments in the 1970s (Shotton 1993).

Second, the apparent transfer of invested power is often an illusion. Observation of the dynamics of collaborative groups of pupils showed that some groups organised themselves as microcosmic invested power hierarchies, with group leaders reporting to the teacher if group members were not fulfilling their tasks. All that had happened in such cases was that some pupils (the 'collaborative' group leaders) had been subsumed into a lower level of the existing class-teacher chain of command. The result for the invested power base is a strengthening of the status quo.

Third, there may be a limited and temporary transfer of power to groups of pupils, but without the support they need to succeed. The group 'fails', their dependence upon the teacher is re-established, and once again the invested power of the familiar class-teacher relationship is reinforced.

The final conclusion was that the transfer of invested power was not a relevant issue to independent learning projects because the nature of invested power is antagonistic to the development of global citizenship. What is needed to enable pupils to empower themselves is not a transfer of invested power but for a transformation of power, to a form of divested power.

The independent learning projects undertaken in the study LEA that were regarded by the participants as successful were those that achieved such a transformation of power, alienating neither the teachers nor the pupils, so that the teachers felt they had a valuable role to play within the co-operative group and the pupils were supported as they explored their new responsibilities. If a state educational system is structured as a model of invested power, then the opportunities for pupils to use the resource of their education to empower themselves are likely to be few. The fieldwork research showed that educational institutions of invested power are unlikely to structure the curriculum and the timetable to make provision for the collaborative and co-operative practices associated with the divested power of independent learning projects. Even if such an institution flirts with the idea of a shift in the balance of power (transfer), it is still likely to fail in providing empowering opportunities because either it will create an all-round sense of failure or it will produce a limited number of pupils who become leaders of the collaborative groups – homonculi of invested power.

When schools have attempted to break from the predominant invested power system of state education they have been vilified (Wright 1989; Shotton 1993). If attempts to introduce libertarian practices failed in the liberal climate of the 1960s and 1970s, what chance is there in the 1990s?

Whilst many would agree with Shotton (1993) that the Conservative Government has sought to strengthen its centralised power over state schools, it can be argued that its approach has been inconsistent (six different Ministers for Education since 1979 have all brought different emphases to the job) and some of its measures have had unintended effects so it is also possible to sketch a scenario in which individual schools are in a stronger position than ever before to develop as empowering institutions. The clumsy consumerism of the Parents' Charter does offer the opportunity for parents to be more engaged in, and more critical of, educational opportunities at a local level and to feel they have a decision-making role to play in the neighbourhood school. Local management of schools and the erosion of the stature of local educational authorities has placed more responsibility, but also greater freedom, in the hands of headteachers and heads of department. Changes in the legal responsibilities of governing bodies and different procedures for their election and constitution have meant that the role of governor is no longer a comfortable sinecure for the traditional holders of invested power.

All of these changes, generally believed by left-wing commentators to have been intended to make schools directly accountable to the local community and so to check any libertarian degeneration, have actually led to the greater autonomy of schools and their communities to institute libertarian policies of educational empowerment, to transform their management structures to a model of divested power, and to unite with similar communities in articulate campaigns to protect or extend their independence. Examples that this is increasingly happening are the nation-wide campaigns against National Curriculum Tests at 14 (1993), for universal nursery education (1994) and against proposed cuts in government funding (1995). (This is particularly interesting in view of Shotton's belief that many of the embryonic libertarian state schools succumbed to external pressures because they were isolated and could not draw upon any support network.)

Analysis suggests that condemnation of state and free schools that attempted to introduce a system of divested power in the 1960s and 1970s was not based upon ideological grounds (for most state schools continue to embrace the *rhetoric* of empowerment) but upon practical perceptions of an appropriate libertarian pedagogy. It is the practice, not the philosophy, of libertarianism that has been the stumbling block – a point made by the only free school teacher to write a book about free schooling:

> If the free schools' preliminary pronouncements have little indication of what free schools were actually going to do when they got started, description of what happened once they were established showed that they were floundering – in some cases badly. (Wright 1989, p.107)

Thus it may be that the route to developing schools as empowering institutions is via practice that is effective in implementing libertarian aims, but is also acceptable to a conservative audience of parents, media and educational officialdom. The findings of the fieldwork research in the study LEA demonstrate that independent learning is an effective pedagogy of libertarian education that is well-regarded by pupils, teachers, parents and other observers, including LEA advisers and inspectors. It was during the late 1980s and early 90s that the independent learning projects took place, successfully and publicly, throughout a conservative, rural shire county. The success of these libertarian initiatives in a transformation to a divested power system was based upon three critical features: creating or strengthening a non-hierarchial partnership between parents, pupils and teachers, exploiting the published rhetoric of empowerment, and instituting an effective pedagogy (of independent learning) to realise that rhetoric.

Schools and other educational institutions must be honest in examining their actual practices and policies in the light of the philosophic rhetoric promulgated in their aims. A school's aims must be apparent in its activities if it is to claim that it is fulfilling them. Too often, enlightened aims disappear under the exigencies of day-to-day expediency. This chapter has sought to argue that the disparity between intention and execution – between rhetoric and reality – is caused primarily by a state educational system of invested power that has a content-laden, rather than a child-centred, view of education – a view exemplified by the National Curriculum. Such a view leads to a didactic presentation of the curriculum that precludes the development of the qualities of citizenship that empower not just the individual, but the collaborative and co-operative groups to which every individual belongs. Typical features of the didactic presentation of a content-laden curriculum are: subject specialism requiring discrete lessons in different rooms, the division of the timetable into short, unconnected lessons, the grouping of pupils in such a way that alienates them from peer contact and support and a lesson structure that discourages group-work, talk, research and activity in favour of silent, individual short tasks usually associated with a worksheet distributed by the teacher. No matter how well-intentioned are the school managers, the underlying ethos of such schools – as experienced by the pupils – is competitive, untrusting and dictatorial.

There is an undeniable rhetoric of educational empowerment and global citizenship that can be capitalised upon to transform schools to divested systems of power and so provide a climate of opportunity for pupils to empower themselves as the citizens of a global future. Those involved in education should move forward to greet these new ideas rather than cower in the institutional bunker of invested power; and move forwards with arms extended in welcome rather than raised in surrender. Goethe wrote – and his observation applies to international, national, local and school government – that 'That government is best that teaches us to govern ourselves.' Such government, at whatever level, requires the transformation of power relationships and the emergence of new understandings of the nature and purpose of power:

> We declare our firm belief in the principles enunciated in the Universal Declaration of Human Rights that everyone has the right to education; and that education shall be directed to the full development of human personality and to the strengthening of respect for human rights and fundamental freedoms. It shall promote understanding, tolerance and friendship among the nations, racial or religious groups and shall further the activities for the maintenance of peace. (Mandela 1953, p.38)

REFERENCES

Bruner, J. (1990) *Acts of Meaning.* Cambridge: Massachusetts; Harvard University Press.

Cassin, R. (ed) (1991) *The Challenges of Human Rights Education.* London: Cassell.

Corrigan, P. (1990) –Social Forms/Human Capacities: Essays in Authority and Difference. London: Routledge.

Council of Europe (1985) *Recommendation No R (85) 7 of the Committee of Ministers, Appendix 3.2.* Strasbourg: Council of Europe.

Davie, R. (1989) 'The national children's bureau: Evidence to the Elton committee.' In N. Jones (ed) *School Management and Pupil Behaviour.* Lewes: Falmer Press.

Education Reform Act 1988. London: HMSO.

Franklin, B. (1992) 'Children and decision making: Developing empowering institutions.' In M.D. Fortuyen and M. de Langen (eds) *Towards the Realisationns of Human Rights of Children; Lectures given at the Second International Conference on Children's Ombudswork.* Amsterdam: Children's Ombudswork Foundation and Defence for Children International-Netherlands.

Freeman, M.D.A (1988) 'Taking children's rights seriously.' *Children and Society 1,* 4.

Giddens, A. (1991) *Modernity and Self Identity: Self and Society in the Late Modern Age.* Oxford: Oxford University Press.

Giddens, A. (1994) *Beyond Left and Right: The Future of Radical Politics.* Cambridge: Polity.

Griffith, R. (1996) *Independent Learning and Educational Citizenship.* Ph.D thesis: Exeter University.

Gray, J. (1983) *Mill on Liberty: A Defence.* London: Routledge and Kegan Paul.

Harre, R. (1983) *Personal Being.* Oxford: Blackwell.

Hart, R.A. (1992) *Children's Participation: From Tokenism to Citizenship; Innocenti Essays No 4.* Florence: UNICEF International Child Development Centre.

Havel, V. (1986) Living in Truth. Twenty-two essays published on the occasion of the award of the Erasmus Priz to Václav Havel. ed. J. Vladislav; London: Faber and Faber.

Herbert, C. (1992) *Sexual Harrassment in Schools.* London: Fulton.

HMSO (1991) *The Parent's Charter.* Bristol: HMSO.

John, M. (1993b) 'Children's Rights in a Free Market Culture.' In S. Stephens (ed) Childrens and the Politics of Culture. Princeton: Princeton University Press.

Jones, N. (1990) 'Reading the world.' In R. Carter (ed) *Knowledge About Language and the Curriculum: the LINC Reader.* London: Hodder and Stoughton.

Kandel, I.L. (1949) 'Education and human rights.' In UNESCO *Human Rights: Comments and Interpretations.* London: Wingate.

Kohlberg, L. (1971) 'Stages of moral development as a basis for moral education.' In C. Beck., B. Crittenden and E. Sullivan (ed) *Moral Education.* Toronto: University of Toronto.

Langford, G. (1985) *Education, Persons and Society: A Philosophical Enquiry.* London: Macmillan.

Mandela, N. (1953) 'No easy walk to freedom: The presidential address by Mandela to the ANC conference.' In R. Mandela (1978) *The Struggle is My Life.* London: The International Defence and Aid Fund for Southern Africa.

Marie, J-B. (1985) *Human Rights or A Way of Life in a Democracy.* Strasbourg: Council of Europe.

McCluhan, M. (1968) *The Medium Is the Message.* Harmondsworth: Penguin.

Measor, L. and Sikes, P. (1992) *Gender and Schools.* London: Cassel.

Mulgan, G. (1991) 'Citizens and responsibilities.' In G. Andrews (ed) *Citizenship.* London: Lawrence and Wishart.

Neill, A.S. (1960) *Summerhill: A Radical Approach to Child Rearing (1926).* New York: Hart Publishing Company.

Priestley, J. (1778) *Miscellaneous Observations Relating to Education. Most Especially as it Respects the Conduct of the Mind. To Which is Added, An Essay on a Course of Liberal Education for Civil and Active Life.* Bath: R. Cruttwell.

Raz, J. (1986) *The Morality of Freedom.* Oxford: The Clarendon Press.

Rousseau, J-J. (1762) *Emile.* (trans. B. Foxley 1911). London: Dent.

Science in the National Curriculum; DES and the Welsh Office 1989. London: HMSO.

Shiman, D. (1991) 'Teaching human rights: Classroom activities for a global age.' In H. Starkey (ed) *The Challenges of Human Rights Education.* London: Cassell.

Shotter, J. (1984) *Social Accountability and Selfhood.* Oxford: Blackwell.

Shotton, J. (1993) *No Master High or Low: Libertarian Education and Schooling 1890–1990.* Bristol: Libertarian Education.

Speaker's Commission (1990) *Encouraging Citizenship: Report on the Speaker's Commission on Citizenship.* London: HMSO.

Starkey, H. (1991) 'The Council of Europe recommendation on the teaching and learning of human rights in schools.' In H. Starkey (ed) *The Challenges of Human Rights Education.* London: Cassell.

Steutel, J.W. (1991) 'Discipline, internalisation and freedom: A conceptual analysis.' In B. Spiecker and R. Straughan (eds) *Freedom and Indoctrination in Education: International Perspectives.* London: Cassell.

United Nations General Assembly Official Records, Resolution 25, 44th Session (1991) *The United Nations Convention on the Rights of the Child.* New York: UN.

White, J. (1991) 'The justification of autonomy as an educational aim.' In B. Speicker and R. Straughan (eds) *Freedom and Indoctrination in Education: International Perspectives.* London: Cassell.

Wright, N. (1989) *Assessing Radical Education.* Milton Keynes: Open University Press.

The Contributors

Monica Cockett is a Research Fellow at the Department of Child Health, Postgraduate Medical School, University of Exeter. In recent years Monica has been conducting research about families, children and the effectiveness of divorce mediation services. She has been involved locally and nationally in the evaluation, management and supervision of mediation training and practice. The Joseph Rowntree Family Study about the effects of family breakdown was completed in 1994 and was carried out with Dr John Tripp.

Niki Davis is Professor of Educational Telematics at the School of Education, University of Exeter. She has undertaken extensive research and development in the areas of communication and information technologies in teacher education in the UK and overseas. Niki is also a British Telecom Research Fellow.

Rhys Griffith was formerly Senior Advisory Teacher in English for a Shire County. He is now a full-time researcher, researching independent learning.

Andrew Hannan is a member of the Runnymede Trust Working Group on Equality Assurance, Reader in Education at the Rolle School of Education and Director of Research of the Faculty of Arts and Education at the University of Plymouth.

Viv Hogan is presently a freelance researcher in Early Childhood Education and Training. She was formerly Assistant Director with Children Today, Devon. She is currently working with the Council for Awards in Children's Care and Education (CACHE). As a result of the Children Today Project, a number of play initiatives have been developed and are still continuing after the Project finished in October 1990. These have included the setting up of a County Play Forum and co-ordinated training for playworkers around the county.

Cathie Holden is a Senior Lecturer in Education at the University of Exeter, where she co-ordinates the Primary PGCE programme. She has taught in primary schools for many years and now lectures in humanities and educational studies. She is currently involved in an Erasmus curriculum development project on Educating for Citizenship in the new Europe: teaching about justice, democracy, human rights and global responsibility.

Mary John is a psychologist whose research work has largely been with minority rights groups. Early work was with John and Elizabeth Newson as part of their longitudinal study on child-rearing. Since then she has acted as a psychological consultant to Head Start in the United States, an expert adviser to the Centre for Educational Research and Innovation, OECD, Paris and later on disability matters to the EEC. She is a Professor of Education at the University of Exeter and Dean of the Faculty of Education.

Munene Kahiro is National Executive Officer for the Child Welfare Society of Kenya which is a non-governmental organisation founded in 1955. The Child Welfare Society of Kenya is in the forefront of promoting the Rights of the Child in Kenya and has hosted the National Conference and four regional seminars on this theme.

Gerison Lansdown is Director of the Children's Rights Development Unit. She has a background in social work/social policy and is currently on the management committees of the Family Rights Group and Child Poverty Action Group.

Jana Ondráčková is a member of the Czech Helsinki Committee's Education Section and its Executive Team. This committee is part of the Helsinki Alliance, Prague. Jana initiated, and now co-ordinates, a new project entitled 'Citizen' which focuses on learning about human rights, the rights of the child, global inter-relations, and involves children and their teachers. A summarised case study on the project is forthcoming as a Council of Europe publication.

Alan Peacock is Senior Lecturer in Primary Science and Chair of International Affairs at the School of Education, University of Exeter. He has been involved in teacher education research and evaluation in numerous African states for almost 20 years.

Juan Miguel Petit is a lawyer and a journalist and works for the Centre for Innovation and Development, Montevideo, Uruguay in several programmes concerning education and policy development.

Rosemary Rae is Senior Lecturer in Social Work and Applied Social Studies in the School of Health and Human Services at the University of Huddersfield. Her work mainly involves teaching on the Diploma in Social work course and her own research. She was previously a social worker for several years in London and Bradford. Her commitment to young people comes generally from a concern about injustice.

Margaret Ralph is a General Inspector of Education with the London Borough of Bromley and a registered Inspector for OFSTED. She served on the all-party committee for Romania, set up by Emma Nicholson in 1991, and was a founder member of the British Romanian Trust for Education and Cultural Exchange. The teaching strategies behind much of the work undertaken in Romania have resulted in the publication of a book and video – 'Fundamental Activities' – to which Margaret has contributed both as a writer and editor.

David Regis is a Researcher in the Schools Health Research Unit in the School of Education at the University of Exeter. This Unit aims to support and promote effective health education in primary and secondary schools. The services it provides promoted co-operation between teachers, parents, children, governors and health care professionals.

Jeremy Roche is a lecturer in the School of Health and Social Welfare at the Open University. He has written widely on Children's Rights and is co-author of *Children's Welfare and Children's Rights* (1994: Hodder) and *The Children Act 1989: Putting into Practice* (1991: Open University).

Michael Singer is a psychologist who, at the time this paper was presented in September 1992, was working at the Ombuds office in Vienna as Child Ombudsman.

Bob Snowden is Professor of Family Studies, University of Exeter. With an academic background in social administration, psychology and sociology, he has applied this knowledge to research into reproductive behaviour, founding, in 1971, the Family Planning Research Unit at Exeter University. In 1982 this became the Institute of Population Studies of which, until recently, he was Director. In 1988 this Institute was designated a Collaborating Centre for Research in Human Reproduction by the World Health Organisation, one of only two social studies centres to be so recognised in the world. He is a member of the Human Fertilisation and Embryology Authority set up by Act of Parliament in 1990. In addition, Bob was the founder chairman of the local branch of the Child Poverty Action Group.

John Tripp trained at Guy's Hospital and the Hospital for Sick Children, Great Ormond Street and is now a Consultant Paediatrician and Senior Lecturer in Child Health at the Postgraduate Medical School, University of Exeter. His research has included a number of clinical projects and his main present research activities are concentrated in two related areas of social paediatrics, namely the effects of family breakdown on children and a novel sex education programme for adolescents in schools.

Colin Wringe read Modern Languages at Oxford and obtained his PhD in philosophy of education at the London Institution of Education. His publications include *Children's Rights – A Philosophical Study* (Routledge and Kegan Paul), *Democracy, Schooling and Political Education* (George Allen and Unwin) and *Understanding Educational Aims* (Unwin Hyman), as well as numerous articles in the field of philosophy of education. He has taught in secondary schools and Further Education and is currently a Reader in Education at Keele University.

Subject Index

References in italic indicate figures or tables

Author Index